THREE FEET ABOVE THE GROUND

THREE FEET ABOVE THE GROUND

HEATHER GODDIN

Matador
9 Priory Business Park,
Wistow Road, Kibworth Beauchamp,
Leicestershire. LE8 0RX
Tel: 0116 279 2299
Email: books@troubador.co.uk
Web: www.troubador.co.uk/matador
Twitter: @matadorbooks

ISBN 978 1788036 405

British Library Cataloguing in Publication Data.
A catalogue record for this book is available from the British Library.

Printed and bound by CPI Group (UK) Ltd, Croydon, CR0 4YY
Typeset in 11pt Minion Pro by Troubador Publishing Ltd, Leicester, UK

Matador is an imprint of Troubador Publishing Ltd

To Christer
and in memory of Dickie Stevens (1920-2010)

Acknowledgements

My grateful thanks to Celia Rhys-Evans, Helen Reeves and Denise Vanston who printed the poems out for me and to Irene Beager who assisted with the proof reading.

Three Feet Above the Ground

The day we met my life began.
What went before is void.
The world became more beautiful,
A wild enchanted place.
There was a brightness in the air
I had not known before.
You opened up your heart to me,
Showed me the treasures of your mind.
My heart leapt at the sight of you.
I walked three feet above the ground.

Now you are gone life must go on
But never again a void.
The world is still as beautiful,
I know it better now.
The brightness lingers in the air,
I see it clearly still.
The treasures that you gave to me
Will not be thrown aside.
But only in my dreams
Will my heart leap at the sight of you.
Only in memory
Shall I walk three feet above the ground.

1980/Revised 2011

Beginnings

This is my season of despair
When all that is bad seems worse.

The mist lies low at the edge of the bare, brown field,
Furrows still filled with the recent snow.
Within the coppice branches drip ice on frozen ground.

And then, amongst the dead leaves underfoot
I catch a glimpse of green.
The first frail snowdrops of the spring.

Stooping, I clear an island in the leaves
And lift the small, brave flowers with gentle hands.
Even if it snows again they will survive.
If they can do it so can I.

For them it is a new beginning.
So must it be for me.

2014

Dog

I am all dog,
None of the cat about me.
Patient, persistent,
Loving my master,
Faithful 'til death.

What kind of dog?
Something quite small and quite noisy.
The kind that gets under your feet
And sooner or later gets kicked
Or trampled under foot.
Then what does it do?
Bite a chunk out of a leg
Or fly to the jugular?
No, it picks itself up, wagging its tail
And starts up all over again.

Cats are so vain.
Washing and grooming for most of the day.
Hunting and eating and sleeping the rest of the time.
(They won't go for walks.)
They use all their wiles to seduce and enchant
And if you don't suit
They'll take themselves off.

I really don't like them
But I do like to chase them
But I know if I did
I'd come off the worst.

I am all dog,
There's none of the cat about me.

2016

Flirting

The table in the restaurant was small,
My leg leaned close to yours.
"Are you flirting with me?" you cried.
"No,"
I replied,
"My knee just found its way to yours,
Liked what it found,
Its comfort and its warmth
And didn't want to leave."

You raised your eyes to heaven,
Tried not to smile,
Without success,
But you didn't move your leg away.
We sat like that throughout the meal
Until we paid the bill and left.

2015

The Mote of Mark

Once there was a settlement
High above the Solway Firth,
Long since gone.
Destroyed in Viking raids, perhaps.
The Mote of Mark,
Now just a clearing in the woods.

Two paths run parallel around the hill.
One to the shell beach
Where the cockle boats anchor
Off the island in the bay.
The other takes you high above the woods
And leads to Rockcliffe down below.
But another path connects the two
And crosses the Mote of Mark.

I hated that path,
Walked through as quickly as I could,
Felt I was watched
By unseen prescences amongst the trees.
I didn't want to linger on my own.

I went there once with Sandy
When he walked the dogs.

We said nothing on that path,
The dogs subdued with downcast ears,
Their tails between their legs.
Once on the upper path
The dogs became quite different,
Their usual boisterous selves.
I mentioned how I felt as we walked along.
"The eyes," he said,
"They watch you from the woods.
The dogs can feel it too.
You saw just how they were.
They hate to take that path."

It is a strange, uneasy place
The Mote of Mark.

2016

Fly in Amber

Bourne on the breeze from the courtyard
Drift the perfumes of summer,
Jasmine and rose.
We lie, close-clasped, drowsy with heat,
In the soft, sweet aftermath of love.
Lovers and friends in wordless harmony,
Lapped in the golden, silken light.

Idly, I watch the patterns of light
On the high-beamed ceiling and the white-washed walls,
Feeling the texture of your skin,
Breathing your body's scent,
Whilst sunlight fades
Through gold and amber into rose
As the bright day dies.

Oh, let me keep this moment to my grave.
My amulet against the dark.
Fly trapped in amber
Held for eternity.

1983

In The High Hills

I have walked further than I thought
For far below, amongst the toy-box sheep and cows,
I see myself stride out amidst the shimmering grass,
The foaming may and meadowsweet.

Climbing the hill I had you at my side.
We walked together for a while
On summer-gold and autumn-russet days
Until I stopped to view the hills
And pick the brambles in the lane.
You went ahead and left me there
To reach the summit on my own.

Here, on the highest hill, winter has come.
Frost stipples the earth beside the drystone wall.
The ground is hard and cold beneath my feet.
The view is beautiful and worth the climb.
The rolling hills and woods, the villages
Lit by a glorious sunset light.

Yet, as I watch, the mists roll down,
Blotting out light and the way ahead.
I cannot go back along the track
For I have walked too far.

I must go down between the hostile trees
To reach the village far below.
I must go carefully, I do not want to fall
But I think of the lights and warmth below,
The welcome I may find.

Will it be winter or will it be spring?
Will you be there?

1987

Rainy Day

What did we do that day?
You took me on a journey through your life.
You showed me places that you loved.
The house where you were born.
Showed me islands, palaces and lakes.
Led me over cobbled streets.

"A pity that it rained," you said,
At the end of that lovely day.
But *did* it rain?
If so, I never noticed it.
When you are there, when you are near
The sun will always shine.

2009

The Unexplained

How can one explain the inexplicable
When it isn't understood?
But nothing has ever seemed so right,
A sense of order and everything in its place,
As though I have known you all my life.
The recognition of a kindred soul.

There was no warning.
No stronger surge of blood.
No faster beating of the heart.
Only a sense of deep and lasting peace.
The need to be near,
To look, to talk, to touch
And give to you my life.

2015

Icarus

I am poised on the cusp of joy.
Flexing my wings
Ready to fly.

I want to soar with the eagles
And rise above the mountain peaks.
Swoop down upon the valleys
And panic the sheep and cows.
Soar up again above the trees
To greet the mountain snows.

I want to rest upon the thermals.
Drift amongst the billowing clouds.
I want to breast the stormy seas,
Sullen and dark below.
I want to circumvent the winter stars.
Encircle the moon.

One day soon when Spring explodes around me
I shall fly with the geese across the northern seas
To reach the lands of fire and ice.

I must not fly too near the sun.

2008

IMPASSE

You pride yourself
That you have never hurt a fly
And I, dumb fool,
Support you in your self-deceit.
You, with your twisted logic
Punishing me
For something you have done.
Because I never make a fuss
You never hear me screaming
Silently.

Perhaps if I behaved badly,
Giving you cause for complaint,
Sulked and made scenes,
Kept you in fear of me,
You would respect me
And value me higher.
How could I then respect
Myself?

And so I act perfectly,
Turning the other cheek.
Meekly submitting
To your blind, unthinking cruelties.

Wounded within.

Could you but hear me,
Could you but open your eyes,
Then, only then, might I find
The courage to speak.

1994

AUTUMN IN NORTH UIST

I am stunned by the beauty of this place.
Water lies upon land. More water than earth.
Mahogany inlaid with silver.
Drowned wilderness, seemingly endless,
Stretching away to the rim of the world.
A network of lochan and loch
Studded with wild swans and the winter geese.
Plover and dunlin, like late flowers of the *machair**,
Cluster in the grass,
Whilst lapwings rise to meet the salt mouth of the wind.

Vast skies swallowing up the land.
Bastions of cloud, fast flying,
Layered in white upon grey, outlined in gold.
Torn by the winds as easily as paper.
A black dot on an outsize canvas
The falcon circles, then plummets like a stone.

The watercolour landscape quickly turns to oils.
Touched by the sun, the red-brown grass turns to flame.
Green-gold islands, splashed with purple,
Rise against a storm-blue sky.
Shell-shaped beaches, blinding white,
Cradle a turquoise sea.

The long dead sleep in their chambered cairns
Or do they still walk?
Passing the passive cattle and the curious sheep,
Do they stand with the crofters in the fields
At the building of the haystacks and the cutting of the peat?
Are they there beside the living on the lochans
For the landing of the salmon and the fat brown trout?
In this timeless, treeless, haunted place
Anything is possible.

Sky, wind and water.
Water. Everywhere water
And always the wind.

1997

Machair: a plain, level or low land, an extensive beach.

Green

In the scorching heat of summer I think of green.
In this land of white-hot rock and dazzling light,
Where the slightest movement drenches
And the parched earth burns my feet,
I think of ice-cold streams and waterfalls
And in the stifling August nights
I think of gentle cooling rain.
In the burning gold of afternoon
I rest within the shuttered shade
And, lulled by the droning of the fan,
I drift into a dream of green.

I take the path through the glen,
Grey mist hiding the mountain peaks,
A milky sky filled with drizzling rain.
I see the snake-like tendrils of the new green fern,
The emerald grass along the track
And the deeper green of dark and ancient trees.
I see viridian moss upon the boulders of the burn,
In noisy peat-brown spate,
Full of the wealth of mountain rain.
I smell the moorland wind,
Heady with heather, pine and peat,
The green-spiced scent of bluebells

And the sharp, dank scent of earth.

I wake confused but for a while
The cool green spills over into the gold.
Then, as the hot day fades
Into a cooler night,
I count the days to autumn rains
When the first flowers spring from the barren earth
And this land, too, grows green again.

1985

Bread

Once there was bread for us.
So many loaves of it,
Fragrant and fresh, warm from the oven,
Temptingly new, smelling of heaven.
Eager to try it, we tore it apart.
We took what we wanted
And wasted the rest.

When times grew hard we laughed and said
That half a loaf was better than none.
We ate it in secret, each precious slice,
Keeping the freshness, tasting our heaven,
Making the most of the rest.

What we have now are the crumbs.
To those who are starving crumbs are a feast.
Remember the good times and savour them well.
They are all that is left.

There will be no more loaves,
For us.

1990

A German Requiem

As we drove through leafy Swedish lanes,
In the hot, blue haze of summer,
You played me Brahms.
"A German Requiem."
In happy, close, attuned companionship
We heard it to its end.
Behind my eyes the tears began to form
But stayed unshed
And, thankfully, you never knew that they were there.
The moment passed. We talked of other things.

And still we drove in summer heat
Under a blue, unclouded sky.
A tranquil landscape in the sun,
Small, blue lakes and shady trees.
Red-painted wooden farms and houses
Trimmed with white
Set amongst empty golden fields
And deep enfolding woods.
A dozen gem-like churches
And fleeting glimpses of the sea.

Now, when I play "A German Requiem"
On the darkest days of winter,

When the frost and fog lie deep upon the grass,
I shall remember summer heat
And that lovely day with you.

2010

Love Song

You are light lying upon water.
A field of ripening corn.
Birdsong at sunrise.
A tree in full bloom.

You are the song of the wind in the trees.
A moonlit path across a midnight sea.
A warm room on a cold, raw day.
The sunshine after storm.

You are the fire at the core of the earth.
The pull of the tide on the seas.
The voyage of the earth around the sun.
The other worlds beyond the stars.

2008

Late-Night Movie

I blunted the edges of grief with life in the fast lane,
Making new friends and travelling the world.
I built up my life again, brick upon brick,
Carefully plastering over the cracks.
I walled up the past.

At last, my daylight world stands firm and strong
And, if I think of you at all,
I smile and say
That what is past is dead and gone.
Now I am free.

But when night comes and I try to sleep,
Then starts again, my late-night movie show.
The flickering, moving pictures of the past.
The well-remembered scenes and those grown dim.
The full-supporting cast, the minor roles
And you, at the centre, glittering star,
Hogging the limelight, stealing the show.
Making me laugh, making me cry.
Crumbling my world into dust.

Now I am free of you.
Who am I kidding?

1998

All Souls Night

I dream of a past that is present.
Cloud-riven moon in the courtyard,
November wind at the door.
Your step in the shadows, your voice on the stair.
Smile meeting smile in the moon-splintered darkness.
Hands searching, caressing,
Mouth seeking mouth.
Flame-winged joy, soaring and circling,
Love piercing darkness with light.

I wake to the bleakness of winter.
Cold glimmer of stars, impervious moon.
The present erasing the past.

Far away in an old, walled city
An ancient house with empty rooms.
Cloud-riven moon in the courtyard,
November wind at the door.
Ghosts of remembrance.
Smiles of the dead.

Deep in the dark at the heart of the house
Do I still wait for you?
Do you still come?

1999

THE PASS OF DRUIMACHDAR

Above the hard, dark shoulder of the hill
The shrouded moon throws off her veils,
Flooding the pass with ghostly light.
Beside the track the swollen burn,
Filled with the snow-melt of an early spring,
Circles and swirls through lace-work snows.

Below the black, time-haunted hills
The train glides, smoothly on.
A monster, gentled by a master's hand,
Seeming to float above the silver track
In this desolate place.
The cloud swoops down upon the frozen hills
Blotting out moon and mountain snows.
Drawing down darkness, banishing light.

Weary at last, I lower the blind
And settle to sleep.
Drifting away on a river of sound
As the night train flows on
Through the Pass of Druimachdar.

1994

The Forsaken

You have stripped all the leaves from my tree,
Stolen the flowers from woodland and field,
Taken the sunshine away.

You have blown icy winds through my house,
Extinguished the fire on the hearth,
Buried me deep in the earth.

You have set me adrift in a boat without oars,
Left me to swim in a sea full of sharks,
Cast me ashore in a desolate place.

You have shattered my world into pieces,
Left me alone without hope,
Trampled my dreams in the dust.

2010

Phoenix

You came from the old men sitting in the sun,
Walking slowly but with purpose,
Fixing your gaze on mine
Until we came together face to face.
"I'm sorry," you said,
"For the hurt that I gave you.
I know now I was wrong."

Love rose then, from the ashes
And sped, a homing bird,
Straight to your outstretched hand.
Your hand was cold, an old man's hand
But your eyes were young in your lived-in face
Reflecting the love in mine.
Nothing had changed
For love had cheated time.

We stood, hands clasped,
Islanded in sunlight,
Amongst the watching eyes and listening ears.
So many things still left undone.
So many words unsaid.

After the fire rebirth.
I am alive. I am reborn

But as I rise and soar towards the sun,
I carry away a burden of sorrow
For the bitter waste of years
And an ache of longing
For the stillborn kiss,
That for a second, hung between us

2000

Question and Answer

You said to me,
"I'd like to see you cry.
I want to know how you'd look."
Why did you say that?
You're not a sadist.
More of a masochist.
Do you think I am so hard
That nothing troubles me?

I should have answered
But failed to do so,
"If you cracked the shell that I have grown
You would see the pain.
If you looked into my eyes
You would see the tears
But all you would see on my face
Is a smile."

Sometimes you baffle me.

2012

LOBSTERS

Grave news from Sweden.
The west coast lobsters are at risk
From distant cousins from America.

Not that that matters much to lobsters,
Their fate is sealed.
They just can't win, whatever transpires.

But I like to think that given the choice
They'd rather die for people like us.
Surely that's better than battling to death
With an alien horde?

It would be nice to think
That native lobsters
Could stage a rebellion
And banish the foe.
Then long could we both enjoy
The sweet, rich, succulent flesh
Of West coast lobsters.

2016

VASA

She looms out of the half-dark,
This ghost ship from a vanished age.
Vainglorious symbol of ambition and power.
Even above the noise of countless tourists,
French, Japanese, Americans,
She threatens from beyond the grave,
Caught out of time. She shouldn't be here.
And the hairs on the back of my neck
Begin to rise.

Later, when the crowds were less,
I went back to see this towering wall of wood,
Top heavy with guns and gold.
No wonder she sank on her maiden voyage.
I thought of the love and skill of those who rebuilt her,
Brought up from her grave on the floor of the sea
But I also thought of those who created her
And those who went down with her
Sacrificed for a monarch's vanity.

Now, when the museum is closed,
I think of her standing so tall and proud
As though ready to sail.
Brooding and silent, waiting in darkness,

Filled with a deadly menace
And I shudder.

2008

Pride of the Swedish Navy, 'Vasa' sank on her maiden voyage, in Stockholm's harbour in 1628. King Gustav Vasa's pride and ambition had caused her to be overloaded with guns and decoration. She would never have been seaworthy. 50 men drowned.

In 1956, 'Vasa' was discovered underwater almost intact, preserved by the brackish waters of the Baltic. Then began a 17-year project of salvage and conservation. In 1990 the museum housing her was opened to the public.

Dementia

They brought you to the bar today,
An old tree, rocking in the wind.
Your eyes met mine
But in your absent face your eyes were dead.
I saw that you thought that you knew me
But not who I was.

Amidst the noise and clatter
I watched you secretly.
You plucked at your sleeve again and again.
Lost in your world of silence.
Divided from us all.

But when I rose to leave
And the friendly farewells said,
You took my hand and smiled.
"Must you go yet?" you said.
Then I knew that you knew me,
A gleam of sunlight in the dark
But I had a flight to catch
And could not stay.

Perhaps it's better this way.
Never having to say goodbye.
    Maybe not.
        Either way it's heartbreak.

2006

Kilnave

Here in this place of treachery and death
I should sense evil within the ruined church,
Hear the clash of steel on steel,
The shouts and groans of dying men,
Smell the blood upon the ground.
Under a leaden sky, perhaps
But not today.

Under the clear, blue sky and summer breeze
The landscape opens wide.
Silver on tranquil blue, gold on green,
The sea, the earth, the sky,
A distant view of mainland hills.
I hear the bubbling curlew cry
And watch the tumbling dance of choughs.
Here I find healing, calm and peace.

Scatter my ashes here, below the kirkyard wall
And let the winds take them where they will.
One with the seasons, night and day.
One with the land, the sea, the sky.
I ask no place in Heaven.
Only this.

2001

AQUARIA

We had survived the hazards of the dark and scary forest,
Lit only by the lightning flash and gleaming waterfall.
Fumbled our way along the rail and up the steps.
Imagination held me in its grasp
And I thought of snakes and the poison-dart frog
Out amongst the tropical trees.
Not in reality, of course
And the poison-dart frog looked innocuous enough
In his small, glass-fronted cave set in the wall.

In the hot dark of the museum rooms
We saw sharks and pirhanas,
A host of fish like brilliantly coloured jewels,
Waving corals and the dance of lethal jelly-fish.

The biggest peril here
The screaming children round our knees.

We came into the sunshine of the restaurant,
Hot, damp and tired, in need of tea.
The place more like a crèche than eating place.
Resigned young mothers with their noisy babes,
Too young to join their siblings in the dark,
In charge of dad or grandmama.

I saw the thoughts pass through their infant brains.
"Well, this is food. What do I do with it?"
"I'm not sure that I want it."
We watched them hurl their sweeties on the floor
And turn their ice-creams upside down
To pour them on the ground.

You said, "I am glad I don't have children."
All I could think of was,
"I am glad I don't work here
And have to clean this mess up everyday."

But we both agreed, in retrospect,
We had enjoyed it all
Enormously.

2015

JOURNEY'S END

Is this then, the end of the road?
After the years of loving
Is this the place where we must part?
You, striding off along your chosen path,
Leaving me here to find my way alone.
When I look back I see the sunlight.
For you the sunlight lies ahead.

Standing here at the crossroads
I crave the impossible.
Longing to have again
That which I now have not.
Put back the clock
And let me live it all again
But play it differently.

The things you have forgotten
Are the things I can't forget.
I thought that love would end with death
But never that love could die.
That I loved you was never in doubt
But did you ever love me?
Did I see what I wanted to see?

If I went back along the road
Would I find the sunlight, too,
Was just an illusion?

1995

In The Argotti Gardens

The south wind blows, raising the ghosts of things long past.
Sweeping the shady paths between the lean and drowsy cats,
Whilst sharp against the milky sky
The fronded palm trees wave.
Above the city traffic, in cloying humid air
The dusty garden sleeps.

I walk between the crumbling bastions
Amongst the round, grey pots of cacti and of winter herbs.
Passing from sun to shade and back again
Beneath the flowerless jasmine in the pergolas.
Like small, white shreds of paper
The almond blossoms fall.
Torn letters in the dust.

I am filled with a strange, deep sadness,
Wanting I know not what.
Blown by the wind like the winter trees
Swung between darkness and light.
The voices of my dead are all about me
Drawing me back to a life long lost.

Give me the north-west wind
With its ice-edged discipline,

Sweeping away, the cobwebby memories,
Wiping my life's slate clean.
Blowing me into the future.
Slamming the doors on the past.

1987

DEDICATION

You made me what I am.
Showed me how to grow.
To see the other side of things.
Taught me to know myself,
The good things and the bad.
Through loving you I learnt to love myself
A little better.

You taught me the nature of love,
Showed me its secrets and its power.
Let it fly free if you want to keep it.
Ask nothing of it and it's yours
A hundredfold.

We, who have no future
Have, at least, the past.
I will carry you with me to my end
In body, mind and heart.

To you, my dearest love,
My better self, my friend,
I give my thanks.
I am what you have made me.

2006

A Culinary Tale.

He plucked me from the flock.
Skinned me and boned me,
Turned me inside out,
Prepared me for his table.
Oven-ready chick.

He served me up with his own special sauce,
Called me his "Dish of the Day."
Jazzed up my leftovers,
Swirled me in feasts of delight,
Fricassees, curries and soups
Until he got tired of the taste.

Then he dropped me from the menu.

1980

Wood

After the storm, the fallen trees
Lie in the wood like lifeless soldiers
On a battlefield.
I grieve for them
Lost in the prime of life and leaf.

But when I hold within my hands
Some small but tactile artefact,
Carved and shaped from wood
Or see some medieval sculpture
Made by a gifted long-dead hand
From some gigantic fallen oak,
I feel that the trees
Haven't died in vain
And I catch a fleeting glimpse
Of immortality.

2008

Hilda

She greets me at the breakfast bar.
Young, beautiful and black.
Graceful, slender,
Walks like a queen.

I help myself to meat and cheese,
Herring and salad, fruit.
My usual selection.
She stands beside me at the bar,
Topping up dishes,
Refilling bowls.

"And how are you today?" she says.
"Fragile," I say,
"I ate and drank too much last night."

She smiles her warm, bright smile.
"It's good to know," she sighs,
"Old people, too, can sometimes overdo it."

What can I say to that?
Nothing at all.
Because, of course, she's right.

2016

GOEPPINGEN

In memory of Elaine Israel, whose story this is.

I have been to a place where I never meant to go.
The town my mother knew before the Holocaust.
I buried my head in the sand like an ostrich,
Refusing to face the horrors of my family's past.

Now I have seen the streets my mother knew,
The house where she was born.
I have been to the school to which she went,
Walked where she walked in the hills above the town.

And with me walked the ghosts of family,
The ones I never knew. So many of them died,
Their names recorded on small cobblestones
Along the streets of Goeppingen.

My mother escaped, survived, began again in America.
Others of the family did not. Parents, sister, cousins.
All their rich legacy was lost
As though it had never been.

But I am glad I made this pilgrimage
Although there are horrors I would rather not have known

For I have found the roots from which I came.
I know now who I truly am.
My life is changed for ever.

2011

From the Ferry to the Capital

For a long time, when I boarded the bus
From the Ferry to the Capital,
I took a journey through my life.

The memories would wound,
Stab me to the heart.
The places that we knew and loved.
Memories of sunshine and of cloudless moon.

This was the bar where once we drank.
That restaurant was where we often went.
Paths where we walked. Roads where we drove.
The sprawling towns, the open fields, the sea.
Here you said this...there we did that...
But we laughed in the sunlight.
Sometimes we cried
For there are darker memories, too.
By journey's end I felt as though
I bled inside.

But life has begun again
And if I take this route
From the Ferry to the Capital
The memories remain

But what I feel is joy.
I have moved on.

New memories now but I am well aware
That these, too, have the power to wound.
Loving this place and you, my friend, so much
Would I have the strength to return
If the dark clouds form again?

2013

Caro Nome

I love your name
Two syllables. Eight letters.
Perfectly balanced. Winged.
I skim with it over the waves,
Swing it from the stars,
Fly it like a kite
And sleep with it under my hand.

Over and over I say your name.
Whisper it into the echoing corridors of night,
Softly like a prayer.
And under clear blue skies
I hurl it into the wind,
Watching it circle and dive
Like a hawk or a falcon.
Then I call it back to me
To settle on my arm.

2007

Waiting for Yesterday

Sometimes I am confused,
Sitting in the darkness, listening to voices in the street,
With the flicker of candles,
The wine and the glasses on the table
And the scent of freesias.
Is it now or is it then?
When you come, will you be as once you were
Or as you are now?

Out of the darkness a chilling thought strikes me.
Has time moved on another ten years?
Is the future now present yet past?
Nothing has changed.
The pattern is still the same.
The light of candles and strangers in the street
And I sit here with the wine and the freesias,
Waiting for yesterday.

1992

Quandary

You said, with a twinkle,
"How many more
Have you told about me?"
I, laughing, replied,
"Oh, just two or three."
Never mentioned the hundreds.

Wanting to tell them
How special you are.
Reluctant to say it to you.

2009

RODEL – ISLE OF HARRIS

Once before I came to Rodel,
Shrouded in mist and rain,
Its small church crouched upon a mound,
Its graveyard dark with ruined tombs.
Within the rough-hewn sandstone walls
Slept Alasdair Crotach, Macleod of Macleod,
Black effigied in gneiss,
Beneath his wondrous recessed tomb
Carved with things of a world that he knew,
His castle, his galley, scenes of the chase,
Angels and saints.
Fear struck me there in brooding half-light.
An ice cold shiver ran down my spine.
It felt as though the dead watched in the shadows.
Coward that I am, I fled.

Today, under cloudless skies and larksong,
Opening its arms to heaven,
The small church proudly stands
Poised amongst the high, green hills
Beside a turquoise sea.
I walk amongst the kirkyard stones,
Reminders of mortality.
Ship's carpenter lost at sea.

The young boy drowned in the ice.
The woman who lived to one hundred and five
And ancient stones too old to bear a name.

Within the church itself, shafted by sunshine,
With the voices of the living all around me,
Still I feel that prickle of fear.
Far from the things of this world that he loved,
His horses, his ship, his home and his kin,
Alasdair Crotach walks.

1996

Steps

Some things are still daunting.
A flight of steps up which I'd once have run,
Delighting in my power to do so.
Well, I can climb them now
But slowly
Without the lightness of heart.

Some things still frustrate me.
Watching the movements of a Scottish dance,
Longing to join the crowd as once I did.
Now I can only tap my feet in time,
Remembering the grace
And the gaiety of long ago.

Some things still cause me pain.
Wanting to run to you whenever we meet
And although my heart runs fast ahead of me,
Physical self walks slow and carefully,
Upright and smiling but watching the ground.

Well, maybe some day…?

2012

Ants

This year I had a plague of ants
Finding a way in through chinks and cracks.
"Poison them," they said,
"You don't want them indoors."
But I can't do that
They have a right to live.
More so, perhaps, than me.

The soldier ants present no stress,
They march right in, in well-formed rows
And march right out the way they came.
The only hazard here
The risk of squashing some
Beneath my feet.

The winged ones are a problem 'though.
They seem to have no sense.
I sweep them up in endless droves
And throw them out the kitchen door.
But still some fly around in mindless woe.
And sometimes, in the morning,
When I draw the blind
The last few remnants lie upon the sill
Clustered together for comfort or for warmth?

There's something endearing in that,
Almost human, in fact.

2015

Warning

I have been a fighter all of my life.
I am the champion of all lost causes.

I have fought in adversity to survive.
I have fought against pain and loss,
Loneliness, heartbreak and despair.
I have fought jealousy that cuts to the bone
And anger that corrodes.
I'll fight to the death for those I love.

I have fought for the underdog.
The old, the sick and the lonely,
For poor dumb beasts
And those who cannot fight for themselves.
Time and again I have been told
To mind my own business.

I never fight harder than when my back
Is up against the wall.
I don't take no for an answer.
I am a true friend
But a dangerous enemy.
So be warned.

If you want a fight you can have it
For even if you win
I won't go quietly.
I'll go down fighting.
All guns blazing.

2014

Gulls

Out of the night they came
In the bay of Trieste.
A snowstorm of gulls,
Fishing by the lights of the ship
And an autumn moon.

Following the ship, this ballet of birds,
Wheeling and dipping,
Riding the waves, and diving below.
Ethereal silver with gossamer wings,
Black in the darkness, out of the light,
Then turning again to a brilliant white.

And then we docked
Amongst the city lights.
As though they'd never been,
The gulls were gone.

2008

Walking on Eggs

Trying to forget
Is like walking on eggs.
One careless step
And the fragile shells shatter
Spewing forth pain.
Butterfly bright,
I skim through my days
Bottling up feeling.
Fire cased in ice.
Brittle as glass.

Sleep is a dark, tormented place
Ravaged by storms and a savage sea.
I wake, exhausted,
To a day without meaning.
Going through the motions,
Picking up the pieces,
Mastering the art
Of walking on eggs.

1995

Planting Wallflowers

High against the darkening autumn sky,
Uttering their harsh, insistent cries,
Southward fly a skein of geese.
Head cocked, bright eyed,
The robin sits in the strawberry tree,
Russet and brown against the cream-belled flowers.

Taking the sturdy plants
I ease their tortured roots into the ground.
Like them, I feel the comfort of earth,
Feeling the warm, dark texture,
Smelling its acrid scent.

The robin comes, companionably silent,
Cautious but keen, watching for worms.
Swiftly I plant, settling and smoothing.
Anger and pain flow out through my fingers
Into the soil.

There is no problem that cannot be solved.
There is no hurt that cannot be healed.
In the strength of the earth lie the memories of summer,
The promise of spring.

1996

White Linen

She placed the food in front of me,
Stopped and said,
"Is your perfume "White Linen?"
"Yes," I replied.
"I gave some to my mother
Not long before she died
And when I smell it now
I think of her," she said.
And I saw the sadness and the loss,
Still raw, written on her face.

When I got home I took the bottle out.
Not much left.
Not enough to cause embarrassment.
Next day I took the bottle
To that friendly, small café
And put it in her hands.
She hugged me then and cried.
"Put it in a drawer," I said
And every time you open it
You'll think that she is near."

Now when I come to town
And go there for a coffee

She comes and kisses me.
She has become a friend.

2016

Moonlight

The full moon unsettles me.
Turns me inside out
And upside down,
Draws me into the street.

Lapped in light, the silvered city sleeps
Under a quiet moon.
Deep in the shadows by the wall,
Like stars, their eyes shine out,
The little ghosts, the city cats,
Watching me pass
Or scurrying past me in a rush of air
On soundless paws.

My feet will draw me on
To the place where once,
Drunk with the wine of love,
I danced in the square
And curtsied to the moon.
No living soul is here.
Only my ghosts,
In the cathedral's shade.
Those I knew and loved,
Long gone before.

Then I run back along the silvered streets,
Scattering the waiting cats,
Back to the house.
I climb the stairs and draw the blinds
To shut out the moon
And wait for dawn
To bring back normality.

1999

A Prospect of Hills

I am tired of this pleasant place.
The golden fields, the endless skies,
The picture-postcard villages,
The lazy rivers snaking to the sea.

I hunger for the hills,
The hump-backed hills, leviathans,
Breasting their seas of cloud.

I crave the cry of eagles,
The autumn gales along the shore,
The violent waters, tumbling from on high.

I want the winter fire of bracken,
The acrid smell of peat,
The glory of the mountain snows.

I seek the scent of heather,
The blue and turquoise waters of the sea,
The gentle days of sun and rain.

Grant me, O Lord, before I die,
A small house near the sea
With a prospect of hills.

1993

Fear of Loss

I've lived with fear all the days of my life.
It's always lurking in the wings.
It strikes me in the small hours of the night
Depriving me of sleep.
It comes in the warmth of the day
When I am busy and untroubled.
It hits me in winter and summer alike
Without rhyme or reason.

I look at your face as you sit beside me,
Each line and blemish dear to me,
When I flower beneath your smile.
But in those moments of happiness,
I think how frail the body is
And how, between this time and the next
You could be gone forever from my life.
When the bottom will fall out of my world.

Why can't I just live for the moment
Instead of fearing what might lie ahead?
But however hard I try
I continue to live with the fear of loss.

2015

Commitment

I knew it at its source,
A gleam of silver in the grass,
Singing its siren song.
In the first, pale warmth of spring
I lay upon its banks,
Sailing my paper boats of dreams
And in the first, hot days of summer
I lingered in the shallows,
Carefree and wild, laughing at life.

But the stream is now a river.
The time for playing games is past.
I must launch my small craft into the current
And let the river take me where it will.
The river sings inside my head.
I do not know what lies before me,
What hidden rocks or sudden squalls,
Deep whirlpools or unfriendly shores.

Here, in this place where sea and river meet,
I can no longer see the land.
An endless stretch of water lies ahead,
Vast and deep, serenely calm.
The music in my head is now a symphony.

I tremble yet am unafraid.
Joyous and strong I reach towards the light.
There can be now no turning back.
This is my choice.
This is my fate.

1981

Tempus Fugit

Long ago when we were parted
You seemed light years away
And six months was eternity.
Time dragged its feet, reluctant to move on.
Life slowed and slept.
The days stood, marking time, row upon row
Waiting to be counted, in orderly lines.

Now you are gone time hurtles by
Gathering momentum.
Undisciplined days tumble over each other,
Squabbling and brawling, in haste to be gone.
Life stands at my shoulder
Hustling me on.

Could I but stop the clock,
Push back the walls of darkness
To let in light and space.
Then would I gather up the jumbled days,
Sort them into order in regimented rows,
Turn them around and march them back
To where you seemed light years away
And six months was eternity

1998

Two Sides of a Coin

(She)
The sunlight has blinded me.
I peer into the shadows seeking your face.
The others greet me with their smiles and friendly words,
Welcome me in, making a place for me
At your side.

You do not speak, lost in your silent world
But your eyes reach out to mine.
The conversation ebbs and flows,
The drinks pile up in front of us.
I value my friendship with these men.
I hold them in affection and respect
But all the time we laugh and talk
I am aware of no one else but you
And in the moment when the others cannot see
I lay my hand on yours
And, although I know you cannot hear me,
I softly say,
"I love you."

Then I leave quickly
Without looking back.

(He)
She stands in the doorway,
Framed by the sun,
Still beautiful to me.
Lighting the room.

I cannot hear their greetings
But I see their faces light in happy recognition,
As they make way for her
And place her next to me.

Lost as I am in silence,
I cannot talk and laugh
As once I did when I could hear
But I see her hands upon the table
And feel her warmth.

The food and drinks flow back and forth
Across the bar.
They laugh and talk together,
Setting the world to rights
But when the others cannot see
She turns and lays her hand on mine.
I watch her lips forming some words.
I cannot be sure but I think she said,
"I love you."

And then she is gone in a swirl of silk,
Taking the sunlight with her.

2004

Times Change

We came here for the peace and quiet.
For village life, the open fields.
Lark song at morning, owls at night.
The vast, wide skies.
The clarity of stars on moonless nights.
A minimum of traffic on the roads,
We knew each person in the place
By name or sight.

But the old ones died or moved away.
The place is full of strangers now.
The traffic whizzes up and down the lane.
It's a while now since I heard the larks
Although, I sometimes hear, an owl or barking fox.

They've built an urban ghetto at the end of the street.
Big houses crowded in where once were open fields.
And if sometime they want to have street lights
We'll have to lose the stars.
Suburbia has come to stay.

2016

SCHOOLGIRLS

It feels like sitting in a field full of starlings.
Islanded amongst these little girls of nine or ten.
They run to and fro, screaming and shouting,
Scattering pigeons and outraged cats.
Some have the promise of beauty.
Others have not.
Pigtails and pony tails, curly cropped heads.
They wear black tights and pleated tartan skirts.
They dazzle me with friendly smiles.
All so polite.

They eat their packed lunches.
Tantalize the resident cats
And then they are gone, with their teachers,
To continue their cultural tour.
Leaving the Gardens to pigeons and cats
In tranquil, sunny peace.

2009

Vegetables

I cut into last week's leeks for supper,
Stripping off layers to find the fresher parts
That are buried deep inside.
I'm still not used to cooking for one,
Still buy too many vegetables
And leave them far too long.

My carrots grow limp and potatoes grow shoots,
Broccoli wilts in the box in the fridge
But I usually manage to eat all the spinach
Before it all turns into mush.

When I have cooked them and some are left over
There isn't a problem with all that is left
But I do get tired of bubble and squeak
And endless containers of soup.

You'd think that by now
I'd have learnt how to judge it
But I fear that I haven't
And still have to race against time
To finish them up before they all rot.

2016

Distant Thunder

Laughing, we ran out into the night
Filled with brilliance and tumultuous noise.
Before we reached the car the drenching rain began.
Slamming the doors behind us, we shook ourselves like dogs,
Laughing still, then falling silent,
Excited by each other and the storm.
We sped away through empty streets
Into the hot October night.

Lightning sheeting pinkish-white
Limning the distant domes of churches,
The square, flat shapes of farms
And the bare, bleached rocky hills.
Forked lightning split the skies apart
Whilst the deafening thunder all about us
Clamoured and beat above the thirsty land.
Drumming and blinding, the curtaining rain
Bounded from rocks and dry stone walls
Turning our road to a river in spate.
Powerless against the flood
We stopped and waited for the storm to pass.

Inside our warm cocoon we turned to one another,
The air between us charged as the night outside,

The beating of our hearts one with the pounding rain.
Then here, our own sweet storm began.
With gentle hands you smoothed the wet hair from my eyes
And kissed my rain-washed face.

Now as I lie in the sultry summer night,
As the dark waits, holding its breath,
Crouched like an animal waiting to spring,
The sky sparks white against the sky
And distant thunder growls.
Memories of that other storm in another time, another place
Flood through my mind.
Again my face is wet
Not this time from the rain.

1996

Autumn Odyssey

I missed you when the ship set sail
On a night of salty, north-west wind.
In the motion of the sea beneath my feet
And the gentle throb of engines down below.

I missed you when between the squalls
A fitful sun shone on yellow leaves.
On sheep-grazed lawns, on silver lakes
And ancient greystone walls.

I missed you when the eagle soared and dived,
Scattering the mountain deer.
When in November sun, the basking seals
Lay on the rocks along a sandy shore.

I missed you when a small boat sped
Across an oiled silk, opal sea
In sunset light and hint of frost
Towards a small and friendly ship.

I missed you midst the laughter and the pleasant talk,
Dining on finest food and choicest wine
And in the comfort of my cabin's warmth,
Lulled by the movement of the sea.

When did I miss you most?
Impossible to say.
I missed you all the time.

2011

Island

You cannot be an island
However hard you try.
For our lives will always touch
The lives of others,
Linked to a mainland
By bridges and boats.

Ferries come and go
But the bridges stay strong.
Don't blow them up
Or let them rot away.

The winter seas are wild and cold
And even if you wanted to
You couldn't swim ashore.
Boats can be caught in ice
But the bridges still remain.
You cannot be an island
However hard you try.

2013

Water off a Duck's Back

It's all so long ago,
That irritating woman, with the fatuous smile,
With whom I worked.
Can't even remember her name.

"You're always so happy," she said,
"Nothing ever bothers you.
It's just like water
Off a duck's back."

I could have hit her but I didn't.
Just smiled. Said nothing.

It wasn't her fault.
It was I who wore the mask.
She knew nothing of the broken engagement,
The stresses and strains
Of caring alone
For old and ailing parents.

How could she have known?

2016

HIGH MASS AT STORKYRKAN

A Russian anthem sung at Högemässa
That almost stopped me in my tracks
As we went to take communion in the nave.

A lone soprano voice that rose above
The low hum of the choir
And soared around the ancient
Red-brick arches,
The great gold pulpit
And the medieval treasures of the nave.

Later, I said to you, "That voice."
And you agreed
How beautiful it was.
I hadn't seen the singer
From amongst the ladies of the choir
And I may never know
Whose voice it was
But for a moment the doors of Heaven opened wide
And I caught a glimpse inside.

2016

Storkyrkan: literally 'Great Church.' In this context the Cathedral in Stockholm.

Orkney Summer

Stark next the sky stand the black hills of Hoy
In the white-water nights.
In the quiet, grey town, the midsummer wind
Whistles and moans in the echoing wynds,
Like the keening of gulls.
Out on the Sound, circling and wheeling,
Fulmar and gannet weave patterns in silver
On burnished grey sea.
Pale blows the thrift in the tangle of grasses.
Pewter-grey seals dive in translucent light.

Smiling, you walk at my side on the shoreline,
Invisible prints in the milky-white sand.
For here, in my heart, to this place I have brought you,
Showing you beauty you never will see.
This garland of islands
Of wind and of seabirds,
The dark hills at sunset, the silent grey town,
The deathless-day wonder of white-water nights.

1992

Renaissance

I am in calm waters now.
Safe haven after storm.
These are uncharted shores
And I must learn their contours as I go
And yet, I seem to know this place.
I have been here in dreams
Or in another life
But never quite like this.

Here in this place I will put down roots and grow,
Striving to be the way I should have been.
You have melted the ice around my bones,
Brought warmth and comfort to my heart.
Now life begins again.
I am reborn.

2013

I Have Been Here Before

When we met I knew you.
Almost as well as I know myself.
I remembered you.

When did we meet before?
Two hundred years ago or so?
I had begun to think that in this life
You would never come.

Stupidly, I thought we would pick up
From where we had left off
But I had reckoned without
The intervening years.
You had forgotten me.

And that is why
It's been a long, steep climb
Back to the place
Where once we parted.

2016

Wolves and Bears

Long ago, when first we met,
You took me to the Zoo at Skansen
To see the wolves and bears.

The bears behaved perfectly,
There in full view
But the wolves, in their pit,
Refused to appear.

"Shall I climb down?" you cried,
With that mixture of mischief and charm
I have grown to know so well.

I fell in love with you that day.
Fell in love for ever
And over the years that love has grown
And still continues to grow.

"Shall I climb down?" you cried.
I'm glad that you didn't.

2016

Graffiti Artist

She stood beside me in a shop,
Not much younger than myself.
"Do you sell spray paint?" she asked.
I couldn't resist the challenge,
Turned to her and said,
"Are you into Graffiti?"

She blinked, then smiled and said,
"No. I've a dead tree in my garden, a conifer.
I thought it might look better
If I painted it green."

Now I've heard
Just about everything.

2016

MYSTERIOUS YORKSHIRE

RUPERT MATTHEWS is a noted author on folklore, ghosts and other aspects of that parallel universe which sometimes intrudes on our own. Rupert has spent a lifetime investigating the paranormal and the bizarre. He has written over 100 books for adults and children including *Mysterious Cornwall*, *Haunted Places of Devon*, *Haunted Places of Kent* and *The GhostHunter's Guide to England*.

MYSTERIOUS YORKSHIRE

RUPERT MATTHEWS

First published in Great Britain in 2011 by The Derby Books Publishing Company Limited, 3 The Parker Centre, Derby, DE21 4SZ.

ISBN 978-1-85983-946-1

Printed and bound by Melita Press, Malta

CONTENTS

Introduction

Yorkshire is stunning. Quite simply stunning. It is not only the good people of Yorkshire who think so, though they are justifiably proud of their county. Outsiders are bewitched by its charms and appeal. That most Yorkshire of vets, James Herriot, was a Durham man by birth, but found his home in Yorkshire.

The county is vast; it covers some 6,100 square miles, or at least it did before the unpopular local government reforms of 1974. This book deals with the historic county of Yorkshire – God's Own County, as it has rightly been nicknamed. That county has some of the most distinctive and obvious natural boundaries of any English county – boundaries that would do justice to an independent country. And Yorkshire once held that title, too.

To the west are the rolling waves of the North Sea. The waters have provided careers for generations of Yorkshiremen. Some have been fishermen, others have worked the coastal ships, and a few travelled much further overseas. James Cook, explorer of Australia and the Pacific Islands, was the most famous of the many Yorkshiremen to seek a life on the high seas.

To the north is the Tees Valley, running inland from the sea. The mighty Tees is 85 miles long, and was once one of the wildest and grandest of English rivers. The lower reaches have been

A narrow, unnamed road wriggles through Oxnop Ghyll on its way from the high moors of Askrgigg Common down into Swaledale at Gunnerside. The mists of Yorkshire hide more than sheep in their mysterious embrace.

tamed over the past three centuries, as increasing industrialisation of towns such as Middlesborough, Thornaby and Redcar have made it necessary to make the river straighter, deeper and easier to navigate. The upper reaches, by contrast, remain as wild and desolate as they ever were. These turbulent miles of river are marked by waterfalls and rapids as the river falls down from the Pennines.

It is those towering Pennine Mountains that form the western boundary of Yorkshire. The northern Pennines are made of a form of limestone, which produces some of the finest turf for sheep to be found anywhere in Britain. The grass is dark-green and highly nutritious for almost all of the year. Here, the Pennines are marked by dales where rivers have cut deep into the hills. The soil in the lower valley floors produces grass as ideal for cattle as the hill grass is for sheep. No wonder Wensleydale has produced premier cheeses since at least the 12th century. South of Airedale, the hills are made of millstone grit, which produces heather and thin, weak grass. Few sheep live here, and dairy products are almost unknown.

The southern boundary of the county is marked in the east by the great Humber Estuary, in the central region by the lower stretches of the River Aire, and in the west by what, in medieval times, were extensive swamps and marshes, now drained to hold the industrial conurbations around Huddersfield and Holmfirth.

Within these natural borders, Yorkshire has developed a character all of its own. That applies as much to its mysterious aspect as it does to its human or natural faces. The Barguest roams the woods, fields and even the cities of Yorkshire on its eternal, supernatural patrols. It terrifies any human who meets it with its ferocious snarl, blazing eyes and monstrous teeth, although exactly what it is really up to is anyone's guess. Nor is it the only mysterious animal to roam Yorkshire: the Church Fenton Tiger hit the national headlines in 2006 and led police a merry dance around the River Ouse as they tried to track this fierce and elusive beast. And Yorkshire had more dragons of more fearsome habits than any other county in England.

Constantine the Great, Emperor of Rome, was proclaimed ruler by the legions at York, but how many of the other tales told about him in Yorkshire are true is unknown. Nor is the identity of Old King Cole entirely certain, although his base of power at York is beyond doubt. King Arthur rode this way after the Romans left and, if local legend is to be believed, he is here still, sleeping beneath Richmond until his country needs him once more.

The saints of Yorkshire have been a mysterious bunch. One saint may even be a Christianised version of the local pagan goddess Brigantia. Another, the mighty miracle-worker St John of Beverley, was real enough, but almost nothing is known of him. As for St Ailred of Rievaulx, he had some dark and mysterious sin in his youth that he hid from those he knew in later life, but which has guaranteed him fame in places as diverse as California and the Philippines.

Witches, warlocks and wizards have inhabited Yorkshire since time immemorial, and few denizens of Yorkshire's mysterious world have been so misunderstood. Old Mother Shipton worked wonders in her lifetime and foretold the future with uncanny accuracy, but many of the her best-known sayings were invented generations later by people with their own motives and agendas. Some wicked people have used the pretence of witchcraft as a cover for very human crimes, as did Mary Bateman in 1809, who was hanged for her trouble. Others indulged in very real forms of 'magic' – hypnotism and medicinal herbs – to achieve good things and gain fame. Wizard Wrightson was a spectacularly successful magic-worker of the 19th century.

Giants have also walked in Yorkshire, as has the Devil himself and numerous lesser demons. Springs and wells have miraculous powers, and some have their ghosts. And the fairies and assorted little people dance about on business of their own.

Other aspects of the mysterious in Yorkshire are more conventional. The county has its phantom white ladies, spectral cavaliers and ghostly monks, as does every other county in the kingdom. It also has its poltergeists, with the infamous Black Monk of Pontefract being one of the best-documented and most-investigated poltergeist mystery in the record books.

There is an intangible quality about Yorkshire that is uniquely mysterious. It cannot be touched and it cannot be pinned down. Some locals and more visitors miss it altogether. But for those who are able and willing to pause and look about themselves, the magical and the supernatural are never far away. There is much to gaze at in Yorkshire, be it the splendours of the City of York, or the wild, remote heights of the Pennines. And everywhere there is something odd and mysterious, sometimes caught in the corner of the eye, but gone as soon as it is looked at.

Yorkshire is simply stunning. So are its mysteries.

CHAPTER I

Mysterious Giants and Devils

Giants loom large in Yorkshire. They were enormous beings who lived many centuries ago, at a time when the world was young and humans were still trying to find their way. Traditionally, giants are said to have lived in Britain before humans came along, and they are said to belong to some older and more powerful race of beings. Some are said to have been so vast that they could make hills by scraping mud off their boots and their strides were three miles long. Other giants were more realistic in stature, standing some 20 or 30ft tall.

Either way, giants are usually credited with prodigious physical strength, but severely limited brain power. Many stories about giants show them to be wicked, evil or greedy, and able to overcome all opposition due to their great strength, although most are eventually outwitted and defeated by some local sage.

It is interesting that in Yorkshire the deeds and feats of giants are often matched by those ascribed to the Devil. Quite why this should be so is something of a mystery; perhaps stories that were originally about the Devil have changed over time to be about less demonic giants, or perhaps the tales were really about giants, but have been made more frightening by being putting the Devil as the protagonist. Some have looked for a common origin for the stories. In early Christian times the old pagan gods were routinely dismissed as demons or devils, and many stories concerning pagan gods have survived in the guise of tales about the Devil. It may be that at least some of the giants that are to be found around Yorkshire were originally pagan gods.

One such may be the giant that once lived at Sessay, above the Swale, south of Thirsk. This gigantic man was in the habit of eating the local sheep at the rate of one a week, and of scoffing the shepherds at the rate of one a year. Such a regular appetite sounds more like a routine sacrifice rather than the irregular cravings of a huge appetite, and this pattern has led some to suppose that the Sessay giant was some local pagan deity.

Be that as it may, the giant one day fell into a deep sleep beside the stream that flows past the southern end of the village. There, he was sighted by a local man named Dawnay, who decided to take advantage of the wicked giant's slumbers. He grabbed a pickaxe, crept up on the giant and smashed in his skull with a single, mighty blow. News of the feat spread far and wide, coming to

The Devil in his traditional appearance as a horned and cloven-hoofed demon. When the Devil pays his occasional visits to Yorkshire he sometimes comes in this hideous guise, but may also disguise himself as a wealthy gentlemen to mislead the unwary.

the ears of the king, who was visiting York. The king sent for young Dawnay to hear the tale first-hand. The king then gave Dawnay the manor of Sessay and all the lands around.

That family is still around, for the 12th Viscount Dawnay succeeded to his title in 2002. Some suspect that an ancestral Dawnay hijacked the existing story of the local giant killed while asleep to enhance his family's reputation and explain how they came to hold their estates.

A very similar tale is sometimes recorded about a giant that lived in Dalton. The Dalton giant is said to have been one-eyed, but otherwise was very similar to the Sessay giant, with a regular appetite for local sheep. In this case, the giant fell asleep beside the watermill below Eldmire Moor. There, he was spotted by a Dalton lad named Jack, who sprang into action by whipping out his knife and plunging it into the giant's solitary eye. The blinded giant then was then easy prey for the local men. The lane leading from the village to the mill is now known as Blind Piece Lane. It must be said that Jack's efforts sound suspiciously like the exploits of the Greek hero Odysseus, who blinded a cyclops in similar fashion.

Given that Dalton lies barely two miles west of Sessay, it has been suggested that the two stories relate back to the same origin. Perhaps the original tale was adapted in Sessay by the Dawnay family, while in Dalton it was altered by some local who had a classical education and so grafted the details of Odysseus onto the local story.

One Yorkshire giant whose fame eclipses all others is Wade. Tales about the great Wade are found scattered far and wide, particularly in the northern part of the county, where he seems to be particularly linked to moors and the bleak uplands. Wade is said to have been the son of a land giant and a sea giantess, and stories about him often mention that he had a boat named Wingelock. It is quite clear that there were originally many more stories about Wade than have survived down to the present day. In his famous work *Troilus and Criseyde,* the 14th-century poet Geoffrey Chaucer wrote:

With sobre chere, although his herte pleyde:
And in the feld he pleyde tho leoun;
He song; she pleyde; he tolde tale of Wade.

Clearly, Chaucer expected his audience to know what 'tale of Wade' he meant, so we can assume that the tale was widely known. From such hints it would seem that Wade was a tricky chap, much given to practical jokes of a violent character. He also seems to have been linked closely to fords and rivers, although his boat seems to have been a seafaring craft.

The link between giants of old and the pagan gods is clear in Wade's family. He is said to have been married to a giantess named Bell and to have had three sons, the eldest of which was Wayland. Bell may be the same as the Celtic solar deity Belenos. Wayland, however, is definitely known to have been Norse god. Wayland has a long and convoluted legend all of his own, which involves a vicious feud and a bloody revenge, as well as a cast of other gods and heroes. If Wade is the father of Wayland, then he too must be a pagan deity of some kind.

Be that as it may, Wade's appearances in Yorkshire are widespread. At Eskdale, it is said that Wade helped in the construction of Mulgrave Castle, while Bell worked on Pickering Castle. The two powerful giants worked the stone with ease, but they had only one hammer between them. When Wade needed the hammer he would bellow at Bell, who would throw it to him across the many miles of moorland between the two building sites. When Bel needed the hammer she would shout and Wade would toss it back.

Meanwhile, the giant couple kept their cow on Egton Low Moor, also in Eskdale. Wade was always thirsty for milk and constantly sent his wife up to Egton Moor to milk the cow. Young Wayland, then a mere babe, got fed up with his mother's absences and one day shouted for her return. Bell ignored the infant's cries, so Wayland picked up a boulder and hurled it at her head. The rock hit Bell's head with such force that it broke neatly in two and fell to the ground. The boulder in two halves remained a notable local landmark until the 18th century, when it was smashed up to provide stones to make the foundations of a new road over the moor, now the A171.

South of Eskdale rise the windswept heights of Wheeldale Moor. Wade decided to build a road over Wheeldale Moor to link Pickering and Mulgrave. He set to work, splitting stones and carefully laying them out to form a smooth surface for his road, and digging drainage ditches on either side of the road. Bell helped Wade by gathering up suitable rocks from across the moor and carrying them to him in her apron. On a couple of occasions the apron strings broke under the strain, and each time Bell left the great heap of stones where they fell. They remain to this day as cairns on the high moor.

Also still there is the road, known as Wade's Causeway. In places it has been overgrown by bogs and heather, and elsewhere the stones have been taken by farmers to build houses and shelters. The most complete section that can be easily visited stands just off the road from Newton on Rawcliffe, over Wheeldale Moor to Egton Bridge. The road is signposted off the road about 400 yards north of the Wheeldale Beck.

This road is something a mystery in itself. Local stories ascribe it to Wade, but historians and archaeologists have sought a more rational origin, though without much success. From the late 18th century onwards it was widely assumed that the road was Roman in origin; it began near Cawthorn, where there was a small Roman fort, then ran north over the moors to end close to Lease Rigg, the site of another small Roman military site. Moreover, if the road had originally continued south, it would have met a known road running from the city of York, Eboracum in Roman times, to the larger legionary fort at Malton.

In addition to its route, the road had some key Roman features. It was flanked on either side by a drainage ditch and was more or less straight. It had clearly taken a huge amount of effort to build, with many thousands of hours of hard work going into its construction. Such an effort would have required a strong authority with the ability to muster together large gangs of workmen and pay, or persuade, them to do the work. Not only that, but the authority needed to have a very good reason for wanting a road over the bleak moors. The Roman military seemed to fit the bill perfectly; they had forts in the area, faced a hostile barbarian enemy a few miles north at Hadrian's Wall and certainly had the manpower to construct a road of this type.

But, in the later 20th century, archaeologists re-examined Wade's Causeway and began to have their doubts. First, the road may have followed a roughly straight course, but it had some

Wade's Causeway is the most mysterious road in Yorkshire. Legend has it that this beautifully surfaced road over the high moors at Wheeldale was built by the giant Wade. Archaeologists have sought a more rational origin for the road, but have failed to find any explanation on which they can agree.

decidedly un-Roman bends along the way. Furthermore, it did not seem to run to the Roman sites at Cawthorn and Lease Rigg, but only close to them. Finally, the construction techniques were clearly not standard Roman military practice. Roads constructed for marching men were almost always composed of layers of graded gravel and sand, with the finer layers on top. These were then pounded flat to compress them and give a firm, dry marching surface. Roads in towns or those intended for heavy carts were made of compressed gravel topped by smooth, usually square, flagstones.

Wade's Causeway, in contrast, was made of flat stones of irregular shape, rather similar to those used today to make drystone walls. These had been put on top of a layer of black peat, which had been spread out to produce a flat surface over the irregular moorland ground. These materials are to be found in large quantities all over the moor, so they would have been very easy to gather and use. Roman military road builders, however, are not known to have used this technique anywhere else.

By the 1990s the general opinion had been reached that Wade's Causeway was not Roman. That left the problem of when it had been built, by whom and why. Before the Romans came the area was ruled by the Celtic Brigantes tribe. This was a rich and powerful kingdom that could certainly have mustered the manpower to build Wade's Causeway. Why they would have wanted to do so, however, is unclear. The Celts of Britain did not go in for building roads, and there does not seem to have been any pressing economic or military reason for the tribal rulers to want to cross the moors with a road apparently designed for marching men.

After the fall of Roman Britain, the area came under the rule of the English Kingdom of Northumbria. Again, the early English did not build roads, although they did make great use of Roman routes and repaired them from time to time. By the time of the Viking invasions, roads were even less likely to have been built, as warfare disrupted the government of the area and made it unlikely that anyone would be able to muster enough men to build Wade's Causeway, even if they had wanted to do so.

The answer to the riddle may lie in the poorly known period that followed on from the withdrawal of the regular Roman legions in AD 410 and the establishment of English rule about 550. This is a true Dark Age for Yorkshire, with very little written history and little more archaeological remains. It would appear that auxiliary troops were left behind when the legions left. They had the task of manning Hadrian's Wall and countering raids coming in from the sea. Sometime around AD 500, the central authority of post-Roman Britain collapsed and the northern part of the province split off into one or more independent states. It may be that Wade's Causeway belongs to this period. The auxiliaries would have known something of Roman military engineering, while the pressing need to protect the coast and river valleys may have provided a need for a marching road over the moors.

Then again, perhaps it was the giant Wade and his wife, Bell, who built the road. They seem to have been busy elsewhere in Yorkshire. Wade is also said to have erected the gigantic standing stone just south of Goldsborough, although no reason is given for this exploit.

Wade is said to have died at a ripe old age, and in some sources is called Wade the Old. He is usually said to lie buried overlooking the Sandsend Beck near Mulgrave. According to a writer in the 1540s, 'Mulgrave Castle standith on a craggy hill, and on each side of it is a hill higher than that whereupon the castle standeth. The north hill on the toppe of it hath stones commonly called Wade's Grave, whom the people here say to have been a giant and the owner of Mulgrave.' Approximately 20 years later William Camden came this way and recorded an extra detail. Wade (whom he calls Wada) was a Duke before the Norman Conquest who was defeated in battle and returned to Mulgrave, where he fell ill and died: 'And here between two solid stones about seven foote high he liethe entombed. Which stones because they are 11ft asunder the people doubt not to affirm that he was a mighty giant.' Of the two stones marking Wade's Grave, only one now remains, and that is on private land and not easily accessible to the passerby. What happened to Bell is unknown.

Wherever the Yorkshire giants went and whatever they did, it seems that the Devil was close on their tracks. Just as the giants are credited with erecting standing stones, so is the Devil. At Rudston is the largest prehistoric monolith in Britain. It stands in the churchyard, just yards from the west door of the church itself. The monolith is just over 25ft tall, although until 1861 it stood at 30ft. In that year the sloping churchyard was levelled off and 5ft of the stone covered up with soil. The top is now covered with lead sheeting to protect what is clearly a top broken by frost damage. Assuming that the stone tapered to a point, it would have been around 5ft taller. With a broken top and buried base, the stone must have been around 35ft tall and over 42 tons in weight when originally erected.

The stone is thin, with two flat faces. One face has fossilised dinosaur footprints going up it, while the other faces toward the midwinter sunrise. There is a second, smaller stone of a similar type in the churchyard. This was moved during the ground levelling, but is thought to have originally stood very close to the larger monolith.

The stone was excavated in the 1780s by a local gentleman and lately has come in for more recent study. It is now believed that the stone was erected during the Bronze Age, about 1600BC, at about the time that Stonehenge was reaching its largest size. The stone is composed of a type of cayton sedimentary rock, the natural source of which is about 10 miles away. The presence of a number of human and animal skulls around its base may mean that it had a sacrificial role, but the skulls remain undated, so this cannot be confirmed. Interestingly, Rudston stands near the Gypsey Race, a stream which flows past several other ancient monuments, such as the Argham Henge and Cursus, on its way from the wolds to the sea at Bridlington.

According to local legend, the stone was thrown by the Devil as he walked over the wolds. Apparently, he saw the villagers building the church and was so angry that he picked up the huge stone and hurled it at Rudston in an effort to demolish the church. He missed, but the stone remains as a mark of his anger. Presumably, this tale is an indication that the stone was sacred to the pagan gods. These gods were routinely described by early Christian missionaries as being demons or devils, and have survived in this form in folk tales and legends.

A rather similar tale tells that the Devil was one day walking over High Moor, northwest of Richmond, when he sat down for a rest on a huge stone. As he eyed the landscape malevolently, the Devil chanced to see the villages of Hartforth and Gilling. Suddenly angry,

The great standing stone at Rudstone is said to have been thrown by the Devil, angered by the devotion of the Christian villagers. In fact, it is a prehistoric monolith dating to approximately the same period as Stonehenge, although what its original function or purpose may have been is obscure.

the Devil stood up, picked up the rock on which he had been sitting and hurled it at Hartforth, shouting out:

> 'Have at thee Black Hartforth
> But have a care of Bonny Gilling!'

The stone overshot Hartforth and landed on the slopes of Gatherley Moor, near the appropriately named Rock Farm, where it still lies. The Devil's fingerprints can be seen in the form of deep impressions on the side of the rock. Quite what the Devil had against Hartforth, nobody can tell, nor do they know why he seemed to like Gilling.

The Devil's aim was not much better when walking over Howe Hill, overlooking the River Ure. He spotted the good folk of Aldborough going to church to worship God and took deep offence. The Devil picked up a great stone and hurled it toward the village church. As he did so, he shouted out:

> 'Boroughbridge keep out o' the way
> For Aldborough town
> I will bring down.'

The village of Gilling was apparently favoured by the Devil, although why this should be is quite a mystery. Certainly, legend has it that he sought to destroy Hartforth, while saving Gilling. Credit: James F. Carter jfc.org.uk

The largest of the Devil's Arrows, which stand beside the A1 near Boroughbridge. This huge monolith is over 22ft tall and is flanked by two others, only slightly smaller. It is unclear if the distinct vertical grooves running down these stones were made by humans or by nature.

He missed, so he threw a second, which got closer, but also missed. He then threw a third and got closer still, following that with a fourth. When this final stone also missed, the Devil gave up and stomped off in a black mood. The stones were left standing where they had fallen: in a straight line running almost north to south. One of the stones toppled in the 16th century and was broken up for use building a bridge, but the remaining three Devil's Arrows remain.

Despite the tale, the raising of these stones is, in fact, of Bronze Age date. The tallest of the three is over 22ft tall and is, after Rudston, the tallest monolith in Britain. The other stones are only slightly shorter and stand 200ft and 370ft from the central monolith. Each of the stones is marked by distinctive fluting, which runs from the top to about halfway down the sides. Opinion is divided as to whether the marks are natural or manmade.

A clue to the original purpose might be found in the fact that the stones line up with the most extreme southerly point at which the moon rises. Since at least medieval times, and possibly much longer, a great fair was held around the stones on Midsummer's Day. By the 16th century the fair was dedicated to St Barnabus, whose feast day falls on 11 June. The fair seems to have declined in the 18th century and ceased altogether during the Napoleonic Wars.

The Devil's Arrows are among the best-known Bronze Age monoliths in northern England, since they stand very close to the A1 just south of Boroughbridge and are a well-known landmark. Actually finding them on foot is not so easy, however, as they lie on private farmland and are not signposted.

The similarly named Devil's Stone on Addlebrough Hill near Bainbridge manages to link the Devil with the giants. Apparently, the hill was once the home of a mighty giant. Unlike most giants, this particular one was friendly toward humans and went out of his way to help the shepherds and others who came up to the high lands above the River Ure. The Devil got to hear about this and took offence. He decided to teach the friendly giant a lesson.

The Devil came walking down Raydale, and when he reached Semer Water he halted and bellowed a challenge to the giant, who was sitting on Addlebrough Hill. The giant answered in a belligerent manner, telling the Devil to mind his own business. The Devil then picked up a huge boulder and hurled it at the giant. He missed, as he so often seems to have done, and the rock came to rest just west of the crag on which the giant sat. It is still there, complete with holes said to be the Devil's fingerprints. Angered, the giant picked up a granite boulder in each hand and threw them at the Devil. His aim was rather better, for each boulder hit the Devil on a cloven hoof, causing him to yelp in pain and make off back to whence he had come, thus leaving the giant in possession of Addlebrough. The stones that hit the giant also remain, lying by the shore of Semer Water.

The Devil got on rather better with the giant Horcum, who lived on Lockton Low Moor, beside what is now the A169 south of Saltergate. Horcum was not content with the height of his home and wanted to build a new hill on which to live. He began digging out soil and rocks, piling it up on a ridge to the east. When the Devil came along, he offered to help. With a single scoop of his mighty hand he tore out a vast quantity of rocks and earth, dumping the huge mass on the giant's mound. He thus created the steep-sided hillock of Blakey Topping and the equally steep-sided chasm of The Hole of Horcum.

The great Black Tom Bell that hangs in the church tower at Dewsbury Minster is rung hundreds of times on Christmas Eve to keep the Devil out of Dewsbury for another year. Credit Michael Taylor.

Given his propensity for hurling gigantic rocks about, it is no wonder that the good folk of Yorkshire have come up with various ways to keep the Devil at bay. In Dewsbury Minster there is a gigantic bell named Black Tom, which was donated in the 15th century by local landowner Sir Thomas de Soothill, who had murdered a servant boy in a fit of rage and escaped execution by carrying out a number of penances, of which donating a new bell was one. Every year on Christmas Eve the bell is tolled once for every year since Christ's birth. By tradition, the final ring must take place precisely at midnight in order to keep the Devil banished from the streets of Dewsbury.

Rather more prosaically, the final ring also marks the opening of casks of the specially produced Devil's Knell. This beer is produced by a local brewer each year and is a tasty, reddish-coloured bitter of 4.8% strength.

At Kirkby Malham stands the ancient church of St Michael Archangel. The present church dates back to 1490, but there was a church here at least as early as the 870s and maybe before that. It is the custom to leave open a small door in the North Aisle during baptisms. The idea is that when the Holy Spirit enters the church to accept the soul of the infant, any demons that are present should have a way of escape to stop them hanging about and causing trouble. The door thus gained the name the Devil's Door.

The churchyard at Kirkby Malham is a pleasant spot, but it would be unwise to stop here for a picnic. The Devil is said to have the nasty habit of leaving succulent food lying about, then snatching the soul of anyone foolish enough to eat it. Credit: Immanuel Giel.

Dibbles Bridge carries the B6265 over the River Dibb north of Appletreewick. Nobody knows when this stout stone bridge was built, nor who did the work. Local legend has it that the Devil constructed the bridge as thanks to a local man who had unwittingly helped the evil one to do his work.

It is also said that the Devil himself visits the churchyard once each year. He sets out a spread of delicious foods as if somebody has planned a picnic, but had been called away. The Devil is seeking to tempt passers-by into eating some of the food, whereupon he will be able to pounce and claim them as his own. Local folk are, of course, wise to this trick; back in Victorian times, however, they forgot to tell their new curate. He was leaving the church one day when he spied the demonic food and was tempted to take a bite. Fortunately for him, he had some salt in his pocket and sprinkled this on the food before he ate. This simple action saved his eternal soul, since the Devil, it is said, cannot stand salt.

Strange to tell, but the Devil is not always hostile to Yorkshire folk. When seeking to destroy Aldborough he spared Boroughbridge, and he seems to have been just as kindly disposed to Gilling. Neither village gained much from such demonic favour, but the people of Dibbdale did. The River Dibb flows strongly between steep banks and can be impossible to ford after rain. According to an old story, the old farm beside the Dibb was home to a man skilled in cobbling. One dark night, a tall, well-dressed stranger came knocking at the door. The stranger had broken the heel on his boot and asked the man to mend it, which he did. The stranger grinned in a sinister fashion when asked for payment. He left without handing over a penny, but promised the man something better than monetary gain. Next morning the man woke up to find a new stone bridge over the river.

The bridge has stood ever since, but its existence has not always been without incident. On 27 May 1975 a coach carrying a party of pensioners on a day out to Grassington, Ripon and Knaresborough was coming down the long, steep hill that leads to the bridge from the east. The coach's brakes failed and the vehicle plummeted into the ravine, killing the driver and 31 pensioners. It is the worst coach crash ever to have occurred in the UK.

Exactly how old Dibbles Bridge really is, nobody is sure. It would seem that a ford existed when a map was drawn in 1750, but that the bridge was standing by 1842. The stonework is strong enough to carry modern traffic, as the road over it is now the B6265. Other than the initials 'JG' carved onto one of the stones, there is no clue to its construction. Perhaps the Devil did build it, after all.

CHAPTER 2

Mysterious Fairies and Little People

The fairies, or the little people, are a remarkably mixed group of Yorkshire folk, who are to be found in villages, woods, fields and towns, up on the hills, down in the valleys and capering along the coast or beside rivers. Some are friendly to humans and a few are hostile, although most seem to be indifferent to our activities as long as we stay out of their way. But the fairies must never be trifled with, nor treated with disrespect, for they are a touchy sort and prone to inflict a nasty revenge for any slight.

The word 'fairy' is, in fact, a French term that was imported to England in Tudor times to serve as a catch-all term for the assorted elves, pixies, boggarts, brownies, hobs and pucks that populate the UK. These various folk each have their own character and distinguishing features, as we will see, but they also have a lot in common. The various races of fairy are generally humanoid in shape, but are very definitely not human. They invariably have magical powers of some sort, although some are more powerful than others. The fairies are almost always capricious

A group of fairies flitter through the skies on gossamer wings in a 19th-century book illustration. This romanticised image of the little people is far removed from the often harsh reality of their exploits in Yorkshire.

and unpredictable; they are reliable for being unreliable. The ability to become invisible to humans is another common characteristic, with some fairies being permanently invisible, while others adopt it as a disguise from time to time.

Many fairies have the power to fly, or at least to travel with supernatural speed, but others plod about with a more standard walking pace. Whether they can fly or not, they do not have wings, but rely on magic for levitation. The size of fairies varies enormously. Some are as big as regular humans, others are the size of a 10-year-old child. Only a very few are smaller than that, although there are some that can scamper about down rabbit holes or slip through keyholes.

Most fairies dress in green or, sometimes, red, but rarely in any other colour. Generally, the fairy clothes are similar to those of humans, although fairies do tend to prefer old-fashioned outfits and almost invariably wear a hat or cap of some kind. They certainly prefer the countryside over the town and are most often encountered by lone humans in some out of the way location. They are usually said to be fond of wild plants and wild animals, caring for them or protecting them with fervour.

Although they like moving in our world, most fairies seem to have another world to which they can go. This is often said to be accessed through some local landmark, such as a cave, hill or stream. There, the fairies live in a society of their own, with rulers, weddings, parties, dances, workshops and other features that generally echo the features of human society.

Quite what might lie behind the tales of the little people is open to question. Many stories about fairies state that they once inhabited Britain, but that when humans arrived they were defeated or driven out and fled to another, parallel world where they were safe from humans and human inventions. This widespread account of the origins of the fairies has led some scholars to think that the tales may have originated at the time that farming folk first came to Britain.

Farming as a way of life came to Britain from Europe around 4,500BC, rapidly supplanting the older, hunter-gatherer lifestyle. Whether the new way of life meant that a new tribe of humans arrived to colonise the land or if the natives adopted farming for themselves (or if the reality was a mix of the two), is a historical mystery that has never been solved. If farming did involve a large-scale movement of peoples, then it is possible that the indigenous hunter-gatherers were indeed driven out by the newcomers. They would have lingered on in wilder, more rural areas, just as fairies are said to do. They would also have shared the fairy fascination with wild plants and wild animals, as it was on these that they relied for survival. For how long such folk could have survived once farming became the dominant way of life in Britain is anybody's guess. Perhaps long enough for the shy, retiring hunter-gatherers to establish themselves in popular imagination as fairies.

Another theory looks to the magical powers of the fairies for an explanation. Perhaps, it is said, that the fairies are little-remembered pagan deities. Certainly, the Christian missionaries in England wasted little time in dismissing pagan gods as demons, devils and non-beings. The ordinary folk, however, may well have retained a belief in the old gods which saw these idols demoted from being all-powerful deities to being magical beings. Certainly, some of the powers credited to fairies do seem akin to those of the old gods, although we know remarkably little about the pagan gods of England, so thorough was the Christian censorship of the old beliefs.

A 17th-century woodcut shows fairies dancing in the English countryside. Note the door leading into a hill and a toadstool nearby, both conventional items to be found alongside fairies in traditional tales.

Some scholars single out the King of the Dead as being the most likely deity to have been the prototype fairy. Pagan rulers of the dead tend to live underground in a parallel world, have magical powers, and sometimes come to Earth to mingle with humans. It is as dangerous to eat food in the Land of the Dead as it is to eat food in fairyland, and the rulers of the dead are generally capricious. That said, most of these comparisons are to pagan religions in southern Europe – principally Greece and Rome. There is no reliable record that the English ever had a death god, and the Vikings, who settled in Yorkshire some centuries after the English, had quite different beliefs about life after death.

Others who study folklore explain fairies as simply a convenient explanation for otherwise inexplicable events and items. The stone arrowheads that, in reality, were made by humans in the Stone Age were often said to be fairy weapons. The birth of mentally handicapped children or those suffering from what is now termed cot death was sometimes explained in terms of changelings: babies changed at birth by the fairies. The fairies of Craven had a particularly fearsome reputation in this respect. While this might indeed explain away the existence of fairies, it is unlikely to be able to explain the wide-ranging beliefs and stories about fairies to be found in Yorkshire.

Take, for instance, Diddersley Hill, just south of Melsonby. This is now a smoothly rounded hill that has gone under the plough, but not so very long ago it was topped by moorland and

The smooth slopes of Diddersley Hill, just south of Melsonby, are said to be a favoured haunt for dancing fairies – and woe betide anyone who interrupts them in their nocturnal frolics.

grazed by sheep. When a Yorkshire folklorist came this way in the 1890s he was told in no uncertain terms that he should steer well clear of Diddersley Hill because that was where the fairies liked to dance of a night. And since everyone knew that the little people deeply resented being disturbed, it was best not to go there. Although the hill is now farmed, it is still said to be a favoured place for the little folk.

When he was a young man, the Australian politician Sir Daniel Cooper lived in Kilnsey, where he had been born and brought up. One evening in the 1840s Cooper found himself delayed with farm work until after dark and had to walk home by moonlight. As he crossed a damp meadow, he saw what he thought were small, pale figures dancing and prancing around. He hurried home, but next day returned to the meadow to find a mass of white mushrooms where he had seen the figures. Cooper assumed that what he had thought were tiny, dancing figures were actually mushrooms, but his mother soon put him right. She told him that he really had seen fairies, but that because he had hurried on without disturbing them, they had left the mushrooms as a gift.

Nafferton Wold is another hill apparently beloved by the little people. Humans walking over the hill would often report hearing the sounds of the fairies moving about under the ground, and the little people were often seen in the area.

Another man to encounter dancing fairies was less fortunate or, rather, less wise than Sir Daniel. Elbolton Hill, near Thorpe in Wharfedale, has long been known to be a favourite haunt

Elbolton Hill near Thorpe in Wharfedale is home to a group of the little people who are generally friendly to humans, but only as long as they are treated with due respect.

A field on Nafferton Wold where fairies have been reported dancing, singing and gossiping under the light of the moon.

of the little people. They have been seen several times dancing on the slopes of this curiously shaped hillock, and some people believe that the cave on the southern shoulder of the hill is an entrance to fairyland. These fairies occasionally invited humans to join their dance, and would deeply resent any refusal, so it was considered wise to dance to the beautiful fairy music if invited to do so.

One farmer coming back to Thorpe from Skipton Market in the 1850s chanced upon the fairies dancing on Elbolton Hill. He stopped to watch a while, but when the fairies did not invite him to join in, he decided to drop a hint by singing a song to them. Undoubtedly the man had been drinking in Skipton marketplace, which might explain his boldness and would probably explain his poor-quality singing. The little folk took exception to the farmer's efforts at melody; they stopped their dancing, and turned on him. Punching and kicking, the fairies beat the man badly, and it was only by fighting as he ran that the man was able to get to Thorpe, where the fairies gave up their assault.

Fairies also dance in the Errington Woods, south of New Marske, or at least they used to do so. The woods cover a steep, south-facing slope overlooking Upleatham, and offer stunning views to Guisborough and Saltburn. A car park just off the A174 makes this a popular destination for walkers and families from Redcar seeking a day out in the countryside, and in recent years the area has become popular for mountain biking. Some blame these visitors for the fact that the fairies no longer dance here. Others claim that it was the massive expansion of New

Marske in the 1960s, when hundreds of houses were built on the side of the old mining village. The resulting boom in population meant that there were many more people about, and most of them came from outside the area and lacked the proper respect for the little people. This is a shame, as the fairies here were traditionally a very friendly bunch. They not only enjoyed dancing among the trees, but often invited humans to join in the festivities.

Also welcoming of human contact were two little people found far to the west. The towering rocks of Rainsber Scar near Bolton-by-Bowland now lie in Lancashire, but were historically part of the Craven region of the West Riding of Yorkshire. The tale here concerns one William Pudsey, a member of the prestigious Pudsey family of Yorkshire landowners. So well connected were the Pudseys that William gained Queen Elizabeth I as a godmother, which was to prove very lucky for him.

William had a silver mine on his estates at Rimington, and he used the silver to mint shillings. During the chaos of the Wars of the Roses, in which the Pudseys had favoured the Lancastrian cause, there had been many mints around the country, but the Tudor dynasty had organised a clampdown that meant that only royal mints were allowed to operate. Pudsey simply ditched his own dies, copied the Queen's shilling design and carried on minting coins. This was, of course, illegal. Pudsey did not care, for he was assisted by two elves named Lib and Michael. These two promised Pudsey that they could mint coins indistinguishable from the real thing.

Unfortunately for the three coiners, gossip got out and soon the Queen's officers came riding into Bolton-by-Bowland looking for Pudsey and his illegal mint. Pudsey saw them coming and sprang onto his horse, while the elves slipped away. In his pocket he had a special magical shilling given to him by the elves. With the royal officers on his heels, William Pudsey rode hell for leather for the River Ribble. He reached the banks on the towering bluff of Rainsber Scar and spurred the horse over the edge. Thanks to the magical elven coin, Pudsey floated safely over the river and landed without so much as a bruise. His pursuers, of course, had to give up the chase.

This head start allowed Pudsey to ride south, keeping ahead of his pursuers. He reached Richmond, in Surrey, where he found Queen Elizabeth on her royal barge floating down the Thames toward London. Pudsey urged his horse into the river and swam out to her. He flung himself on the mercy of his royal godmother and received a pardon for his crimes, although he was forced to hand over the magical coin. When he got home Lib and Michael had vanished, never to return.

Coins were again key to the relationship between a human and fairy at Willy Howe, a Bronze Age burial

A silver shilling from the reign of Queen Elizabeth I. It was these coins that William Pudsey was forging with the mysterious aid of the fairies in the later 16th century. His subsequent efforts to evade the forces of justice took Pudsey south, to Richmond in Surrey. Credit: Mike Peel.

mound near Burton Fleming. A tall, handsome farmhand living in the village often caught sight of a pretty girl watching him from the hedges near the Howe, but whenever he want to talk to her she would slip away out of sight and be impossible to find. Then, one day, the young woman did not run off, but waited for the farm boy to speak to her. She told him that sadly she had to leave the area, but that she wanted to leave him a gift. If he would climb to the top of Willy Howe every day at dawn, he would find there a golden guinea as a gift. But if he ever missed a day, arrived late or told anybody else where he was getting his money, the gifts would stop.

For some years all went well, but then the young man decided to marry. After all, with his good looks and new-found wealth he was a good catch for the local girls. On the day of his wedding he decided to confess to his bride where he was getting his gold. He led her up to the top of Willy Howe at dawn, but there was no golden guinea. Never again did he find money on Willy Howe; he had broken his pact with the fairy girl and so she no longer honoured her side of the bargain.

Equally helpful to humans was the hob of Hart Hill, near Whitby. One spring day around the 1790s the workers at a farm near the hill noticed that some mysterious person was doing work about the farm at night. Not being averse to a bit of help, the workers decided not to tell the farmer of their nocturnal assistant. All through the spring and summer the mysterious intruder would come along at night to work hard.

Then, at the height of harvest, one of the workers heard the sound of a flail thudding away in the barn late at night. Curiosity got the better of him, and he sneaked up to peek through a crack in the barn wall. There, he saw a short man with long, straggly hair, hard at work threshing the grain to separate the barley from the chaff. The worker watched in wonder as the little man worked his way through the grain twice as fast as any normal man could achieve. He could not help noticing that the only clothing the man had on was an old, tatty shirt that hung loose down to his knees.

Discussing his discovery later with his friends, the man told them of the old, stained shirt, and the men decided to provide their mysterious helper with something better. The only fabric that they could lay hands on at such short notice was rough, hempen cloth. This they cut to shape and sewed into a smock. They then took the smock to the barn and, before leaving for the night, laid it out next to the threshing floor. The men then made as if to go to sleep, but in fact crept back to the barn to see what happened next.

The strange little man arrived as the moon rose and walked across the barn to pick up the threshing stick. He then saw the smock, picked it up and tried it on. A look of disgust spread over his face, and he shouted out, 'Gin Hob given nowt but a hard, old hemp! He'll come no more, neither to thresh nor stamp.' With that he stalked out of the barn and never again came back to help the farm workers. Gin Hob had obviously taken offence at being given such a low-quality smock. The helpful hobs were notoriously touchy; they often helped humans, but could easily turn nasty.

Very similar was the hob of Hob Hill, near Upleatham. This particular hob favoured the farm that was run by the Oughtred family. It had a particular affinity for cattle, driving them in and out of the fields as required, but would also turn its hand to threshing grain or topping off turnips if such jobs needed doing. The hob worked on the farm for decades, with the Oughtred family taking great care never to offend their mysterious helper. But one fateful summer, illness struck and the Oughtreds had to hire men from outside the area to bring in the harvest. One man took off his coat, as the warm sun made him too hot. Unfortunately, he left the coat hanging on the fence when he finished work for the day. When the hob turned up to thresh the grain that night, he saw the coat and assumed that it had been left as a gift for him. This was the greatest insult that could be offered to a hob, so he turned his back and walked off, never to return.

Another helpful hob who took offence at a gift of clothes was resident at Sturfitt Hall, near Reeth. He worked happily enough for years, but when the lady of the house saw him one night and noticed his tattered clothes she decided to sew him a new suit. When this was left out he inevitably took offence and left.

Not so consistently helpful was the hob known as Robin Roundcap, who lived at Spaldington Hall, north of Howden. This fine, Tudor mansion was the centre of a sprawling farming estate, whose workers needed all the help that they could get. Robin Roundcap carried out all the usual tasks of a hob by threshing the grain, trimming root crops and other tasks. As the years passed, however, the hob took something of a dislike to either the dairymaids or the dairy in its entirety. While the men working the fields would find the hay freshly turned and grain stooks neatly stacked, the dairymaids would find cheese cut open and milk pails overturned.

Eventually, it all got too much for the owners of Spaldington Hall, so they sent for the vicar of nearby Bubwith. That learned gentleman paid a visit to see the problem for himself, and promptly decided that Robin Roundcap was too powerful a hob for him to tackle alone and called in the vicars of Holme and Eastington to help him. Together, the three vicars went to Spaldington Hall and began to pray. They eventually managed to force Robin Roundcap into a well in the courtyard, then sealed the top of the well with a lid made of willow wood, against which the hob was powerless. There things rested until 1800, when the hall was demolished. The old hob well was sealed off permanently and now lies under the flagstoned yard of the farm that replaced the hall.

Another troublesome hob lived on a farm in Arkengarthdale. When its domestic trickery got to be too much, the farm owner left out a Bible and a candle, in to which had been stuck a dozen pins. When the hob saw the objects, it turned into a grey cat and fled. A hatred of iron is a common feature of many tales about the little people.

The wild uplands of Rudland Moor, above Farndale, were home to a hob who lived in a tall cairn perched on the hillside above the crags of West Gill. This hob would sometimes slip down to the nearby farms to help with the farmwork, but just as often would play pranks. In the 1830s or thereabouts the hob took a particular dislike to one farmer and plagued his farm with innumerable tricks. The farmer decided to move to a new farm down the dale, near Kirkbymoorside.

On the day that the move was to take place, the farmer and his family loaded all their belongings onto a cart and set off. Just as they were leaving, a neighbour saw them and called out, 'I see thou's flitting then?' Before the farmer could reply, there came a loud bang from inside

Arkengarthdale, seen here at Calver, is the most northerly of the Yorkshire Dales. The hob here was driven away when the owner of the farm where it lived left out a Bible and a candle stuck with a dozen pins.

a chest, and the hob called out, 'Aye, we'se flitting right enough!' Deciding that he might as well be plagued by the hob in a farm he liked as in one he did not, the farmer turned about and went home.

Rather more ambivalent in its attentions was the hob of Marske-by-the-Sea. Sometime before 1780, the bishop decreed that the church perched on the clifftop east of the village was no longer convenient for the vicar, and it was, in any case, in need of repair. He ordered that the old church be pulled down and the stones reused in the building of a fine new church in the village centre. The move was welcomed by the vicar, but not by many of his parishioners, who rather liked the bracing walk up to their place of worship.

Moreover, the old church was not only much loved, but very historic. It had been built on the orders of Bishop Agelric in 1042, on the site of an old preaching cross that dated back to the very earliest days of Christianity in England. It had thus managed to survive the influx of pagan Vikings, and had played a key role in converting the invaders to Christianity. Agelric had dedicated his church to St Germain, who had been Bishop of Paris from 555 to 576. Germain had played a lead role in stamping out the last vestiges of paganism left over from the Roman Empire in France, and had persuaded King Childebert of the Franks to spend much money on the Church, in particular founding a great abbey near Paris to house the relics of St Vincent. That abbey would later be rededicated to St Germain himself, and St Germain-des-Pres became the richest and most magnificent abbey in France. The Church of St Germain at Marske was not in the same league, but was a popular shrine nonetheless.

Finally, the day came when the workmen arrived to begin work pulling down the old church. All day long the work went on, and by nightfall much of the upper walls had been taken down and the stones carted off to the new site. Next morning, the workmen arrived to find that the stones had been removed from the new site and taken back up the hill to be rebuilt into the walls from whence they had come. The vicar blamed the locals and ordered the work to begin again. Again, the stones were taken down and moved, but next day the same thing had happened. This time, the vicar took no chances: when the workmen finished work for the day, he and the foreman sat up at the new site, so as to catch any of the parishioners who tried to move the stones.

Next morning dawned clear to reveal that, once again, the stones had been taken back and rebuilt into the walls of the old church. The bishop, if not the vicar, knew when to admit defeat. He ordered that the efforts to build a new church should be abandoned; instead, the workmen were put to repairing the old church on the clifftops.

The vicar was more convinced than ever that his recalcitrant flock was to blame, and he preached at them thunderously that Sunday. The congregation, however, knew that they had nothing to fear, for none of them had lifted a finger. It was the hob who lived in the old churchyard who had resented the changes and who had been busy at night replacing the stones. They said nothing to the vicar, doubting that a man of God would believe in such things as hobs.

It must be presumed that the hob has since left the churchyard. The Church of St Germain again fell into disrepair during the 20th century. In the 1960s most of the church was demolished, and today only the tower and spire remain in the graveyard; the tower's use as a marker for sailors along the coast making it worth the cost of repair.

The lonely tower and spire that stands on the clifftop just east of Marske-by-the-Sea. This is all that remains of the ancient medieval church that served the town and, if legend is to be believed, housed a local hob for generations.

The cliffs of Runswick Bay were formerly home to a hob who had the power to cure local children of whooping cough. The cave where he made his home inside the cliff is at the centre of the photo.

Another hob lived in the cliff-side caves of Runswick Bay, not far from Hart Hill. This particular hob had the power to cure whooping cough. If any child caught the disease they would be taken by their mother to the caves, or hobholes as they are known at Runswick. The children would be pushed into the cave, while the mother called out, 'Hobhole Hob, Hobhole Hob. My bairn has gotten the cough. Take it off! Take it off!' Invariably, it was said, the dangerous whooping cough would ease.

Quite distinct from hobs, which were usually found in homes or farms, were the 'old men', who lived in mines. The lead mines of Swaledale were a favoured home for the old men, who could be heard tapping away with their hammers from behind the walls of the mines. It was generally thought to be good practice to work toward the sound of these fairy workings, as the old men were considered to know where the most productive seams of ore were to be found. The miners used to carry small stones with holes in them, which they placed at spots where galleries met or tunnels intersected as offerings to the old men.

More conventional little folk are to be found just south of Ilkley, around the White Wells. In 1878 it was reported that the man who looked after the plunge pool, in which locals could bathe to enjoy the curative properties of the waters, had a very strange experience:

> William Butterfield always opened the door [to the pool] first thing in the morning, and he did this without ever noticing anything out of the common until one beautiful, quiet,

midsummer morning. As he ascended the brow of the hill, he noticed rather particularly how the birds sang so sweetly and cheerily and vociferously, making the valley echo with the music of their voices. And in thinking it over afterwards he remembered noticing them, and considered this sign attributable to the after incident. As he drew near the wells, he took out of his pocket the massive iron key [to the door] and placed it in the lock, but there was something "canny" about it, and instead of the key lifting the lever it only turned round and round in the lock. He drew the key back to see that it was alright and declared that it was the same that he had, on the previous night, hung up behind his own door down at home. Then he endeavored to push the door open, and no sooner did he push it slightly ajar than it was as quickly pushed back again. At last, with one supreme effort, he forced it perfectly open, and back it flew with a great bang! Then "whirr, whirr, whirr", such a noise and sight! All over the water and dipping into it was a lot of little creatures, all dressed in green from head to foot, none of them more than 18 inches high, and making a chatter and jabber thoroughly unintelligible. They seemed to be taking a bath, only they bathed with all their clothes on. Soon, however, one or two of them began to make off, bounding over the walls like squirrels. Finding they were all making ready for decamping, and wanting to have a word with them, he shouted at the top of his voice – indeed, he declared afterwards, he could not find anything else to say or do – "Hallo there!" Then away the whole tribe went, helter-skelter, toppling and tumbling, heads over heels, heels over heads, and all the while making a noise not unlike a disturbed nest of young partridges. The sight was so unusual that he declared he either could not or dare not attempt to rush after them. He stood as still and confounded, he said, as old Jeremiah Lister down there at Wheatley did, half a century previous, when a witch from Ilkley put an ash riddle upon the side of the River Wharfe and sailed across in it to where he was standing. When the well had got quite clear of these strange beings he ran to the door and looked to see where they had fled, but nothing was to be seen. He ran back into the bath to see if they had left anything behind, but there was nothing; the water lay still and clear as he had left it on the previous night. He thought they might perhaps have left some of their clothing behind in their haste, but he could find none, and so he gave up looking and commenced his usual routine of preparing the baths; not, however, without trotting to the door once or twice to see if they might be coming back, but he saw them no more.

It is generally thought that the springs that feed the healing water into White Wells were originally sacred to the Celtic goddess Verbeia. A stone altar dedicated to the goddess now stands in the porch of Ilkley church and shows a woman in a heavily pleated skirt holding two snakes over her chest. Exactly where the altar was found is unclear, but the inscription links it to the soldiers who were stationed in the Roman fort that stood between the springs and the River Wharfe. The iconography on the altar is similar to that found on other Roman altars of water deities, so it seems almost certain that Verbeia was a water goddess, which might also explain why the springs are thought to be beloved by the fairies.

Rather more hostile to humans were the fairies of Flamborough. Just outside the village is a perfectly circular pit. It is said that if anyone were to run around the pit nine times without stopping, tripping or stumbling, then the fairies would come out. This was undoubtedly a silly thing to do, as the fairies would be in vengeful mood for having been summoned up in this way. Not only that, but in the 18th century a young woman named Jenny Gallows committed suicide here for some unknown reason. She too would be summoned up, appearing in a white dress to declare:

'I'll tie on me bonnet
And put on me shoe
And if thou's not off
I'll soon catch thou.'

It might be that a story about the local hob has got transferred to the unfortunate suicide.

At Mulgrave Woods, not far from Whitby, there are said to be two most unpleasant hobs. The first lives in the aptly named Hob's Cave. Anyone seeking to summon the hob need only approach the cave and shout out, 'Hobtrust Hob, where is thou?' A threatening voice would then call out from the depths of the cave, 'I's tying on my left-foot shoe. And I'll be with thee...NOW!', whereupon the hob would spring out to the terror the inquisitive visitor.

Mulgrave Woods, near Whitby, are home to a fairy by the name of Jeanie. She is generally well disposed to humans, but takes deep offence if a mere mortal should call her by her name, so it is best to speak of other things when walking in these woods.

The dark ravine of Trollers Gill, seen from the road over Whithill, towards Skyreholme. This is said to be home to a malevolent tribe of fairies who, in the 1990s, were made into the unlikely heroes of a children's television series.

The second fairy of Mulgrave Woods goes by the name of Jeanie. For most of the time, Jeanie is a placid soul, but if anyone calls her by her name she turns angry. One local farmer tried this in the early 19th century. Being no fool, he had brought with him a fast-riding horse on which to gallop off if Jeanie did in fact appear, but it did him little good. As soon as he had called out Jeanie's name, the fairy appeared. He put spurs to his horse, but could not outpace the vengeful spirit. He got as far as Barnby Brook before Jeanie reached out and stroked the horse's tail, whereupon the horse fell dead. The farmer was sent sprawling into the stream, but managed to get out at the other side. With running water between them, Jeanie was powerless. The terrified farmer fled, sending others to retrieve the corpse of his horse.

North of Skyreholme lies the sombre ravine of Trollers Gill, a rocky slash in the rolling uplands of Whithill. This is the home of a malevolent tribe of fairies who come out to prey on passing humans. Their favourite trick is to hurl rocks down to break legs or skulls and render the humans easy prey to be dispatched at will. At other times, the evil fairies will lure humans into the ravine by calling out as if they are traveller lost and in need of help; once the luckless human has been tricked into the ravine, his fate is sealed.

In the 1990s these gruesome tales were made into a children's television series for ITV. Entitled *Roger and the Rottentrolls,* the series followed the adventures of a schoolboy named Roger who accidentally strays into Trollers Gill, and by way of a misunderstanding is acclaimed king by the Rottentrolls who live there. These Rottentrolls, with their many comic features, were considerably less violent and bloodthirsty than their counterparts in the real Trollers Gill.

Equally unpleasant was the evil fairy of Horbury. The wetlands down by the River Calder were said to be home to a malevolent little man who liked nothing better than to spring out and attack people. He was said to be about 3ft tall and to have large, perfectly round eyes that glowed as if made of burning coals. He was blamed for several drownings, having been presumed to have pushed the victim into the river. The last sighting of this unpleasant character was some 75 years ago, so hopefully he is no longer about.

Tales of 'Awd Goggie' were once widespread around Yorkshire, especially in the East Riding. This elderly fairy man was said to be passionately devoted to apples, pears and other fruits. He spent most of his time in orchards and would chase and attack anyone who did harm to a fruit tree.

Between Piercebridge and Kirklevington, the Tees forms the northern boundary of Yorkshire, and until the much-to-be-regretted redrawing of local boundaries in 1974, much of Teesdale lay within the North Riding. Living in the Tees is a fairy whose behaviour rather supports the idea that these magical folk are pagan deities of old. Peg Powler lives in the river and only rarely comes out onto dry land. When she is seen she wears a long, green dress, as befits one of the little people. She also has green skin, long, green hair and razor-sharp teeth that she bares in a malevolent grin. This Peg Powler has the disturbing habit of reaching out from the river to grab the ankles of anyone walking along the banks. If she can get a good grip, she will pull the passerby into the river and drown them. Apparently, she has the right to claim one life each year, and if she does not get her victim she will cause floods and mayhem. After heavy rain, Peg Powler washes her clothes in the river, causing soap suds to form foam that drifts downstream from the rapids and waterfalls of Upper Teesdale.

This sort of behaviour sounds very much like that of a pagan water goddess. These denizens of the rivers are often very beautiful to behold – something that cannot be said of Peg Powler – but are almost invariably dangerous or tricky to encounter. Certainly, the rivers and many streams had their own pagan goddess before Christianity came to these shores. It would seem that the memory of those powerful ones lingers on.

Another Peg, this time Peg O'Nell, frequented the upper stretches of the River Ribble. According to a story collected in the 19th century, Peg O'Nell had been a servant sent out one bitterly cold winter's night by a heartless mistress to collect water. Peg had slipped on an icy rock and fallen into the Ribble, where she drowned. Thereafter, she came back once every seven years in a vengeful mood. If the locals were sensible they would arrange for a cat or a dog to be drowned by the rocks where Peg had died. If this were not done, the angry Peg O'Nell would grab the nearest human and drown them instead. A clearer account of animal sacrifice to appease an angry pagan deity would be difficult to imagine.

It is not only the Tees and Ribble where such water deities might be found. The upper reaches of Swaledale have a fairy called Kelpie, who will seek to lure men into the dangerous waters of the Swale by appearing as a beautiful young woman in distress.

The Wharfe also has its water fairy. Just north of Bolton Abbey the river flows through a narrow valley with steep sides, which is known as the Strid. In the spring, some say only at dawn on May Day, a fairy riding a white horse appears from the river and gallops up and down the valley, before returning to the waters. Some years ago, on May Day, three sisters named

The Wharfe just above Bolton Abbey. This stretch of river is home to a water fairy that can prove to be surprisingly dangerous, even murderous, to humans.

Mauleverers set out to seek the fairy and her horse. Presumably, these girls were from the Mauleverers of Allerton, a once-prosperous noble family of Yorkshire that provided many soldiers, MPs and diplomats to England before the family became extinct in 1713. Whether the girls had come up from Allerton (now a suburb of Bradford) or were more local, they came to a grisly end. After disappearing into the spring-morning mists, they vanished. Some days later their bodies washed up on the banks of the Wharfe, near Otley. Presumably, they had offended the fairy in some way and had paid the price.

An equally deadly fairy haunted the Hurtle Pot, a natural sinkhole ending in a flooded cave that lies beside the church in Chapel-le-Dale. The fairy here was usually called a boggart: a name often applied to fairies who torment and persecute those guilty of crimes such as theft or fraud. This particular boggart is said to live in the waters of the cave at the bottom of the Hurtle Pot, and to occasionally make its presence known by churning butter, the sounds of which activity can clearly be heard. In fact, the noises are made by pockets of air trapped inside the cave, which set up a sloshing sound when disturbed by the flow of water.

A visitor in 1778 recorded his impressions of this odd phenomenon:

The first curiosity we were conducted to was Hurtle Pot, about 80 yards above the chapel. It is a round, deep hole, between 30 and 40 yards diameter, surrounded with rocks almost on all sides, between 30 and 40ft perpendicular, above a deep, black water in a subterranean cavity at its bottom. All round the top of this horrid place are trees, which grow secure from the axe; their branches almost meet in the centre, and spread a gloom over a chasm dreadful enough of itself, without being heightened with any additional appendages. It was indeed one of the most dismal prospects we had yet been presented with: almost every sense was affected in such an uncommon manner, as to excite ideas of a nature truly horribly sublime. Whenever we threw in a pebble or spoke a word, our ears were assailed with a dismal, hollow sound, our nostrils were affected with an uncommon complication of strong smells from the ramps and other weeds that grew plentifully about its sides and the rank vapours that exhaled from the black abyss beneath.

After viewing for some time, with horror and astonishment, its dreadful aspect from the top, we were emboldened to descend, by a steep and slippery passage, to the margin of this Avernian lake. What its depth is, we could not learn, but from the length of time the sinking stones we threw in continued to send up bubbles from the black abyss, we concluded it to be very profound. How far it extended under the huge pendant rocks, we could get no information of, a subterranean embarkation having never yet been fitted out for discoveries. In great floods, we were told, this pot runs over: some traces of it then remained on the grass. While we stood at the bottom, the awful silence was broken every three or four seconds by drops of water falling into the lake from the rocks above in different solemn keys. The sun shining on the surface of the water illuminated the bottom of the superincumbent rocks, only a few feet above; which, being viewed by reflection in the lake, caused a curious deception, scarcely anywhere to be met with – they appeared at the like distance below its surface, in form of a rugged bottom: but, alas! How fatal would be the consequence if any adventurer should attempt to wade across the abyss on this shadow of a foundation! While we were standing on the margin of this subterranean lake, we were suddenly astonished with a most uncommon noise on the surface of the water, under the pendant rocks. It is called by the country people Hurtle Pot Boggard, and sometimes the fairy churn, as a churn it resembles. It is no doubt frightful to them, and would have been so to us if we had not been apprized of the cause: we found it was effected by the glutting of the surface of the water against the bottom of some rocks, or passages worn into them to a considerable distance, when it was descending after rain, as then happened to be the case. This deep is not without its inhabitants: large, black trouts are frequently caught in it by the neighbouring people. Botanists find here some rare and curious plants.

Another potential link to pagan gods comes from Blea Moor, north of Ribblesdale. This particular hob was in the habit of taking a ride on passing carts, but was otherwise not much of a nuisance. Then in the early 19th century a local shepherd named Jack Sunter found three large metal rings sticking up from a bog. He picked them up and took them home, though he had lost one by the time he got back. He sold them to a gamekeeper, who had them cleaned up and in turn sold them to a gentleman at Kirkby Lonsdale. The rings turned out to be silver and enamel armlets dating from the Iron Age. The hob was never seen again.

No account of the fairies of Yorkshire would be complete without a look at the Cottingley Fairies. The fairies of Cottingley Beck caused a huge sensation in 1919, when photographs taken

The Cottingley Beck, just north west of Bradford, hit the international headlines in 1919 after two teenage girls took photos here and claimed that the images showed real fairies. The tale behind the photos was investigated thoroughly and was taken up by famous author Sir Arthur Conan Doyle.

by two little girls showed them talking to and playing with fairies. The photos and the story behind them were investigated thoroughly, republished around the world and used by advocates of the supernatural both to prove and to disprove the reality of fairies.

The events at Cottingley began in the summer of 1917, when 10-year-old Frances Griffiths and her mother came on a visit from their home in South Africa to stay with their relatives, the Wright family in Cottingley. Frances played often with the 16-year-old Elsie Wright close to the Cottingley Beck, where they got their shoes and clothes both wet and muddy. When Mrs Wright tried to ban the girls from the beck, they protested that the only reason they went there was to play with the fairies. Mrs Wright refused to believe them, so the girls borrowed Mr Wright's camera and trotted down to the beck. Half an hour later they were back, saying that they had photographed the fairies.

The camera in question was a Midg that used the glass plates that were usual at the time. These plates were used one at a time and measured three inches by four inches. They were fragile and clumsy to use, but Elsie had helped her father, who was a keen amateur photographer, and was reasonably proficient at handling the big, awkward camera. When Mr Wright came home, Mrs Wright gave him the camera and told him the story. He took the camera up to his darkroom and processed it. The photo showed Frances looking towards the camera from behind a bush, while four fairies danced in front of her. One of the fairies was playing a pipe as she danced. All of them seemed to be females and were dressed in flowing gowns and sported large, butterfly-like wings. Mr Wright thought the photo to be a fine prank by the girls, but Mrs Wright thought that it might actually show real fairies.

Two months later the girls sneaked the camera out again and took a second photo. This image showed a male fairy with angular features and long, spindly limbs. He was wearing tights and a close-fitting jacket with a neck ruff. The male fairy was prancing across a lawn and reaching out to touch Elsie's hand as she sat on the grass. Again, Mr Wright dismissed the photo as a trick by the girls.

This time, however, Mr Wright firmly banned the girls from touching his camera. Photographic plates were not cheap and his camera was an expensive one. He was worried that they might drop it in the beck and ruin it. He also searched Elsie's bedroom and the area around the beck, looking for the model fairies that he assumed the girls had used. He found nothing.

Over the following months the photos were shown to friends and relatives, who had various reactions to them, but it was not until the summer of 1919 that the pictures caused a stir. Mrs Wright attended a meeting of the Theosphical Society in Bradford, an organisation that had as its stated objectives: to form a nucleus of the universal brotherhood of humanity without distinction of race, creed, sex, caste or colour; to encourage the study of comparative religion, philosophy, and science; and to investigate the unexplained laws of nature and the powers latent in man.

Mrs Wright showed the two photos at the meeting and was asked to bring copies along to the society's annual conference in Harrogate. The photos were displayed at the conference, and the society's secretary Edward Gardner was deeply impressed. Not only were the photos technically good, they also showed the fairies clearly and in detail. Gardner was also impressed that it had been two young girls who had produced the pictures, believing that they would not have been capable of the difficult techniques that would have been involved in faking such good photos.

Gardner persuaded Mrs Wright to lend him the original glass negatives so that they could be analysed. The plates were sent to Harold Snelling, one of Britain's leading photographic experts at the time. He studied them carefully and pronounced that 'the two negatives are entirely genuine, unfaked photographs, with no trace whatsoever of studio work involving card or paper models. These are straightforward photographs of whatever was in front of the camera at the time.' This was not quite the same as saying that the photos showed real fairies, but it was good enough for Gardner, who began a lecture tour on the subject of fairies, in which he used the photos.

The tour brought the photos to the attention of Sir Arthur Conan Doyle, best known today as the author of the *Sherlock Holmes* stories. As well as a writer, Doyle was a noted investigator of paranormal activity. He had the negatives sent for analysis by both the Kodak company and the Ilford company, both of them experts in photographic plates and studio techniques. Kodak pronounced the photos to be genuine originals, untampered with in any way. Ilford took the line that since fairies did not exist the photos must be fakes, but they could not suggest how the trickery had been achieved.

By now, the fairy photos had become internationally famous, and the girls were given false names to preserve their anonymity. In July 1920 Frances again came to visit the Wrights. Gardner took advantage of the trip to lend the girls a camera and ask them to see if they could take any more photos. Unknown to the girls, Gardner gave them specially treated photographic plates that would reveal fakery more easily than ordinary plates. On 19 August the girls took two photos, and a third on 21 August. The undeveloped plates were handed over to Gardner, who had them developed with great care. The results showed three more high-quality photos of fairies. The first showed Frances looking at a fairy as it leapt through the air. The second depicted Elsie looking at a fairy that is standing on the branch of a bush and holding out a posy of harebells. The third showed a group of fairies moving about in the grass.

When Doyle released the new photos to the world via the pages of the top-selling *Strand Magazine* they caused a sensation. Some saw them as proof of the existence of fairies, others saw them as proof of the cleverness of young girls. Either way, the story of the Cottingley fairies spread around the world and led to renewed interest in the subject. In 1921 Gardner tried to persuade the girls to take more photos, but they told him that they had not seen the fairies for some time and assumed that they had left the Cottingley Beck.

As the years passed, doubts began to be raised about the photos. Nobody could find any evidence of trickery of any kind, but the fact that the fairies had hairstyles very fashionable among humans soon began to make them look remarkably dated. The fairies in the pictures also matched the typical picture-book fairy in other ways, such as having flowing robes and delicate wings. This did not match the descriptions of 'real' fairies as they appeared in old stories or eyewitness sightings.

Gradually, researchers adopted the view that the pictures were fakes. This led investigators to concentrate on how two young girls had been capable of producing such convincing false images.

The playing fields off Stonebridge Avenue in Hull, where a policemen encountered some little people in 1977. He reported that the little people appeared to be dancing to music that he could not hear.

Suspicions grew that Mr Gardner had been behind the photos. Meanwhile, the girls had married, moved away from Cottingley and refused to talk about the fairies on the grounds that, as adults, they were no longer interested.

Then in 1983 the two girls, now elderly women, broke their silence. They gave an interview in which they said that they had genuinely seen fairies down by Cottingley Beck and had been annoyed by Mrs Wright's proposed ban on their visits. To persuade her to let them continue to play by the stream, the girls said, they had faked the first two photos. They had used drawings of fairies made by Elsie and copied from a popular children's book of the time, *Princess Mary's Gift Book,* published in 1914. The drawings were then pasted onto cardboard and propped upright using hatpins. The ploy had worked and their childhood games had been allowed to continue.

Elsie and Frances said that when first Gardner and then Doyle got involved they had been too embarrassed to admit the truth. After all, the girls were teenagers from a rural village, while Doyle was one of the most famous writers in the world. The girls had produced the new photos in the hope that the two important men would be satisfied and go away. When this did not work, the girls had told Gardner that the fairies had left in order to get rid of him.

So the Cottingley Fairies were revealed to have been fakes after all. But that does not disprove all the other Yorkshire fairies. Indeed, it should not be thought that sightings of fairies or the little people are restricted to the past, nor to rural areas. Late on the evening of 9 August 1977 residents of Stonebridge Avenue in Hull reported some strange goings-on to the local police. Sergeant David Swift was sent to investigate, arriving just after midnight. He found an unusually small bank of fog sitting in the middle of the playing fields. Walking forward to investigate, Swift saw three figures emerging from the mist, each of which stood about 3 or 4ft tall. They seemed to be dressed in tight-fitting outfits, with hats or headgear of some sort. The figures moved with an odd, jerky motion that might have been some sort of dance. Swift paused, then advanced further. The figures danced back into the fog, which then dissipated, leaving the policeman alone on the now-deserted playing fields.

Such an account reads like a traditional meeting with the little people. Certainly, anyone who had such an encounter before *c.*1900 would have put the incident down to the fairies. These days, people are more likely to interpret short, humanoid creatures as being aliens landing in UFOs from a distant planet.

That, at least, is what Philip Spencer thought when he had a bizarre encounter on Ilkley Moor on 1 December 1987. Spencer was walking over the moor to visit a relative and had with him a camera, as he usually did. As he strolled along, Spencer saw a figure a couple of hundred yards ahead of him on the path. He thought that the figure was about 4ft tall, and took it to be a boy wearing an odd hat or mask. The figure was gesticulating at Spencer as if urging him to go away or stay back. Spencer snapped off a photo and continued forwards. The figure then ran off out of sight into the heather and bushes. A few moments later Spencer saw an object rise silently into the air and speed off.

Wondering what he had encountered, Spencer had his photo developed. It showed a figure that seemed to have arms rather longer and a head rather larger than was normal for a human. Spencer gave the photo to a UFO investigation team, which sent it off for expert analysis. This showed that the figure was about 4ft 6in tall, and was not superimposed or added in any way. The photo showed no signs of being tampered with, and apparently showed what had really been there. What it was, of course, was another question entirely.

A rather more complex case took place about dawn on 28 November 1980 at Todmorden. A farmer had reported some cows missing from his field, and policeman Alan Godfrey was sent out in his patrol car to try to track them down. As he drove along Burnley Road, Godfrey saw what at first he thought was an overturned bus. As he got closer, he saw that the object was actually hovering just above the road. It was almost oval in shape, about 20ft across, and seemed to be rotating. Godfrey stopped his car and began to draw the object. There was a sudden flash of light, and Godfrey found himself and his car parked up about 200 yards from where he had been only an instant before. Checking his watch, he realised that 15 minutes had passed. When he got back to his station he found that another police patrol had reported sighting a UFO in the area, so he filed his own report.

It was not until some weeks later that Godfrey decided to take the matter further. He agreed to undergo hypnosis to try to remember what happened during the 15 minutes when he appeared to have been unconscious. This revealed that the engine on the police car had suddenly stopped, and that the radio had been swamped by static. The hovering object had then become much brighter, until Godfrey had to shield his eyes. He had then found himself in a large room with

A modern sketch of an eyewitness report of 'aliens' who emerged from a UFO. In many respects these humanoids resemble older accounts of meetings with fairies, in both the physical appearance of the little people and their behaviour.

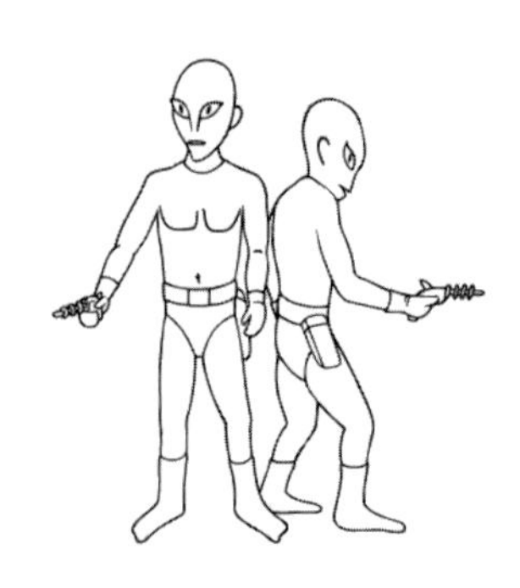

a tall man, who said his name was Yosef or something similar. There were also four robot-like figures, about 4ft tall, that were scurrying about, seemingly carrying out various tasks. Yosef had asked Godfrey a string of questions about the nearby area, then indicated that Godfrey should leave, after which he regained consciousness in his car, as he had originally recalled.

This is not to say that the fairies were actually aliens from another planet, nor that the occupants of UFOs are fairies. It is interesting to note the similarities between the two types of unexplained humanoid creatures: fairies and UFO crew are both said to be about 4ft tall; to frequent remote areas; to fly; to have powers that might indicate magic (fairies) or advanced technology (aliens); and to treat humans with a strange mix of indifference, contempt and hostility.

Perhaps one day we will know the truth.

CHAPTER 3

Mysterious Treasures

If there is one thing everybody loves, it is a tale of buried treasure. The lure of instant wealth has always had a strong attraction, but when blended with the romance of lost gold or ancient jewels it becomes nigh irresistible. There have been endless tales about misplaced treasures, cash found by some lucky local, or some rich man who died without telling anyone where his hoard was to be found.

What makes these stories so much more believable is the fact that, undoubtedly, there really is a huge amount of astonishingly valuable treasure buried in the Yorkshire soil. From time to time these treasures are uncovered and make the finder instantly rich, as well as greatly adding to our knowledge of the past.

On 6 January 2007 retired Leeds businessman David Whelan travelled to a farm near Harrogate, where he had permission from the landowner to search a field before it was ploughed. Using his metal detector, Whelan methodically worked across the field, then stopped when his detector indicated the presence of a large metal object under the soil. Whelan began digging and, at a depth of a little over a foot, found a lead sheet. When that was uncovered it proved to be the lid of a chest, inside which was the gleam of silver coins. Whelan at once alerted the Portable Antiquities Scheme (PAS), the body that lists all finds of ancient objects. The PAS called in the British Museum, which carried out a thorough search of the field and took the finds away for study.

The Harrogate Hoard, as it became known, turned out to include 617 silver coins, plus 65 other silver objects, of which the finest was a bowl of silver with a gilded interior that was decorated with lions, stags and horses. All the objects dated to the period 890 to 925. There was nothing to indicate to whom they had belonged, nor why they had been buried. The context of the burial, however, did indicate an answer to the mystery. It is known that in 927 the Viking Kingdom of York lost its independence and was absorbed into the Kingdom of England. The annexation does not seem to have followed an invasion, but that Athelstan of England moved fast when King Sihtric of York died suddenly, but naturally, leaving no clear heir. Undoubtedly, however, the switch from pagan Viking king to Christian English ruler must have led to a degree of social and political upheaval.

The hoard is undoubtedly that of a Viking; most of the objects came from the Scandinavian world. The only exception was the magnificent bowl that was of French manufacture and seems to have been used for consecrated bread during Christian mass, probably in a monastery. The bowl most likely came to York as a result of a Viking raid on France. Presumably, the vast collection of wealth belonged to a Viking lord or merchant, who buried it for safekeeping when the English moved in. For one reason or another, he was unable to retrieve it and so it remained in the soil.

The Harrogate Hoard was taken to the British Museum for cleaning and study. It was valued at just over £1 million, and was purchased by the Yorkshire Museum and British Museum jointly. It is now on display in the Yorkshire Museum, York.

Rather smaller, but even more mysterious is the Silsden Hoard. This was found in 1998 by Jeff Walbank, who was out using his metal detector in a field near Silsden. The hoard contains 27 gold coins and a single gold ring, in which is set a gemstone engraved with the figure of a man. Almost all the coins were staters issued by the mint of the pre-Roman Catuvellauni tribe, which held sway over the South Midlands and parts of East Anglia. Most were minted by the ruler Cunobelinus, who reigned from *c.*AD 10 to *c.*AD 35. A few of the coins were minted by his brother Epaticcus, who seems to have been a subsidiary ruler to Cunobelin in the AD 30s, although nobody is entirely clear quite what his position really was. A very few coins had been minted by a different tribe, the Corieltauvi, which ruled a swathe of territory from Lincolnshire to Leicestershire, Nottinghamshire and Warwickshire. The ring has been dated to *c.*AD 20 and is of Roman workmanship. None of the objects had been produced by the local Brigantes tribe, which ruled most of what is now northern England, including most of Yorkshire.

Quite how this mix of objects got to be in Yorkshire is unclear. The latest object in the hoard dated to *c.*AD 38, so it must have been buried soon after that date. At first it was assumed that the hoard was the property of a warrior from the Brigantes who had been on a raiding invasion of the Corieltauvi and Catuvellauni. The loot he brought back, it was presumed, was then buried for safekeeping near his home and, for some reason, never recovered. More recently, however, archaeologists have suggested that the hoard might have been left by a refugee from the Catuvellauni. In AD 43 the Roman Emperor invaded Britain and defeated the Catuvellauni in battle. Perhaps a nobleman fled north to the Brigantes to be outside the reach of Rome and brought the hoard with him.

In all likelihood, the mystery of the Silsden Hoard will never be solved. It is not alone, however, as several other equally enigmatic hoards dated to the AD 40s have turned up in what were the lands of the Brigantes. The Silsden Hoard was bought by the Bradford Art Gallery and Museum, and is now on show at Cliffe Castle Museum, Keighley.

Very definitely not on view to the public is the hoard of treasure at Dobb Park Castle. This castle was, in fact, a hunting lodge erected in the early 17th century. It was a three-storeyed tower with a walkway around the roof, from which hunters could admire the views across the Knaresborough Forest. The ground and first floor contained large rooms warmed by enormous fireplaces. These must have provided welcome shelter for hunters coming in off the bleak hills nearby.

The lodge is now in ruins, with the frost and rain taking a heavy toll on the stones that remain standing. Despite being a listed building, Dobb Park Castle continues to crumble away, the impressive lintel over the main fireplace recently cracking in half.

Although at first sight the roofless ruins may appear to be deserted, they are said to be the lair of a most unpleasant creature. This is a black dog with three heads which lurks about the crumbling stones, intent on fulfilling its mission. According to local legend, the owner of the lodge in its heyday deposited a large chest of gold coins under the foundations of the tower, in such a position that only he knew where it was could get access it. He left the hideous dog as guardian, with orders to kill anyone who got too close to the hidden gold. The man died before he could retrieve the gold, but the dog remains.

The great keep of Richmond Castle. According to legend, a fantastically rich treasure lies buried somewhere beneath Richmond, although it would take a brave man to face the dangers that surround it.

Another long-lost treasure is said to lie buried under Guisborough Priory. It is said that a tunnel runs from the priory ruins to a field on the far side of Skelton Beck, close to Tocketts Mill. Why this tunnel was dug is not recorded. Halfway along the tunnel there is hidden a chest of gold, on top of which is perched a raven, who guards it with great, but unspecified magical powers. It has been suggested that this powerful raven indicates that the tale of treasure is somehow linked to the pagan Viking god Woden, who had a liking for both treasure and pet ravens. Quite how a pagan god's gold could get linked to a Christian priory is unclear.

Another legendary treasure in a tunnel is said to lie deep beneath the ground somewhere near Richmond. There had long been a legend that Richmond Castle was linked by an underground passage to Easby Abbey, about a mile away. According to most versions of the tale, the medieval passage had been constructed as an escape route for the castle garrison in case of an attack by the Scots, who were often raiding over the border, although they rarely got this far south. Another version holds that the tunnel was built by the monks of Easby as a way to reach Richmond town, where they could cast aside their monastic robes for everyday clothes and indulge in some decidedly unmonastic activities among the pubs and hostelries of Richmond.

Whatever its origins, it was widely thought that the tunnel had been used by the last monks of Easby as a hiding place for their treasures when the Abbey was closed down by King Henry VIII in the 1530s, during the Reformation. That a good deal of the contents were salvaged from the Abbey is well known: the choir stalls in Richmond Parish Church, for instance, came from there. What exactly became of the Abbey's cash is not entirely clear. Certainly, local belief had it that the money was hidden by the monks who hoped that the Reformation would prove to be a temporary change and that they would soon return to their home. They did not return, of course, and so the treasure remained hidden in the old tunnel.

When, in around 1705, a group of soldiers stationed in Richmond Castle found what seemed to be the entrance to an underground chamber, they at once leapt to the conclusion that they had found the long-lost tunnel. They were equally convinced that a vast treasure was almost within their grasp. It must be admitted, however, that those old monks did not always have the same idea of treasure as would 18th-century soldiers. While the latter imagined the treasure to be gold and silver, it is just as likely that the monks hid away old books or the finger bone of a saint for safekeeping.

It was with huge disappointment that the soldiers found that none of them could fit into the hole they had found; presumably they were all big, burly men of the type the army loves. Therefore, they grabbed the company drummer boy and persuaded him to enter the underground chamber on their behalf. Perhaps they offered him a share of the treasure if he agreed, or promised him a hiding if he refused, either way he went down. He squirmed into the hole and found himself in what seemed to be an ancient cellar. Of treasure there was no sign, but there was a tunnel leading off from the old cellar and heading east towards Easby Abbey. The soldiers threw the boy's drum down to him and instructed him to explore the tunnel while beating steadily on the drum. They would follow the sound of the drum, tracing the track of the underground tunnel and following it to the prospective treasure.

Off set the drummer boy, beating loudly on his drum, with the soldiers trudging overhead. The route led along Frenchgate and past St Mary's Church, down to woods along the banks of

Easby Priory is said to be linked to Richmond Castle by an underground tunnel. Legend has it that the monks used the tunnel to hide their valuables when they received news that the priory was to be closed down in the 16th century on orders of King Henry VIII.

Middleham Castle is still rumoured to be hiding the fabulous treasure of the once-mighty Neville family. One of the richest and most powerful northern families throughout the 14th and 15th centuries, the Nevilles came to grief when they rebelled against Queen Elizabeth I in 1569. Only a minor branch of the family survived the treason trials that followed, and the family line continues today as the Earls of Abergavenny.

the River Swale. All seemed to be going well, but suddenly the drumming stopped. The soldiers waited for the drumming to begin again, but it never did. Nor did the boy ever re-emerge. Exactly what happened to the unfortunate drummer boy has never been explained.

Some say that the mournful sound of the boy's ghostly drumming can sometimes be heard at Easby Abbey, Easby Woods and near the Swale. Of course, the fabled treasure still lies somewhere along the lost tunnel. Each year, the schools of Richmond organise a walk from the town's Market Square to Easby Abbey and back along the route taken by the soldiers. The walk is led by a boy dressed in the uniform of a drummer boy of the Green Howards, the local regiment, which has a museum in Trinity Church Square, Richmond.

Almost 10 miles to the south lies another castle with a hidden treasure, but this time the tale has a modern twist. Middleham Castle was begun as a wooden structure in the 1080s, but rebuilt in stone after it came into the hands of the powerful Neville family in 1270. After 1471 it became the home of Richard of York, who later became King Richard III. During the reign of his brother, Edward IV, Richard served as Constable of England and as Governor of the North. From the fortress at Middleham he ruled the northern counties and guarded the Scottish border. The castle was then a massive and powerful building that contained extensive halls and living quarters within its walls, along with the offices and administration buildings needed by Richard. After Richard's death at the Battle of Bosworth, Middleham passed to the new king, Henry VII, but canon soon made the defences obsolete and it fell into disrepair. After being garrisoned during the English Civil War, it was sold into private hands and fell into ruin. It is now cared for by English Heritage and is one of the largest and most impressive ruins in Yorkshire.

According to local belief, one of the Nevilles buried a vast treasure just outside the walls of Middleham Castle. It is said that a powerful magical spell was cast over the treasure to hide it from treasure hunters. There is a way to circumvent the spell, but it seems ridiculously easy. Anyone seeking the treasure needs to run around the castle three times without stopping, tripping or stumbling, and then dig down wherever they happen to stop. The author tried it when he was at Middleham, but found nothing. Perhaps you will have better luck.

One treasure hunter who got lucky at Middleham was Ted Seaton, who, with two other treasure hunters, was scanning the field beside the castle in September 1985. As evening drew on, the three men were packing up when Seaton picked up a signal. Resting just beneath the turf he found what he thought was a modern ladies make-up compact. When he got the object home and cleaned it up, he found it was made of pure gold and had decoration that he thought looked medieval. Proper study followed; this revealed the piece to be a 15th-century diamond-shaped locket set with a single large sapphire. The front was engraved with a picture of the Holy Trinity, while the reverse has a picture of the nativity. The locket held a piece of silk, in which was wrapped a small amount of soil. One theory has it that the soil may have come from the Holy Land, even from the site of the crucifixion. The jewel was almost certainly made for a woman, and it has been speculated that it was made for Anne Neville, wife of Richard III. The jewel was sold for £1.43 million and is now on display in the York Museum, while a copy is on show inside Middleham Church.

One man who did not get away with the treasure he found was the farm labourer who was threshing corn in a barn close to Kirkstall Abbey in about 1829. Kirkstall was a Cistercian abbey that was founded in 1152 and grew to be one of the richest in Yorkshire, before it was closed down by Henry VIII in 1539 as part of the Reformation. There had long been rumours that the monks had protected some of the abbey's treasures from King Henry's grasping hands and hidden it somewhere locally. The labourer worked hard on the hot summer's day

In 1985 a local man found this magnificent medieval jewel close to Middleham Castle. The jewel is gold, on which is mounted a 10-carat sapphire. The discovery of the gem reawakened interest in the old stories about the lost wealth of the Nevilles.
Credit: Fingalo Christian Bickel.

and, around about midday, decided to stop for his lunch. He left the barn and sat down in the shade of the abbey ruins.

As he munched on his bread, the man spotted what looked like a hole under the abbey walls. Peering into the hole, he saw that it led to a chamber or vault of some kind. Wriggling through, the man found that the chamber was bigger than he had thought. At the far end was a door leading to a second chamber, in which he spotted a large oak chest containing the glimmer of gold coins.

'I'll have some of that,' the man thought to himself, and began walking toward the chest. Suddenly, a cock crowed close at hand. The man span round to see a black cockerel and a black horse standing in a corner of the underground room. The horse then whinnied and stamped its foot. Deciding to ignore them, the man again stepped toward the gold. Again, the cock crowed and the horse whinnied. Now feeling nervous, the man looked around carefully, but could see nothing else in the room. A third time the man stepped toward the chest of gold, and a third time the cock crowed and the horse whinnied. Before the man could look around, he was struck a stunning blow on the back of the head and collapsed, unconscious.

He awoke lying slumped at the door to the barn where he had been doing his threshing. Shaking his head to clear his senses, the man ran back to the Abbey. His bread and cheese lay where he had left them, but of the hole leading to the underground chamber there was no sign. Although he went back many times and searched carefully, he never was able to find the entrance to the chamber again.

The village of Bainbridge in Wensleydale began life as the Roman fort of Virosidum, but it is the much older burial barrow of Stony Raise Cairn that hides the treasure to be found here. The cairn stands on the bleak slopes of Stake Fell, south of the village, and is far from any public footpath, and even further from any road. It is easily the largest prehistoric cairn in Yorkshire, measuring 100ft in circumference and standing over 8ft tall.

According to local legend, a giant was walking up Wensleydale one day and wanted to head south to Wharfedale. He was carrying on his back all his worldly goods in the form of a chest of gold, which weighed a considerable amount, even for a giant. He got past Addlebrough Hill, where another giant (or perhaps the same one) had an altercation with the Devil, but when faced with Stake Fell he stopped in dismay. Setting his jaw grimly, the giant vowed that to spite God, who had put the mountain there, he would carry his load over into Wharfedale.

Instantly, the sack of gold was ripped from his back by unseen hands and thrown down, whereupon vast numbers of stones surged up from under the ground to cover the gold and stop the giant from picking it up again. The giant stomped off in disgust, leaving the cairn and his gold behind. It is said that only a man equipped with a hen and a monkey stands any chance of finding the hidden gold. Even then, he is not secure in his new fortune. Having found the chest of gold, the man must pull it out of the cairn in absolute silence and then carry it down to the River Ure, neither speaking a word, nor letting the chest touch the ground. One man back in 1858 managed to take a hen and a monkey up to the Stony Raise Cairn and promptly found the hidden chest. So great was his surprise that he cried out, whereupon the chest sank back into the cairn.

Some 20 or so years before this failed attempt, another man had an unfortunate encounter with treasure at Sexhow, on the banks of the River Leven. A farmer from outside the village bought up a farm that had gone on the market after the sudden death of its elderly owner – a woman known locally as Awld Nanny. The new owner was a sober and hardworking man, so he quickly licked the rather neglected farm into shape.

As he lay sleeping one night, the farmer awoke suddenly as if he had been shaken awake. Standing beside his bed was an old lady dressed in rough working clothes. The woman told the startled farmer that she was the ghost of Awld Nanny. She instructed him to go out next morning and dig beneath a gnarled, old apple tree in the back garden. There, she said, he would find a chest of gold and a chest of silver. He could keep the silver for himself, but must give the gold to Awld Nanny's niece, who was living in poverty in Middlesborough.

Next day the farmer went out with a shovel to dig, and found the promised chests of coins. Instead of giving the gold to the intended recipient, he kept it all for himself and told not a soul the source of his new-found wealth. His neighbours did soon notice a difference in the man: not only was he now considerably richer than he had been, but he was drinking heavily and had become bad-tempered.

Some weeks after the change came over the farmer, he visited Stokesley Market on business. People who saw him there said that he was jumpy, nervous and distracted, and that he was drinking heavily. After dark his neighbours in Sexhow heard the farmer riding home, galloping furiously on his horse. One neighbour looked out to see the man gallop by, screaming wildly, 'I will, I will, I will!' Clinging to the man's back was the figure of a woman: an old woman wearing a straw hat that the neighbour thought looked remarkably like Awld Nanny. The farmer rode his horse through the farm gate without pausing to open it and crashed to the ground on the far side – stone dead.

The worried neighbours crowded round, then carried the man's body into his farmhouse and sent for both a magistrate and the local woman who laid out bodies. In the farm kitchen they found a rambling note giving the story of what had happened and what was left of the gold and silver. The coins were collected up and sent to the niece, after which nobody saw Awld Nanny again.

By way of contrast, a man from Burton Fleming managed to get away with a treasure that was most certainly not intended for him. According to William of Newburgh, who was writing in the 1170s, the incident took place in his youth, which would have been *c.*1130. The man was walking to Wold Newton, and passed by the round barrow of Willy Howe – an enormous Bronze Age burial mound, around 25ft tall and more than 100ft in diameter.

The man heard the sound of laughing, singing and jollity coming from the direction of the mound. Wondering who could be throwing a party at night in the middle of nowhere, the man walked up to the mound. He noticed, set into the side of the mound a door that he had never noticed before and, becoming curious, peeked inside. There the man saw a party in full swing with feasting, dancing and drinking. A servant spotted the man and offered him a goblet full of what appeared to be wine.

The man took the drink, but he was no fool. He was fully aware that he had stumbled upon a fairy feast and knew well that it would be extremely dangerous to eat or drink anything offered

The church at Burton Fleming gave shelter to a local man who managed to purloin a goblet from fairies holding a celebration at nearby Willy Howe. The cup was later presented to King Henry I.

A M D G
IN LASTING MEMORY OF THOSE BRAVE MEN
FROM THIS PARISH WHO LAID DOWN THEIR
LIVES IN THE GREAT WAR

him by the fairies. To do so would risk him being trapped in the fairy kingdom for years, possibly forever. Instead, the man waited until nobody was looking, then tipped out the fairy wine, tucked the goblet into his jacket and ran for it. He soon heard the fairies in pursuit, but managed to get to Burton Fleming Church before they could catch him. He ran into the church and slammed the door behind him, against which the fairies were powerless.

The fairies left before dawn, leaving the man the proud owner of the beautiful goblet. The man sold it to his lord, who passed it on to King Henry I in an effort to curry royal favour. Henry I, in turn, gave it to King David of Scotland, perhaps as part of the settlement upon the Scottish King's marriage to an English heiress. When King William I of Scotland was captured by the English at the Battle of Alnwick in 1174 he had to hand the fairy goblet back to England's Henry II as part of his ransom. The goblet then passed into the care of the bishops of Rochester, but after 1300 nothing more is heard of it, which seems a shame.

The lost treasure of Bowes goes back further than most. The great Bowes Castle stands here, guarding the route up over the Pennines that uses the River Greta to get as far west as possible, before climbing up over Stainforth Pass. It is the route used by the modern A66, and has long been a route favoured by merchants and armies. Most of the castle to be seen today dates to around 1322, but it was begun in 1136 by Alan the Black, 1st Earl of Richmond. Alan the Black chose the spot partly for its strategic position, and partly because of the ruined Roman fortress on the banks of the Greta, from which his masons could steal stones to build the new castle.

The Roman fortress was named Lavatrae and, as Roman forts go, was large, covering some four acres. The fort began life as a regular army base in around 140, but by the later Roman period was a second-rate base, manned by a shadowy unit called the Numerus Exploratum. This was about 300 men strong, and seems to have been an auxiliary or mercenary unit. When orders came instructing the Numerus Exploratum to abandon the defence of Britain and head to Gaul to protect Rome itself, the men decided to take what they could while the going was good.

Grabbing their weapons, the mercenaries set about looting anything of value from the local farms and villages. Gold jewellery, silver coins and large quantities of bronze household goods were stolen, women raped and men killed. The outsiders had, however, mistaken their victims. These were not humble farmers but members of the Brigantes tribe, a Celtic people with a proud fighting tradition of their own. The farmers sent word through the Brigantes lands and soon Lavatrae was under siege. The cornered mercenaries sent out word asking for help against what they claimed was an unprovoked tribal rebellion, then barricaded themselves in and prepared to fight. The Roman authorities, however, were too preoccupied with the Goths invading Italy and threatening Rome itself to be bothered with an out-of-the-way bunch of mercenaries, and no help was sent to the beleagured thieves. After some days, the Brigantes burst into Lavatrae and massacred the mercenaries. With the bloody work done, the Brigantes searched for the stolen goods and jewels, but could find nothing. The mercenaries must have hidden them before they died.

So things rested for centuries. Then it was noticed that the ghostly Roman soldiers who had long lurked around the abandoned Roman fort were not randomly wandering about, but seemed to be intent on one particular purpose – perhaps burying their stolen treasures. In the 1660s two men from Barnard Castle decided to go to Bowes to sit up for the ghosts, then dig where they appeared in the hope of finding the gold. The two men set off, but did not return.

Next morning one of the men was found slumped dead among the Roman ruins. His body was found beside a deep hole in the ground, and his friend's knife stuck from his back. It was presumed that the men had found the gold, then quarrelled over it with fatal results. The killer, it was thought, must have fled with the treasure. But three days later his body was washed up on the banks of the river at Greta Bridge. There was no gold on the body, but a look of stark terror was on his face.

What happened remains a mystery to this day. Some think that the gold still lies in the Roman fort, others believe that it is now washing around in the bed of the Greta. Nobody knows and, given the fate of the two men who last went looking for it, nobody is much inclined to find out either.

High upon Bilsdale Moor stands the ancient burial mound of Flat Howe. There is said to be a great treasure buried here, but, as at Bowes, nobody is very keen on searching for it. The great golden hoard is guarded by a dragon of immense size and ferocity. Perhaps it's best to stay away then and rely on more conventional means of acquiring money, like working, for instance.

CHAPTER 4

Mysterious Wells and Springs

Life cannot exist without water, and humans need pure drinking water to thrive. Water came to have a huge significance for the people of Yorkshire, especially if it was pure enough to drink straight from the ground.

Rivers and streams that have been contaminated by animal dung, human waste or rubbish tipped out of houses is not fit to drink straight from the beck. Of course, this water is fit to drink if it is treated, but in days gone by this was not fully appreciated. It was known that stream water was safe to drink if it were first brewed into beer. This was because the brewing process involved boiling the water, and so our ancestors took to drinking vast quantities of thin, weak beer. Nevertheless, pure sources of drinking were highly prized, and some odd stories have been told about them.

At Keyingham there was a natural spring on the slopes overlooking the Humber Estuary. This spring was considered to be so important that a stone cross, now long since lost, was erected in the early medieval period. Both well and cross were dedicated to the fifth apostle, St Philip. Philip was always one of the less well-known of the apostles, so why he was chosen as the patron saint of this well is unclear. He came from the town of Bethsaida, the same town as Peter, but his only actions in the Bible come when he translates into Greek for other desciples, and when he asks Jesus about God the Father at the Last Supper.

Perhaps the clue to his appearance in Yorkshire is that, unlike the other Apostles, St Philip was married and is known to have had children. The spring had magical marriage properties. It was firmly believed by locals that if a young maiden could persuade a young man to accompany her to the spring and together gaze into the waters, they would find true love. If the girl then tossed in a silver coin, the man would inevitably marry her, and together they would lead a long and happy life, blessed by many children.

Given that the tale was widely known, it seems highly unlikely that any young man would go to St Philip's Spring with a young woman unless he was already in love and intended to marry her. It may be that the waters of the spring were linked to some pagan fertility cult. Or perhaps marriage ceremonies in pagan times involved a visit to the spring. Whatever the case, it seems most likely that the waters already had a strong role in local love lives.

When the Christian missionaries arrived they will have wanted to banish the pagan gods. It is known that elsewhere the missionaries would adopt any local custom or belief that was too strong for them to eradicate. If belief in the magical love powers of this spring were strong, the missionaries may have taken over the waters and, as patron, given it the first married saint that they could think of: St Philip.

A similar process might have been at work at Roche, south of Maltby. The site is now occupied by the sprawling ruins of Roche Abbey, which was founded in 1147. Unlike many other abbeys, Roche did not have to be built in stages, dependent on finances, having been funded by

The ruins of Roche Abbey near Maltby. The monks who founded the monastery chose to dedicate it to the Virgin Mary, as a local holy well was already given the name 'Lady's Well'. Unknown to the Christian monks, the lady in question may have been quite a different sort of deity. Credit: BPA.

the deep pockets of the wealthy northern magnate, Richard de Busli. The Abbey housed Cistercian monks, but remained the property of de Busli and his heirs right down to the dissolution in 1538. The complex ownership of the abbey led to some unusual payments by the commissioners of King Henry VIII, as they sought to take over the estates of the Abbey. It is by no means certain that the King made much of a profit on the deal.

When the monks arrived at Roche they built their abbey on the east bank of the little stream known as the Maltby Dike. They found, however, that there was a natural spring on the west bank that was widely known locally as the Lady's Well, and which was highly revered by the villagers. The villagers believed that the Lady's Well had the power to grant wishes if a person threw a bent pin into the waters. Perhaps it was no coincidence that Roche Abbey was dedicated to Our Lady, the Virgin Mary, and that it featured a large Lady Chapel. Whether the original Lady Well was, at heart, dedicated to a pagan water goddess, or to the Virgin Mary, it seems that the monks wisely took their lead from a very popular local veneration.

Another well that demanded bent pins if it was to perform its magic is to be found at Thorp Arch, south-east of Wetherby. This spring was sacred to St Helen, but again local scholars believe that it was originally a pagan site. Waters drawn from the spring after a bent pin had been thrown in were said to be highly effective at curing eye infections, but this was not the only use for the well. If a young woman came here at night without anybody knowing what she was up to, she could conjure up an apparition of her future husband. All she had to do was tie a rag to a nearby tree and say a prayer to St Helen.

Another spring sacred to St Helen is that at Kirkby Overblow. The spring is on the edge of the churchyard and empties into a horse trough. These days it is dry if there has not been much rain for some weeks.

At Melsonby there is a natural spring, also dubbed the Lady Well, which pours forth a reliable flow of water that forms the headwaters of the Clow Beck, one of the tributaries of the River Tees. According to locals, a ghostly white lady will appear beside the Lady Well, then walk off downstream towards the village church, which is dedicated to St James the Great. Perhaps this is some faint memory of a pagan water goddess, but, if so, no other belief has been recorded about the spring at Melsonby.

A very clear story about a pagan well becoming a Christian one concerns a well close to the churchyard at Brayton. Many centuries ago, a young woman in Brayton was being courted by a man named Robin, but was uncertain if his intentions were honourable. She therefore went

The Clow Beck at Melsonby as it forms a curve around the churchyard. The spring that feeds this stream is dedicated to a lady, although which lady is unknown.

down to the well with a bent pin, which she dropped into the water, while asking the local fairies for help. Instantly, the girl fell into a deep sleep beside the spring. She dreamed that she met a fairy, who walked down from Brayton Braff, a nearby hill. The fairy told the girl that her tribe of fairies was unable to smelt metal, but could use her bent pin to make an arrowhead. In thanks, she conjured up an image of the man the girl would marry, and the girl was delighted to see that it was Robin. The fairy then told her that if any other maiden wished to see an image of her future husband, she needed only to offer a bent pin in the spring and lie down to sleep. The girl then awoke and rushed home to throw herself into the arms of her boyfriend.

The local vicar was not so pleased as the girl. When he heard of this deal with the little people he donned his robes, picked up a Bible and hurried down to the spring. He began by exorcising the fairies, who he called 'evil spirits', and then dedicated the well to Our Lady. To this day, the place is officially known as Our Lady Well, although locals call it The Pin Well.

Rather more sinister is the Drumming Well of Harpham, which lies a few yards south of the church. This well is, in fact, an artesian spring, which draws up water from deep beneath the ground. The top of the spring has been improved by having a 4ft-wide stone-lined shaft sunk down to a depth of at least 15ft. The water bubbles up out of this shaft and spills out to form a large marshy patch south of the spring, then runs off to form the Kelk Beck. Every now and then the well emits a strange drumming noise, as if somebody is enthusiastically playing rolls on a military drum deep down under the ground.

The story told locally has it that in the 1070s, when King William the Conqueror came north with his army to impose his Norman rule on the northern counties of England, he killed the Lord of Harpham in battle. Fearing that the village might prove to be the centre of discontent or rebellion, William promised the village and estates of Harpham to whichever member of his army could get there first to establish a Norman presence.

Hearing this, a young knight named Sir Ralph de St Quintin decided to ride hard for Harpham and claim the reward. To his great anger, however, when he galloped into the village he found, sitting calmly on the steps of the Church of St John, a drummer boy munching on an apple. The boy had not heard of the offer by King William, and had wandered into the village looking for something to eat. St Quintin, clearly a churlish and violent man, chatted to the drummer boy, then asked him for a drink of water. The boy pointed St Quintin to the spring, but the knight pretended that he could not find it and asked the boy to show him. As soon as the boy was standing over the stone shaft, St Quintin stabbed him dead and threw the body down the shaft, to be followed by the boy's drum.

A local wise woman saw what happened and cursed both St Quintin and the well. She decreed that the boy's ghost would remain to haunt the well, and that he would play his drum whenever death was about to come to a member of the St Quintin family. Given how large and widespread the family became, the poor boy must have been kept busy.

The story was widespread and famous in medieval times, so much so that the St Quintins felt that they had to answer the charges of murder. They therefore put about a different version of the story. According to the St Quintins, the whole thing had been an accident. The St Quintins were in the habit of holding an annual fair at which local men could compete in martial arts,

The Drumming Well of Harpham has a number of legends and stories attached to it. It is said that a drummer was murdered and his body thrown down the well, since which time the eerie sounds of a drum being played have reverberated out of the well from time to time.

such as archery, sword fighting and so forth. This much of the tale is undoubtedly true. As the lords of the manor, the St Quintins were responsible for ensuring that the requisite number of men were ready and available to serve in the royal army in times of war, and offering prizes for fighting skills was a good way of encouraging the local men to be suitably proficient.

This version has it that a local Harpham boy named Tom Hewson served as the drummer for the local troops when they turned out, and was employed at the annual fair to play his drum to call for silence. When it came to the archery contest, the champion put forward by the St Quintins to shoot against all comers fluffed a particularly important shot. Striding forward in anger through the crowd, Lord St Quintin accidentally bumped into young Tom and knocked him down the well. Distraught, the Lord organised a rapid rescue party, but the boy had unfortunately died before he could be pulled out. The boy's mother then laid the curse on the St Quintins in mistaken revenge.

Whatever the truth, the St Quintins are long gone from Harpham, but the drummer remains. Every now and then, the well pours forth its haunting sound. It is assumed that water rushing through some twist or turn in the subterranean passages causes the noise.

A second well at Harpham is worth mentioning, this time it lies half a mile or so east of the church. This well is covered over by a small, domed stone cover that stands about 3ft tall. It is dedicated to St John of Beverley, as is the village church. The well is said to have the power to tame wild beasts and to calm any animal brought there. Writing in the 1120s, William of Malmesbury mentions the well and its properties as evidence of the sanctity of St John of Beverley. He records that the 'most rabid bull became as gentle as a lamb' if it drank the waters of the well.

The drumming well at Harpham is not the only noisy well in Yorkshire. At the western end of Main Street in Newton Kyme is a well covered over by a low, stone-arched structure, which goes by the name of Black Tom's Well. The Tom in question was Sir Thomas Fairfax, who rose to be the commander-in-chief of parliamentary armies during the English Civil War of the 1640s. His first foray into warfare, however, proved to be disastrous. The early months of the war were spent with both sides trying to secure the local arsenals and chests of money held by each county and city to defend the realm against foreign attack. In Yorkshire, Fairfax had the orders of Parliament to grab these, while the Earl of Newcastle sought to do the same for the King. At first, the two avoided each other, each commander grabbing those towns or cities where he knew he had support – which meant that Fairfax spent most of his time in Leeds and the West Riding.

On 30 June 1643, however, Newcastle, with over 10,000 men, ambushed Fairfax at Adwalton. The Roundhead army broke and fled. Separated from his men, without food or water, Fairfax galloped over the countryside with Royalist horsemen on his track. As night fell he found himself at Newton Kyme, and hid himself inside the stone shelter over the well. There he rested while the Cavaliers rode by. Next morning he was able to escape and reunite his scattered forces. To this day, the well will sometimes emit strange noises, like those of galloping horses or a drum being beaten. Locals say that the intense fear felt by Black Tom that night has left its mark on the well.

St John's Well at Harpham is dedicated to St John of Beverley, as is the village church. The magical property of taming wild animals is ascribed to this natural spring.

A well with an altogether more positive image is the Brandon Holy Well, just west of Scarcroft. This long had a reputation for being good at healing cuts and bruises. The waters, however, flowed over the aptly named Holywell Lane and froze in winter, causing problems for drivers. Yorkshire County Council wanted to fill in the well to improve road safety, but the Earl of Harwood, who owned the land, refused point-blank to allow the sacred waters to be blocked off. After some dispute, the Earl got his way.

In the grounds of Copgrove Hall, near to the gamekeeper's cottage, there is a sacred well that traditionally had healing properties. Sir John Flogers, writing in 1697, recorded, 'Cold baths and bathing – the people resort here to be recovered of fixed pains with or without tumour, rheumatism, quartans, strains, bruises, rickets and all weaknesses of the nerves.' For some obscure reason, this well is sacred to St Mungo, the patron saint of Glasgow, who is buried in that city and, so far as is known, never came to Yorkshire. Mungo's real name was Cyndeyrn (or Kentigern), with 'Mungo' being a nickname meaning 'the dear one'. He is credited with converting several tribes in what is now southern Scotland to Christianity and died in 614.

Other healing wells are to be found at Easthorpe Wood near Appleton-le-Street, Coverham, Spittal Hardwick, Hilderwell and Tanfield. At Timble, the Greenwell Spring has the tradition that silver coins must be washed in the water to cure disease

Yet another healing well of some antiquity is the sacred well at Thornton-in-Craven. This well is somewhat unusual as, although the spring is known to have had a reputation for sanctity for centuries, nobody is really sure why. Archaeological studies show that the natural spring is the site of the very earliest Christian presence in the area. Sometime around AD 600 a font was placed here to receive the waters and form a pool in which pagans could be baptised. These early fonts were shaped like shower trays and were set at ground level. Those seeking baptism at this early date were usually adult pagans, not newborn babes, so the fonts were built so that adults could step into them and stand while having holy water poured over them. Later, a small church was built over the font, and this was restored in the 9th century. In itself this was no mean feat, for the area was then ruled by pagan Vikings.

When the Normans conquered England they spurned the small, old church covering the spring and instead built a new church on top of the nearby hill. The old church was demolished and the spring returned to the open air. The spring continued to be used and, if it had not already had such a reputation, gained one for being able to bring relief from pain. In the 17th century an octagonal stone hut was erected over the spring, and the waters collected in a stone basin surrounded by a flagstoned pavement. This structure was restored in 2007, with the addition of a sloping path down to the spring, which for the first time allows disabled access to the dell in which the spring bubbles forth. Healing services are still found here from time to time, usually in the summer months when the water and the weather are warmer.

Another spring inside a church used to be found inside York Minster, that great church of the north. The spring in question originally rose within the garden of the house of the commanding officer of the Roman army in York, and might be the reason why he had his house built on this spot. After the Romans left, the stout stone walls of the house were reused for an early Christian church, which, in time and after many rebuildings, became the minster we know

The natural spring in the churchyard at Thornton in Craven has recently been restored. The 17th century stone cover has been rebuilt and is now surrounded by a flagged courtyard, accessed down a ramp from the road.

today. The spring and church were used during Easter 627 to baptise King Edwin of Northumbria, the first king of that northern kingdom to become a Christian. The spring has now been covered over, but its site is marked by a font at the eastern end of the crypt.

Another mystery surrounds the spring that feeds the Cod Beck at Osmotherly. There are various versions of what is essentially the same story. A typical example has it that many centuries ago a wealthy woman was riding to market at Northalleton with her son, Os. As they trotted along they met a group of gypsies, who offered to read the fortune of the boy. Having been paid the customary silver coin, the lead gypsy prophesied that the boy would one day drown. The distraught mother at once bought a plot of land on the slopes of Pamperdale Moor, where she could build a house far from any deep water. The years passed and the boy grew to be a strapping teenager. One day, he and his mother were out walking over the hills when they became tired and lay down to sleep. As they slept, a spring of fresh water suddenly erupted with such force that it overwhelmed and drowned them both. The locals who found the bodies washed down into the valley below called the place 'Os-by-his-mother-lay', which has become corrupted to be Osmotherby.

The name of the village, however, has nothing to do with such a watery tragedy. It derives from the Viking man's name 'Asmunder' and the suffix 'by', which means 'an isolated farm'. Quite where the story came from, nobody knows, but the spring and the Cod Beck remain.

CHAPTER 5

Mysterious History

Yorkshire has a long, rich history, but although much of the past in the county is well documented, other aspects remain obscure. Some of those mysteries defy solution, but others have tantalising clues that may indicate the truth behind the evidence we are presented with, sometimes hundreds of years later.

One of the earliest mysteries, but one which is now generally thought to have been solved, concerned the Roman Emperor Constantine the Great. It was Constantine who finally made Christianity not only tolerated, but favoured in the empire, although he exacted a price in the form of Christian recognition of the imperial government.

The bald facts that are agreed by all confirm that Constantine was the son of the pagan Emperor Constantius and a Christian woman named Helena. In 305 Constantius was in Britain preparing to fight a campaign against barbarian tribes called Picts, who lived north of Hadrian's Wall. The name 'Pict' means simply 'painted men', and since most Celtic tribes in Britain painted themselves for battle, it is not entirely clear which tribes were to be the target of Constantius. In any case, Constantius mustered his army in the great fortress of Eboracum, now York, and sent for his 33-year-old son, Constantine, to join him on the campaign.

At this point in time Constantius had been joint emperor with Galerius for less than a year, and Constantine was living with Galerius as a hostage for his father's good behaviour. After some discussion, Galerius was persuaded to allow Constantine to travel to Britain. He arrived at Eboracum *c.*June 305. The Roman army marched north, passing through Hadrian's Wall and embarking on a campaign into the northern mountains, which lasted some months. The fighting ended in partial success, with the northern tribes cowed but not beaten. The army returned to Eboracum as winter drew on, and there Constantius fell sick.

The next spring the army failed to set out again on campaign due to the serious illness of Constantius. On 25 July 306 Constantius died. It was then up to the Roman senate, in practice led by the remaining joint Emperor Galerius, to select the next joint ruler. Among the Roman army in Eboracum, however, was a German mercenary named Chrocus, one of the toughest and most successful commanders of the time. He persuaded the army units in Eboracum to declare Constantine the next joint Emperor, and to send messages to the governors of the various provinces demanding that they accept the move. The implicit threat of a prompt invasion by the notoriously ruthless Chrocus and the large army in Eboracum was enough to persuade the governors of Britain and Gaul to accept, but those in Spain refused and sent to the senate for advice.

Galerius then stepped in and advised the senate to grant Constantine the title of Caesar, a rank that gave Constantine the powers of an emperor, but not the same rank. At this point, Chrocus suddenly died. How he met his death is a mystery, but Constantine subsequently blamed Chrocus for the illegal power grab and accepted the deal offered him by Galerius. Constantine

The bronze statue of the great Roman Emperor Constantine I that stands outside York Minster. It was here that General Constantine was hailed as Emperor by his troops.

was given Britain, Gaul and Spain to rule. He then left Eboracum for Gaul, where he established his capital at Trier. It is now thought likely that Constantine had Chrocus murdered as part of the deal with Galerius.

Constantine's status as one of the few men active in Britain to become emperor, and the fact that his later works helped to make Christianity accepted in Rome, meant that a huge of number of stories were soon circulating about him in Britain. How many of these had any basis in truth, it is impossible to tell. The tales were first recorded in the 12th century. According to these, Constantius came to Britain not to fight the Picts, but to put down a rebellion in Britain led by a man named Coel. Constantius arrived in Britain with a vast army, whereupon Coel promptly surrendered. Constantius then married Coel's daughter, Helena, as a move to placate the British. Constantine was a son of this marriage and, when he grew up, inherited rule over Britain from his mother and over Rome from his father. Constantine then appointed a number of rulers to govern various parts of Britain on his behalf. This version of events was held to be true until the early 20th century, when it was found that the supposed proof came from documents written many centuries after the date.

Although the birthplace and ancestry of Helena is not recorded in any ancient source, it would seem that there was something rather disreputable about her background. Being the daughter of a British king does not fit the bill. What little evidence survives indicates that she was the daughter of an innkeeper from Drepanum, now Hersek in Turkey. She seems to have been the long-term mistress of Constantius rather than his wife, and by 305 had been pushed off to an obscure country estate so that Constantius could make a politically advantageous marriage. She almost certainly never came to Britain.

The stories about Helena being British may have arisen from confusion with a lady named Helen who was born in Britain at Caernarfon *c*.340. She married Magnus Maximus, a Roman army officer, and is credited with having introduced the idea of monasticism to Britain. Maximus was raised to be joint Emperor in 383, with control over Britain and Gaul. In 388 he tried to add Italy and Spain to his domains, but was killed in the fighting that followed.

Meanwhile, the King Coel who cropped up as the supposedly British father of Constantius's *wife*, Helena, seems to have been confused with another real person, who lived some years later. Coel is usually referred to as Coel Godebog, meaning 'Coel the Protector', or as Coel Hen, meaning 'Coel the Old'. These days, he is better known as Old King Cole. He is named in the records of several of the small kingdoms that existed in northern England, as it is now, in the 7th and 8th centuries. According to these records, Coel was the ancestor of at least three royal families and he lived *c*.420.

Coel must have been born soon after the collapse of Roman rule over Britain, which took place in 410. The kingdoms whose rulers trace ancestry back to him stretched from the Humber and Ribble and north to the Forth and Clyde. Interestingly, this area was thought to have been under the rule of the Roman military, guarding Hadrian's Wall and operating out of Eboracum (York). It is known that Roman provinces and military districts became independent as the Empire broke up. Perhaps that is what happened at Eboracum in 410. Maybe what Roman occupation was left in northern Britain established itself as independent states under a general, with a name similar to Collerius. That general may have divided the lands up among his sons, and so founded the various historic kingdoms. Alternatively, it may be that the royal families traced their power back to grants made by Coel to local strongmen, not his actual sons. Whatever the truth behind the mysterious Coel Hen, he undoubtedly lived in and around Yorkshire in the turbulent years following the collapse of Roman power.

Another mysterious figure from the decades following the fall of Roman Britain is even better known than Old King Cole. This is King Arthur, best known from a collection of stories that play on his reputation for Christian faith, chivalric honour and magical background. The real Arthur lived around the year 500 or so. His exact status is unclear, and some historians dispute that he ever lived, but he would seem to have been a well-known warrior or ruler, who wielded power across much of what was Roman Britain. Some think that Arthur was an army man who rose to power by military force; others believe that he was a civilian, elected to keep Roman administration going until the Empire recovered. Nobody can now be certain.

It is generally agreed that Arthur was killed in a civil war among the post-Roman Britons *c*.540. That war destroyed the cohesion of Britain, dividing it up into a number of petty states, none of which were rich or powerful enough to survive long on their own. That opened the way for the invading English from northern Germany to take over and create what has become England. As a consequence, later generations of Britons looked back on the rule of Arthur as a golden age. His exploits, and those of his men, were celebrated first in poem and song, then in legend and epics, before being buried deep beneath later additions and changes, so that by the 15th century he was being presented as a romantic medieval knight, not a post-Roman ruler.

Arthur is remembered at Richmond in two ways. In the cliffs overlooking the south bank of the River Swale, just west of the town, is a perfectly round hill called Round Howe, and in its flank is a large cave that is named Arthur's Oven. Anyone baking a cake in an oven that big must have been mighty indeed. There is also an ancient tale that was first recorded in the 17th century, but which was still firmly believed in the 1850s. The story tells of a Richmond potter named Thompson, who was one day walking along the banks of the Swale, perhaps past Round Howe, when he met a strange man dressed in a long robe.

'Will you help us?' asked the man.

'If I can,' replied Thompson. The man then led Thompson into a cave that narrowed to a passage, then opened out again into a great vault or cavern. The cavern was lit by a pale, unearthly light that seemed to come from nowhere and yet from everywhere at once. Spread across the cavern were hundreds of sleeping men. Each of them was dressed in old-fashioned armour and had shield and sword by his side. There were also several stout chests of the sort used to store gold or silver coins in the days before paper money and credit cards took over. Thompson turned to ask his guide how he could be of help, but the man had vanished.

Thompson edged warily into the room, taking great care not to touch or disturb any of the ferociously military-looking men. He then spotted a large table on which rested a horn and a sword. He worked his way to the table and picked up the horn. It seemed to be a perfectly normal horn. Thompson turned it over in his hands a few times, then put it down. Next he picked up the sword, which again seemed to be quite ordinary. But when Thompson began to draw the sword from its scabbard things began to happen. The sleeping men stirred and made signs of waking up. A couple of them reached out for their weapons, and others grunted or groaned loudly.

Thompson dropped the sword and sprinted for the exit, terrified of what the mysterious warriors would do to him for having disturbed them. As he reached the narrow passage by which he had entered, Thompson heard a voice call out from behind him:

'Potter, Potter Thompson,'
'If thou had either drawn
The sword or blown that horn,
Thou'd be the luckiest man
That ever yet was born.'

Thompson did not stop, but blundered on to reach the fresh air. Gasping for breath on the banks of the Swale, Thompson looked back to find that the cave by which he had entered the great cavern was now no more than a shallow depression in the ground. He came back many times, but never again found his way underground, and neither has anyone else.

Although the luckless potter did not learn the name of the men asleep in the cavern beneath Richmond, it seems likely that they were the warrior band of Arthur. A very similar story is told about a farmer at Sewingshields and a knight at Dunstanburgh, both in Northumberland, and about other places in Britain.

One of those places is Freeborough Hill (sometimes spelled Freeburgh), just east of Guisborough. Like the Round Howe at Richmond, this is an almost perfectly conical, but entirely natural hill. The tale told here concerns a farmer from Dimmington named Edward Trotter. Trotter was out looking for lost sheep up on the moors where Freeborough Hill stands when he spotted a hole in the ground. He at first thought it to be a badger sett, but as he got closer he realised that it was much larger than he would expect a sett to be. Getting on his hands and knees, Trotter crawled into the hole, which gradually became taller as he progressed, until he could stand up and walk quite easily.

After about a hundred yards of so, Trotter found himself confronted by a large, oak door with ancient, iron hinges and studded with iron bolts. Trotter gave the door a push and found that it opened slightly. He gave it a hefty shove and fell through the doorway. He was instantly grabbed by the scruff of the neck and hauled to his feet by a tall, muscular man clad in chain mail and holding a spear in his hand. Now thoroughly frightened, Trotter glanced around to see he was in a vast chamber set with long tables and dozens of chairs, in each chair sat an armoured man sleeping.

The large doorkeeper shook Trotter and scowled into his face. 'Silence!' growled the man. 'You dare to disturb Arthur and his knights?' Trotter was lost for words and said nothing. The doorkeeper glared and went on, 'Is it time for us to arise yet?'

Trotter thought quickly and decided on what he thought was probably the safest answer. 'No,' he ventured.

'Then get out!' roared the doorkeeper. He threw Trotter out the door and slammed it shut. Trotter crept back along the passageway, grateful to be back in the fresh air. Like the potter in Richmond, Trotter tried several times to find the hole again, but never did.

One of the small states that emerged from the chaos that engulfed Britain after the death of Arthur was Deira. This state takes its name from Derventio, the name of a small, fortified Roman town that stood where Malton is now. Before the Romans arrived, the area from the Humber to Scarborough and inland to Easingwold had been home to the Celtic Parisii tribe. This area was then turned into a local government district by the Romans, and it was this district that seems to have become independent as Deira *c*.540.

Late Roman practice was for local districts to be ruled by a council made up of the richer local landowners and merchants, who then elected men to carry out specific tasks, such as commanding the local militia, maintaining roads or clearing out drains. It is likely that Deira began its life as an independent state under this sort of a system, but, if so, all records have long since been lost.

In about 581, however, Deira was converted into a kingdom ruled by an Anglian warrior named Aella. Exactly how an English invader came to seize power in a post-Roman Celtic state is a mystery. Nor is the year in which the change took place certain: it could have been almost any time between 565 and 585. Neither is it clear whether the change from British to English rule involved any great change in the population. It may be that Aelle brought in large numbers of English settlers and exterminated or enslaved the native British. On the other hand, he may have been the leader of a small band of warriors who imposed their rule on a much larger British population by force. What is known is that within a generation or so Deira had expanded to stretch from the Humber to the Tyne, and inland to the Pennines. In doing so, Deira took over two mysterious and poorly known small British states, Elmet and Craven, which covered what is now the West Riding. Effectively, Deira had come to cover what is now Yorkshire, and may be considered to be the origins of the county.

Deira was to remain an independent kingdom until *c*.616 when King Edwin of Deira inherited the Kingdom of Bernicia, which stretched from the Tees to the mouth of the Forth. He thus created a new kingdom, Northumbria. For some generations, Deira continued to be administered separately. As late as 679 Alfwine, a son of the Northumbrian King Egfrith, is recorded as ruling Deira on behalf of his father. Thereafter, Deira vanishes from history.

At some point in its history, Deira was attacked by an alliance of northern British kingdoms. This campaign culminated in the Battle of Catraeth (Catterick), and is usually dated to *c*.600. This would place the battle soon after Deira was taken over by the English, and so it would seem that the campaign was part of an attempt by the British to regain control of what is now Yorkshire. The battle is known primarily from a poem called *Y Gododdin*. This was first written down *c*.900, although it is certainly older than that, and might have been composed within a few years of the battle itself.

The poem is an elegy to the 300 British warriors who assembled at what is now Edinburgh, before marching south to attack Deira. The title refers to the Kingdom of Gododdin, which covered the Forth Valley and provided most of the fighting men for the invasion. The invasion came to grief in a battle that lasted from dawn until dusk. The poem recounts the heroic deaths of more than 100 named warriors, and concludes with the survival of a single man who carried the news of defeat home again.

In recent years, however, this interpretation has been questioned. There are clues in the poem that it may have been composed *c*.560. This early date would make the attack on Deira a war between post-Roman Britons in which the English played no part. This would make it a battle fought as part of the civil wars that followed the death of Arthur. Historians know that men from Strathclyde lost a struggle that they called Gwen Ystrat at about this time, but have never been able to identify where Gwen Ystrat was. Perhaps Gwen Ystrat and Catraeth were one and the same.

Whatever the truth behind the Kingdoms of Deira, Elmet and Craven, the area now covered by Yorkshire was firmly part of the Kingdom of Northumbria by 793, when a terrible event took place. Savage raiders arrived in ships from the north to attack the peaceful monastery on the island of Lindisfarne, in the northern part of Northumbria. The monks were slaughtered, their treasures stolen and the English learned a new word: 'Viking'. In 867 a huge army of Vikings arrived, smashed the Northumbrian forces and carved up the old English kingdom between themselves. What had been Deira became the Kingdom of York, or Jorvik, under a ruler named Halfdan.

Halfdan did not last long, for in 877 he was expelled and replaced by Guthred. Exactly how Guthred came to be King of Jorvik is something of a mystery, for he seems to have begun life as a slave in Denmark. Even more bizarre, it seems that it was the Christians in the kingdom who made the pagan Guthred ruler of Jorvik. According to one very early version of events, the Vikings had expelled Halfdan for unspecified crimes, before deciding on a successor. The Vikings then met to debate who should be the next king, or if they even needed a king at all when they could manage with an assembly of freemen meeting from time to time to make decisions.

Into this meeting walked Abbot Eadred of Carlisle, who had a strange story to tell. Eadred announced that he had been resting in his monastic cell when he experienced a vision of St Cuthbert. This Cuthbert had died in 687, after a long career as hermit, monk, bishop and scholar. He had risen to be the Bishop of Northumbria, and after his death had become the most revered saint in Northumbria. Carlisle had long been the capital of the British Kingdom of Rheged, becoming part of Northumbria through a dynastic marriage *c*.730. It is unclear if, at that time, the Vikings ruled what had been Rheged, so whether Eadred came as a conquered subject or a citizen of a rival state is unclear. Come he did, however, and he made a curious request.

Eadred said that St Cuthbert had instructed him to ask for a slave named Guthred, son of Hardacnut, who belonged to a widow. After a bit of searching, the Vikings found that such a slave did exist and brought him to Eadred. The widow was none too pleased to have her home help taken away, so Eadred paid her the going rate for a young male slave. He then announced that St Cuthbert had said that young Guthred should be made ruler of Jorvik, and that he should be given a totemic bracelet to wear on his right arm. These events might seem surprising, but even more amazingly the army of Viking warriors did as Eadred asked and made Guthred King of Jorvik.

What lies behind this mysterious story it is difficult to know, but there are clues. Unlike Halfdan, Guthred ruled more or less securely over all of what had been Northumbria. He also gave lands to monasteries, and received the support of the monks when Jorvik was invaded by the Scots, a Christian nation; it seems likely that Guthred may have been a Christian himself. At any rate, he seems to have been far more acceptable to the native Northumbrians than Halfdan had been. This factor may have been what persuaded the Vikings to choose him as their new ruler. As for his slave status, it was not unknown among the Vikings for a slave to fight as a warrior and so win his freedom. Even so, it is a mysterious tale that no doubt hides some strange truth.

The Viking Kingdom of Jorvik flourished for almost a century. Further south, however, the Christian English Kings of Wessex had been gradually recapturing territory lost by other English kingdoms to the pagan Vikings. As land was captured, the Kings of Wessex began claiming to be the Kings of the English, and set about creating a united England. By the 940s King Eadred of England had reached the River Humber. At a meeting held in Pontefract in 947, King Olaf of Jorvik promised to become subject to Eadred, on condition that the Vikings could continue to run their own internal affairs.

In 952 Olaf was expelled by the Vikings, who installed in his place a prince with the grim name of Erik Bloodaxe, who promised to restore full independence. Erik Bloodaxe was a colourful character. He was the younger son of King Harald of Norway, and killed his elder brother to gain the throne. He was then overthrown by the nobles in favour of another brother, and fled west to grab power in Orkney, then part of Norway, before going raiding down the western coasts of Europe and into the Mediterranean. He then went to Denmark by way of Ireland, engaging in various feuds and raids along the way. By the time he appeared out of the blue in York he was a famous warrior, but an infamously violent man.

The sources are vague, but Erik seems to have started putting together an alliance of Viking kingdoms in Britain to resist the growing power of Eadred. Certainly, the Kingdom of the Isles (the Hebrides) joined his cause. There is also some evidence that he made friends with the King of Scots. If so, this would have been a formidable alliance that must have disturbed Eadred.

What happened next is mysterious. According to one version, Erik, with his brother Ragnald and son Haeric, was travelling over the Pennines in summer 954, by way of Bowes and Stainmore on the old Roman road now overlain by the A66. Why he was travelling from one part of his kingdom to another is unknown, but he was travelling light, with only a small bodyguard. It would seem that he was persuaded to make the journey by Earl Oswulf, an Englishman who governed much of the northern part of Jorvik for Erik. The journey was a ruse to lure Erik into a trap.

At Stainmore, Erik and his men were ambushed by a large warrior band led by Earl Maccus Olafson. Erik and all of his men were killed, with the treacherous Oswulf hurrying back to York in safety. Within weeks, the warriors of Eadred were spreading throughout the land to enforce his rule. Oswulf did well out of the killing, becoming the Earl of Northumbria and governing all of what had been Jorvik for King Eadred. The independence of Northumbria was over, and England was united as a single kingdom. It would seem that Erik had been murdered to clear the way for an English takeover of Jorvik.

Things may not have been so straightforward, however. Maccus Olafson may have been the son of Olaf, who was ousted by Erik, making the killing more a revenge attack than a political assassination. If so, then maybe Eadred and Oswulf simply took advantage of the situation, rather than having engineered it. Yet another version states that Erik was killed in a large battle, along with five other kings, at a place in southern England. Still another chronicle records that Erik left Jorvik to travel to Spain and was killed there for unexplained reasons. We shall probably never know the truth.

Eadred died without leaving a son, but he did leave a daughter, named Elfflaed, and she features in another Viking tradition to have left a mysterious mark on Yorkshire. Just off the A1079 east of York is Siward's Howe, a domed mound that is usually said to be a Bronze Age burial mound, but according to local tradition is more closely linked to Elfflaed's husband, Siward Ulffson.

Siward was, the tale goes, a famous Norwegian warrior, and the son of a princess and a polar bear. He had gained fame by killing a dragon in Orkney. He then heard that another dragon was on the loose in Yorkshire and set out to hunt it down. He and his band of warriors landed in the Humber and were approaching York along the Hull Road when they came to what is now known as Siward's Howe. Sitting on the mound was an old man dressed in a grey cloak, who beckoned to Siward. When Siward approached, the old man told him to give up his quest for the dragon and instead to go to London, where he would meet a king who would make him rich and famous. Siward glanced nervously at his men and said that he could not do as instructed as his men might think him frightened of facing the dragon. The old man then gave Siward a banner embroidered with a black raven flying over a landscape, which he said was called 'Ravenlandeye', meaning 'Raven Land Terror'. Seeing this, Siward's men agreed to follow him.

Landing in London, Siward entered the city carrying his banner. This was spotted by King Cnut (Canute), who had in turn been told by a mysterious stranger to appoint as Earl of Northumbria a stranger who entered London carrying a banner of a black raven flying over green fields. Siward was promptly made Earl and sent north to rule the northern counties from York. Siward ruled the area wisely and well for many years. He drove off a Scottish invasion, then in 1054 invaded Scotland to defeat and kill King Macbeth (of Shakespearean fame).

During the course of this invasion, Siward's eldest son, Osbjorn, was killed in a skirmish. When the news was brought to Siward, he sat silently for a while, then asked the messenger to describe the wounds that had killed his son. Nervously, the man did so. When he had finished Siward broke out into a huge smile. 'All in the front!' he declared. 'I rejoice, for his death was worthy of him.'

Siward himself would die less than a year later. According to an almost contemporary chronicle:

> Siward, the stalwart Earl, being stricken by dysentery, felt that death was near, and said, "How shameful it is that I, who could not die in so many battles, should have been saved for the ignominious death of a cow! At least clothe me in my impenetrable breastplate, gird me with my sword, place my helmet on my head, my shield in my left hand, my gilded battleaxe in my right, that I, the bravest of soldiers, may die like a soldier."

His surviving son, Waltheof, helped Siward get dressed in his armour and lifted his father to his feet. The old man stood leaning on his spear for some minutes, then gave a great sigh and fell down dead. He was buried in the hill that bears his name.

Despite the tales of dragons, bears and strange men in grey, Siward is an undoubtedly genuine historical figure, despite being enigmatic in the extreme. Although he was probably not the son of a polar bear, no record survives of his background. He arrived in London in 1019 with a band of warriors and his famous banner, and almost at once was promoted by Cnut, and by 1030 was Earl of Northumbria. The story of his meeting with an old man on Siward's Howe is probably an attempt to explain his meteoric rise. In pagan Viking myth, the great god Odin often walked the earth disguised as an old man dressed in grey. He would then interfere in human affairs, favouring bold and brave warriors over cunning, sneaky weaklings.

Siward's death is recorded in 1055, and his insistence on being given his weapons to hold was widely known at the time.It seems unlikely that he was buried under Siward's Howe, however. He is recorded as having a tomb in St Olaf's Church in York.

At some point in the Viking wars, Ripon acquired a unique tradition. The usual version of events is that King Alfred the Great of Wessex (ruled 871–899) came to Ripon as part of a tour of England inspecting defences against the Vikings. Alfred approved of the defences of Ripon and so granted the city a royal charter. He was, however, less impressed with the readiness of the militia, and so instituted the office of Wakeman, giving him a special horn. The Wakeman had the task of patrolling the city streets and city walls from dusk until dawn every night to keep a watch for Viking armies or Viking infiltrators. He had to blow his horn in the marketplace four times at 9 o'clock each night to signal to the citizens that his duty was being carried out.

To this day, the Wakeman, dressed in his ceremonial garb of long, grey coat with red trim and a black tricorn hat, marches into the market place at 9 o'clock every evening to blow his horn. The original horn is now in the town museum, and a modern replica is used for the ceremony.

There are, however, a number of problems with this traditional tale. For a start, the famous Alfred the Great did not rule further north of the River Thames, never mind north of the Humber. And the only real danger to Ripon in those years came in 947, when the Christian English King Eadred attacked the city and burned Ripon Minster to the ground. Perhaps the Wakeman is a Viking innovation aimed against the English, which later generations changed to being an invention of Alfred's once Ripon became part of a united England. Others suggest that the Wakeman dates to 1108, when Ripon was granted a charter by King Henry I.

As with so many mysteries, the truth remains obscure. But the Wakeman continues his ceremonial horn blowing night after night.

Some years ago a Wakeman of many years standing, Hugh Ripley, died suddenly. That night, his place in the nightly ceremony was taken by a temporary substiture. As the horn was sounded, there came a gasp from the small crowd that always gathers for the event: Hugh Ripley's ghost had put in an appearance. He was seen by the crowd peering from the window of his house, which overlooked the market square. More than a dozen people saw him quite clearly, but when the house was searched there was nobody there.

In 1066 England was once again invaded by a vast Viking army. This time, the army came from Norway and was led by the formidable warrior Harald Hardrada. It came to reinstate the renegade Earl Tostig of Northumbria, who had been expelled from England the previous year. The Vikings came with 300 ships, making their army some 15,000 men strong, which was large for its time. The army cruised up the East Coast of England, landing to raid and pillage from time to time. They turned into the Humber Estuary and headed up the Ouse. They landed at Riccall and, leaving a small guard over the ships, the Vikings marched on to York.

The local English were not idle all this time. Earl Morcar, who had replaced Tostig as governor of Northumbria, mustered his men for war and sent urgent messages south asking for reinforcements. Earl Edwin of Mercia arrived first, while messengers came from King Harold of England that he was hurrying north with troops from further south.

The Vikings were sighted from the walls of York long before King Harold's army was anywhere near Yorkshire. Earls Morcar and Edwin decided not to wait inside York, but to march out to face the invaders. They marched their army south out of the old Roman gate, along the banks of the Ouse to Gate Fulford. What happened next is something of a mystery.

Beyond doubt, a great battle was fought somewhere south of Gate Fulford, but nobody knows where. The contemporary chronicles are silent about the course of events, recording only the outcome. Later Norwegian accounts give a reasonably detailed picture of the fighting, but they do

Ripon Marketplace. It is here that the Wakeman of Ripon has sounded his horn four times every evening for centuries. Quite why he should do this is something of a mystery, as the traditional accounts are historically inaccurate.

not match the landscape particularly well and may be unreliable. According to these, the English attacked first, having a river on one flank and a marsh on the other. Harald Hardrada had only half his army with him at this point, and the Vikings began to fall back. When the remaining Vikings arrived, a fresh counter-attack was made through the marsh, which pushed the English towards York. The English army then broke up, and collapsed into a band of fleeing fugitives.

This view of events does not quite match the aftermath of battle. Earls Edwin and Morcar both survived the battle, returning to York and slamming the city gates shut in the face of the Vikings. Talks then took place, which ended in a truce, under which the Vikings retreated to Stamford and the English promised to meet them three days later to pay an unspecified sum of money. This gives the impression that the English retired in good order, and certainly had enough men and discipline left to hold the city in such strength that the Vikings dared not attack. Clearly, the battle had not been a rout.

In any event, King Harold of England arrived two days later with the main English army. He marched to Stamford and inflicted a massive defeat on the Vikings. So great was the carnage that Harald Hardrada and Tostig were both killed, and only 24 ships were needed to take the survivors back to Norway.

As for the battlefield of Gate Fulford, the most sensible place for the English to have tried to stop the Vikings was on the banks of the Germany Beck, just south of Gate Fulford. If they had lined up here, they would have had the Ouse on their right flank, but their left flank would have rested on West Moor, not on a marsh. The marshes would have been further south near Naburn, but the English always called the battle 'Gate Fulford'. Archaeological investigations have been made widely around both Gate Fulford and Naburn, and at other locations. None of these have turned up the usual debris of medieval battles: arrowheads, broken weapons and pieces of metal armour.

The course of the fighting and the location of the battle remain mysteries. The solving of the problem is becoming urgent, as developers seek to cover the land south of York with housing and commercial developments. If the battlefield is to be saved, the first task is to solve the mystery of where it is.

At Skipsea there was once one of the mightiest castles in northern England, although nothing remains today except extensive earthworks. The castle was built by a Flemish knight, Sir Drogo de Bouerer, who had fought alongside William the Conqueror at the Battle of Hastings in 1066. Young Drogo was obviously a dashing and important man, for he married a cousin of the newly crowned King William and was granted the lands of Holderness, stretching from the Humber to Bridlington. Sir Drogo and Lady de Bouerer settled down to a life of apparently happy domesticity, having several children and no known arguments.

It was in 1086 that Drogo built the vast, sprawling castle at Skipsea to serve as both a fortified stronghold and as administrative headquarters for the governing of his spreading estates. He enjoyed high favour with William at this time, but then things went wrong, and even today it is impossible to know the truth.

As Christmas approached in 1086, Drogo appeared at King William's court. He had clearly ridden hard and had only a small escort of men. Drogo marched into William's presence and

The earthen ramparts are all that is left of the once-mighty castle at Skipsea. This castle was home to a succession of powerful barons, but it was the first baron, Sir Drogo de Bouerer, who is rumoured to have murdered his wife here before fleeing abroad. This incident would lead indirectly to the death of King William the Conqueror in 1087.

announced that the time had come to show his wife the de Bouerer estate in Flanders. William agreed that this was a good idea, but Drogo had an odd request. He said that he was temporarily short of cash, having spent all his ready money on Holderness, and asked if William would lend him some travelling expenses. Again, William agreed, handing over a handsome purse of gold. Drogo bowed, smiling, then mounted his horse and set off at full speed for Dover.

Three days later a mud-spattered messenger arrived at the royal court from Yorkshire with the routine news from the county for the royal court. Among the news was the announcement of the unfortunate death of Lady de Bouerer after a short illness. William at once smelled trouble; he sent officials north to Yorkshire and south across the Channel to Flanders to investigate.

The men sent to Yorkshire came back first. They reported that Lady de Bouerer had died suddenly with odd symptoms. Local gossip had it that she had discovered that Sir Drogo was having an affair, and had acquired a love potion from a local witch that would ensure her husband's affections returned to her. The lady had taken the potion home, intending to put it in her husband's meal at a private dinner one night. It had been that very night that she had fallen ill, and she died at dawn next day.

The messengers sent to Flanders came back a few days later to report that Sir Drogo had refused to see them. Count Robert of Flanders had failed to help them in any way, and seemed to be protecting Sir Drogo. William suspected that Drogo had murdered his wife, William's cousin, and mustered his armies to march to war in spring 1087. King Philip I of France supported Robert of Flanders, so William began his vengeful hunt for Sir Drogo by marching into Paris. William died in battle at Mantes when his horse stumbled and threw him against the pommel of his saddle, causing massive internal bleeding. The new king, William's son, William Rufus, at once forgot the war and allowed Sir Drogo to return to Skipsea. Perhaps he knew something that indicated Drogo's innocence, or maybe he had not liked his cousin.

Whatever the truth, a ghostly white lady was widely believed to haunt Skipsea Castle ever after. She was reported as recently as the 1890s, but does not seem to have walked the grassy mounds of Skipsea since then. Hopefully, she has found peace at last.

Rather more respectable was Sir Leonard de Reresby, Lord of Trybergh. In the early 13th century he went off to the Holy Land to fight on crusade against the Moslems. While there, he was captured and sold into slavery. No news came back to Yorkshire for seven years and it was assumed that he had died. His widow was a handsome and wealthy lady, and it was not long before she attracted the notice of local knights. Having obtained permission from the Church, she decided to remarry.

On the morning of the wedding of Lady Reresby a peasant was walking out to work in the fields near Trybergh. In a field he found a bearded middle-aged man, covered in dirt, clad in rags and bound by iron chains. Amazingly, it was the missing Sir Leonard. Even more amazingly, he had absolutely no idea how he had got there. He had fallen asleep the night before in a filthy Moslem prison in Damascus, but had woken up in a chilly field. The wedding was promptly called off and the event hailed as a miracle. After his death, some years later, Sir Richard was canonised as St Leonard of Reresby. A stone cross was erected to his honour and remains to this day.

A couple of centuries later another death in Yorkshire led to more mystery. A man named Robin died at Kirklees and was buried in the graveyard of the Cistercian Priory there. These days, only the gatehouse remains, just off Junction 25 of the M62, but the grave is there still. The reason why this obscure grave has survived, while the rest of the priory was swept away in the Dissolution of the Monasteries and the centuries that followed, is that the Robin in question is widely believed to have been the famous outlaw Robin Hood.

According to Yorkshire legend, Robin Hood left his usual haunts around Nottingham to come to Kirklees Abbey when he fell ill. His aunt was the prioress at Kirklees and was famed for her healing skills. Unknown to Robin, however, his aunt had a lover in the shape of the wicked and avaricious Sir Roger of Doncaster, who was determined to get his hands on the reward for Robin's head. Waiting until Robin's comrades Little John and Will Scarlett were absent, Sir Roger slipped into the room and stabbed Robin on his sickbed. Robin grabbed a sword and slew Sir Roger, before dying himself.

Another version says that it was Robin's aunt herself who killed him with a potion while pretending to heal him. As Robin felt his life ebbing away, he called Little John to his side and asked for his bow. Robin then shot an arrow out of the window, asking to be buried where it fell. Little John found the spot and buried Robin accordingly.

Thomas Gale, Dean of York in the late 17th century, recorded that he had visited Robin's grave and found engraved on it a script in medieval English, which he translated as:

'Here underneath this little stone
Lies Robert, Earl of Huntingdon,
No archer was as he so good
and people call him Robin Hood.
Such outlaws as he and his men
Will England never see again.'

No such inscription can be found today. The stone marking the grave has the single word 'Robin'. It is widely thought that Gale invented the inscription, or perhaps was told by a local that this is what the stone had once said.

Of course, the true identity of the Robin buried at Kirklees Abbey is wrapped up in the mystery of whether there ever was a real Robin Hood or not. Although today Robin Hood is firmly placed in Sherwood Forest, the earliest stories about him are less specific, and have him ranging widely across Nottinghamshire and Yorkshire. Nor does he rob from the rich to give to the poor in the early tales, instead he campaigns against corrupt officials and unfair treatment of the poor. Nor does he live in the times of King Richard the Lionheart and his treacherous brother Prince John, instead living in the reign of 'King Edward', which would put him in the 14th century, whichever Edward is meant. Finally, Robin is not an outlawed Earl of Huntingdon, nor any other sort of nobleman, but a yeoman farmer. He is thus, in origin, a rather different figure from the popular image he has in the 21st century.

Whether this outlaw was a real man is a mystery. Some scholars believe that the large number of real places, real people and real events mentioned in the early stories indicate that there actually

Robin Hood's Well, beside the A1 near Skellow. The well was almost demolished when the road was widened, surviving only because it was the work of famous architect John Vanbrugh. Although most modern versions have Robin Hood active around Nottingham, the earliest versions make him a Yorkshire figure.

was an outlaw called Robin Hood. Others point out that most of the stories are so far-fetched that they cannot really be true. Perhaps there had been an outlaw called Robin who became something of a hero across Nottinghamshire and Yorkshire. If so, it may be that a series of tales were told about him, which, while firmly rooted in real places and characters, had fabulous details added to make them more exciting. None of which solves the mystery of who the Robin buried at Kirlees might have been.

Be that as it may, many of the earliest references to Robin Hood also call him 'Robin of Loxley'. In the terminology of the 14th century, this would mean that he had been born in Loxley, or at least had grown up there. Loxley is now a suburb on the western outskirts of Sheffield and firmly in Yorkshire. A traveller in 1637 recorded that he was shown a ruined stone cottage on nearby Rodney Hill that he was told had been the birthplace of Robin Hood. The site is now occupied by Loxley Primary School.

Another Yorkshire link to Robin Hood is to be found just north of Skellow, beside the A1. Here stands Robin Hood's Well. This rustic stone structure was erected in the 18th century to cover the well. This was no mere whim by a local man, but was put up by the great architect John Vanbrugh when he was in Yorkshire working on Castle Howard for the Earl of Carlisle.

When the A1 was made into a dual carriageway, some road planner with no sense of history decided to widen the eastern side, which meant covering the actual well with tons of concrete and tarmac. The stone structure was shifted 50ft or so, and now covers not a well but solid ground. It seems to have been the link to Vanbrugh, not to Robin Hood, that saved it from oblivion.

The well has ancient links to Robin Hood, having been known by his name as long ago as 1422, when the spring was marked by a stone chair, which was popularly believed to have been made for Robin Hood himself.

An ancient tradition that apparently refers to another outlaw is the Burning of Bartle, which takes place in West Witton every year on the Saturday nearest to 24 August. The ceremony begins at 9 o'clock in the evening, when a larger-than-life figure of a man dressed in old-fashioned rural clothes is hoisted onto the shoulders of local men and paraded down the main road of the village. The effigy is halted outside the two pubs in the village, and outside particular houses defined by tradition. At each stopping place, the crowd chants the traditional verse:

'On Penhill Crags he tore his rags.
At Hunters Thorn he blew his horn.
At Capplebank Stee he brake his knee.
At Grassgill Beck he brake his neck.
At Wadhams End he couldn't fend
At Grassgill End we'll make his end.
Shout, lads. Shout!'

The places referred to in the verse are all to be found close to West Witton. The Penhill Crags are the steep, rocky slopes of a mountain south of the village, which rise to heights of over 1500ft. The route traced by the verse follows a zigzag path down the mountain, through the village, to a small field just outside. The procession follows the last part of this route, ending in the field south of the main street. There, the verse is chanted once again, before the figure is put down and set on fire.

Exactly what this ceremony celebrates is a mystery. The local version told most often is that Bartle was a notorious medieval sheep rustler who operated across Wensleydale, much to the chagrin of local farmers. One day, it is said, the villagers of West Witton spotted Bartle up on Penhill Crags and set out in pursuit. The chase followed the course set out in the verse, ending with the great thief being killed in the field of Grassgill End.

The local church is dedicated to St Bartholomew, however, whose feast day is 24 August. The name 'Bartle' was a common version of Bartholomew, so some have suggested that Bartle may originally have been St Bartholomew. In medieval times it was not unusual for statues of saints to be paraded through the streets on their feast day. Perhaps the Burning of Bartle is some survival of this medieval custom. It has certainly become something of a tourist draw, and today has grown to be a fairly important festival that attracts substantial crowds to the jollity and partying that takes place.

Yet another old-time bandit once frequented Bulmer, near Malton. This was Hugh de Pontchardon, better known in Yorkshire as Black Hugh. Although a notorious robber and possessed of a viciously violent temper, Black Hugh did not go the way of most such men by being outlawed. The reason for this was that he carried out useful services for the almost equally notorious Bishop Antony Bek of Durham. Bek may have been a bishop, but that did not stop him from being excommunicated in 1293 by John le Romeyn, Archbishop of York. The excommunication followed a string of high-profile events in which Bishop Bek behaved in a remarkably secular way for a supposedly celibate cleric. King Edward I stepped in to back Bek, forcing Romeyn to rescind the excommunication.

Black Hugh, meanwhile, was carrying out Bek's orders in Scotland. War between England and Scotland broke out in 1295. As a leading landowner in the north, Bek was expected to send men to fight in Scotland, but as a cleric he was not obliged to lead them himself. He sent Black Hugh instead, and before long the Bishop of Durham's men had earned an enviable reputation for skilful fighting, and an unenviable one for butchery, rape and pillage. The war ended in 1300, and Black Hugh came to England to be rewarded by Bishop Bek with lands around Thickley in Durham and Bulmer in Yorkshire. Black Hugh now proved to be as violent and vicious a landlord as he had been a soldier.

Black Hugh was not to be unemployed for long. In 1301 Bek fell out with his own cathedral chapter and the Prior of Durham. He sent for Black Hugh, who went through the priory with his thugs, throwing the monks out into the street and seizing their treasures for Bishop Bek. This time the king sided against Bek, and ordered him to make restitution. Black Hugh was sent away to kick his heels at Bulmer, making life a misery for his tenants. When Edward I died his weak son, Edward II, came to throne, and Bek took advantage to pursue his old feuds, with Black Hugh as his instrument of violence. But in 1309 Black Hugh dropped dead. He may have suffered a heart attack, but local gossip soon had it that the Devil had come for his own.

Be that as it may, the estates granted to Black Hugh reverted to the Bishopric of Durham, and Bek took to hunting in the lands around Bulmer. One day over Christmas 1310, Bek was out hunting when he was confronted by a man dressed in black and mounted on a white stallion. The local huntsmen knew who he was, and so did Bek. 'Hugh,' gasped the Bishop. 'What maketh thee here?' The phantom of Black Hugh merely smiled and beckoned. Bek blanched, put his spurs to his horse and galloped off. A few days later he was dead.

Since then, the ghost of Black Hugh has been seen many times, galloping over the lands around Bulmer. He is always dressed in black and mounted on a white horse; and woe betide anyone that he notices and beckons to join him.

Not long after the Bishop was beckoned to his grave by Black Hugh, two sisters decided to fund the building of a new church at Withernsea on the Holderness Peninsula, a few miles north of the mouth of the Humber. The money was donated, masons brought in, workmen hired and all was going well, until the chief mason asked what he thought was going to be a fairly straightforward question: was the church to have a spire or a tower. 'A tower,' replied one sister. 'A spire,' replied the other. The two sisters fell to bickering, then to arguing, and work ground to a halt. In desperation, the mason suggested that the sisters consult the abbot of Kirkstall Abbey, a cleric noted for his tact, wisdom and judgement.

The two sisters travelled to Kirkstall Abbey, now a picturesque ruin on the western outskirts of Leeds, and explained the dispute to the abbot. That learned gentleman listened carefully, consulted his own master mason and sent for the priests of neighbouring parishes. He was no nearer to finding an answer to the dispute when he happened to overhear a pair of merchants discussing the dangers to sailors of navigating the mouth of the Humber. What was needed, they said, was a clear and distinctive landmark north of the river mouth, to warn sailors of the treacherous shoals and sandbanks. Finally, the Abbot of Kirkstall had his answer.

He sent for the sisters and told them that they were both right. The sisters grinned. He instructed them to build a church each, right next to each other, with one having a tower and the other a spire. That way, both sisters would get what they wanted, the parishioners would get two lovely churches, and the sailors would get an unmistakable landmark that would visible for miles out to sea. And so the sister churches of St Mary's Withernsea and St Peter's Owthorne were built.

Unfortunately, the coast here is gradually eroding – more than 30 villages recorded in the Domesday Book of 1087 have vanished. A great storm in 1816 washed St Peter's into the sea and unroofed St Mary's. The good folk of Withernsea built a new church, but only one. The maritime landmark was lost, so a 127ft-tall lighthouse was built instead. That lighthouse is now redundant, so it has been converted into a museum dedicated to the actress Kay Kendall, who was born in Withernsea.

During the 1450s, the simple-minded King Henry VI had allowed government to fall into the hands of his unscrupulous French wife, Margaret of Anjou, and her corrupt henchmen. The Duke of York led a faction calling for the return of honest government. England was torn apart, and many families found their loyalties torn between the rightful king (Henry) and the better man (York). War had broken out between the two factions in 1455, and John, the 9th Baron Clifford of Skipton, decided to back King Henry, and so marched to Towton with the Lancastrian army.

In 1460 Clifford fought at the Battle of Wakefield, playing a major role in gaining the victory for the Lancastrians. The Duke of York was killed in the fighting, and his 17-year-old son, Edmund, was wounded and captured. Convention at the time was that prisoners could be either imprisoned or ransomed. But when Clifford spotted the wounded Edmund of York, he drew his sword and hacked the boy to death. Margaret of Anjou approved of the butchery, which turned many people against the Lancastrian cause. The new Duke of York, Edward, the elder brother of Edmund, vowed revenge. He got his wish the following year, when Clifford was killed at the Battle of Ferrybridge.

The main Lancastrian army was utterly destroyed at the Battle of Towton on 4 March 1461. As a result, Henry VI was deposed and Edward, Duke of York, became King Edward IV. One of the new King's first acts was to confiscate all the Clifford lands and order the arrest of the entire Clifford family. It was widely assumed that the Cliffords were to be executed as revenge for the death of young Edmund of York.

News of the orders reached Skipton Castle before the King's men arrived, and Lady Clifford took swift action. Her baby daughter, Elizabeth, was given to a local farmer to be passed off as his child. The middle child, Richard, was sent to live with relatives in Flanders. The eldest, and the new Baron Clifford, was seven years old, and the King's men at the ports had a good description of him. He could not flee the country, and instead was sent to Londesborough, a

The tower of the church at Withernsea. This is a modern replacement for the medieval church, which fell into the sea centuries ago as a result of coastal erosion.

remote part of the Clifford estates. There, he was passed off as a relative of a local shepherd and put to work tending the sheep. There he stayed, working as a humble shepherd, while Edward IV remained king. Edward died in 1483 and was followed onto the throne by his brother Richard III, who was no more inclined to forgive the Cliffords than Edward had been.

Finally, in 1485 Richard III was killed in battle, and the Lancastrian Henry VII became king. He at once reversed the orders for the arrest of the Cliffords. Richard came back from Flanders, while Elizabeth and Henry revealed their true identities. Henry became the 10th Baron Clifford and was given back Skipton Castle and most of his lands. The 25 years as a shepherd had left an indelible mark on the man, however. He became known as the Shepherd Lord, and was known to be much kinder and more charitable to poor folk than were many other lords. The Shepherd Lord did not take well to life in Skipton Castle. He spent much of his time in the countryside, chatting to shepherds and farmers. The title is now held by the 27th Baron Clifford.

Another medieval cleric left his mark at Sessay, south of Thirsk. One day in 1463, or perhaps 1464, a newborn baby was found in the porch of St Cuthbert's church in Sessay, nestled in blankets and placed in a wicker crib. The blankets and the baby's clothes were of good quality, indicating that he came from a good home, but nobody ever admitted ownership. The baby was christened Thomas, and was widely nicknamed 'Thomas Found Amang Us'. He was brought up by the charity of local farmers, but at a young age showed both a devotion to God and a keen intelligence, so he was sent off to a nearby monastery to be educated.

At the monastery, the boy was entered into the register, not as Thomas Found Amang Us, but as Thomas Magnus. He did very well for himself, and by 1504 was Archdeacon of the East Riding. By 1520 he was a privy councillor, and three years later was made treasurer of the king's forces in the north, responsible for maintaining an army in case of war with Scotland. In 1530 he was rich enough to found a grammar school at Newark for the education of other poor boys like himself, and in 1534 became Warden of Sibthorpe College. Around the year 1540, the position of vicar of Sessay fell vacant, and Thomas Magnus, now a very respectable 76-year-old, decided to take up the position and retire. He died on 18 August 1550 and was buried in the church where he had been found so many years before.

On his tomb, Magnus instructed should be written 'Here lyeth Mr Thomas Magnus, archdeacon of the East Riding in the metropolitan church of York, and parson of this church, which died the 18th day of August, *anno domino* 1550, whose soul God pardon.' What need such a leading, eminent and respectable churchman had for pardon from the Lord is not clear. Perhaps Thomas Magnus knew something we do not.

In 1588 a schoolteacher from Pontefract volunteered to join the militia that was summoned to guard against landings by soldiers from the Spanish Armada. No such landing took place, and the Armada was soundly defeated, but the Yorkshire militia spent many anxious weeks patrolling the coast. On one such patrol, the schoolmaster found a bundle of twigs washed up on a beach. When he went home, the man used the bundle of twigs to inflict corporal punishment on any of his boys that misbehaved. In time, the twigs fell apart, so he threw what was left into his garden. There, the pieces took root and grew. A schoolboy one day tried chewing on a twig from the new bush and discovered that it had a fantastic flavour.

What the schoolmaster had unwittingly picked up was a bundle of liquorice roots, lost from a sinking Spanish ship. The liquorice became hugely popular in Pontefract, and before long the town was turning out a steady supply of liquorice sweets, dubbed 'Pontefract cakes' by locals, or so the story goes. In truth, nobody is really certain how liquorice came to Pontefract.

Austwick, near Settle, has a rather more jovial reputation. The folk there are, according to those who live in nearby villages, an amiable bunch of fools. The stories told about the foolishness of the Austwick folk are many.

One day, it is said, a group of Austwick folk were resting on the banks of the Austwick Beck when one of the man decided to go for a swim to cool off. He jumped in, but did not come back up. Instead, a stream of bubbles surfaced, which when they burst seemed to sound like 'The b-b-b-b-best is at the b-b-b-b-bottom.' Promptly, another man jumped in, only for him to disappear in turn and the bubbles to rise again. One by one, the men of Austwick all jumped in and drowned trying to find out what was so wonderful at the bottom of the beck. This led to a Yorkshire saying 'The best is at the bottom in Austwick', meaning that things might seem better somewhere else, but you were, in fact, better off where you were.

Another time, an Austwick farmer was having trouble with his haymaking. One day the sun would shine, so he dashed out to spread the hay, only for it to rain the next day. He then gathered in the hay because of the rain, only for the sun to come out. In the end, he decided that if he could not take his hay to the sun, he would take the sun to the hay. He stacked the wet grass in

Semer Water is said to cover a town whose inhabitants were too evil to be allowed to survive, and so the town was destroyed by God.

his barn and waited for the next sunny day. He then took his wagon out to the field and let the sun shine into it for several hours. He then threw a great canvas sheet over the wagon to trap the sunshine and hurriedly drove the wagon into the barn. He whipped off the canvas to release the sunshine and allow it to dry the grass into hay.

It was not foolishness, but sin and greed that did for the citizens of Semer. This town once stood in a side valley of Wensleydale, but no more. Almost 2,000 years ago, Joseph of Arimathea came to Britain after the crucifixion of Jesus Christ. Joseph of Arimathea was the man who donated his own tomb for the use of Christ's body. He was a rich man, most likely a merchant. There have long been persistent legends that Joseph came to Britain, most often he is said to have come to Cornwall and the West Country to trade tin. One version says that Christ himself came to Britain as a young man, working on one of Joseph's ships. Another has it that Joseph fled to Britain to escape early persecution of the Christians. It was presumably on this later journey that he came to Wensleydale.

Joseph was journeying up the dale when he found that night was drawing in, and he stopped at Semer to ask for shelter. Nobody was willing to give him so much as a scrap of food, never mind a bed for the night. In desperation, Joseph knocked on the door of a hovel halfway up a hill and was delighted to be welcomed in by the elderly, impoverished couple there. They gave him a bit of cheese, some biscuits and some milk to drink from their meagre store, and allowed him to sleep by the fireside. Next day, Joseph left to continue on his journey. As he left the ramshackle cottage, he turned to stare down towards the town where he had found nothing but hostility. He shouted out a curse:

'Semer water rise, Semer water sink,
And swallow up all but this little home
Where they gave me bread and cheese
And summat to drink.'

At once a mighty flood arose and drowned the city beneath a lake. The lake is still there and is known as Semer Water, after the ruined town that lies beneath its waters.

If greed destroyed Semer, it was a passion for plants that made the fortune of Sir Thomas Chaloner *c.*1600. Chaloner was a well-connected gentleman, as his father had been a famous poet, but he was not overly wealthy. The family's main assets were the lands around Guisborough that they had acquired when the great Guisborough Priory was closed down during the Reformation.

In 1598 the 40-year-old Sir Thomas set off on a journey through Europe, in the course of which he visited Rome. While there, he went to see the alum mines that belonged to the Pope, and were the source of much of his income. At this time, alum was a very important mineral, as it was almost the only way in which many vegetable dyes could be fixed to woollen cloth, and it was useful in the leather-tanning process as well. There were only three sources of alum in the entire world: one was in Turkey and exports to Christians were banned; the second was in Spain, then at war with England, and exports to England were banned; the third was just outside Rome, and the Pope demanded enormous prices from English merchants.

As Sir Thomas was being shown around the papal alum mines, he spotted an unusual little plant. He knew that it grew on some hills near Guisborough, but had seen it nowhere else. The Italian guide noticed his interest and told Sir Thomas that the plant was very rare and grew nowhere in the world except on the hills around the alum mine. Sir Thomas at once leapt to the conclusion that if the same plant grew on the hills near Guisborough, then there was probably alum somewhere in those hills. He was delighted, but his excitement was quickly dashed. The guide explained that extracting alum from ore was a complicated process, and boasted that only craftsmen skilled in the craft could manage it.

Sir Thomas did some serious thinking. If there was alum near Guisborough and if he could extract it, then he would have a seriously impressive source of income. His first problem was to confirm that he had alum ore there, and the second was extracting the mineral from the ore. For both he reckoned that he would need a skilled craftsmen. The pope, however, had made it a capital crime for his alum workers either to leave the papal states or to give their knowledge to a foreigner. Sir Thomas appeared stuck at an impasse.

Just six months later, however, Sir Thomas started the production of alum at Guisborough. Helping him was a highly skilled mine manager with swarthy skin, who spoke only broken English with an Italian accent. Quite how Sir Thomas had managed to get the man out of the papal states, across Europe and to Guisborough, is a mystery. Neither man ever told the secret.

Locals came up with their own theory, however. Sir Thomas, it was widely known, had come back from Italy with a huge quantity of Italian red wine transported in several dozen large wooden barrels. It was thought that the alum man had been sealed into one of the barrels, together with a large quantity of food and water, then shipped out with the wine. The truth will never be known. What is known is that Sir Thomas and several other landowners near Guisborough promptly became very rich. Whitby stopped being a small fishing port and became one of the premier ports of Yorkshire, as alum was shipped out and coal brought in to power the refining process. Whitby, and the Chaloner family, never looked back.

Not long after the Chaloners made their fortune from alum, England was torn apart by civil war. Most of Yorkshire declared their support for the King, although some towns preferred Parliament, and fighting was quick to break out across the county. At Skipsea, two brothers fell out with each other about which cause to support. They drew their swords and began fighting in the moat of the abandoned Skipsea Castle. The struggle lasted all day and into the night, when both men fell down dead from exhaustion. The footprints left by the fighting brothers proved impossible to fill in and remained visible well into the 19th century. So did their ghosts, continuing their deadly struggle in spectral form whenever the moon shone on Skipsea castle.

The war ended with victory for Parliament. Charles was captured at Newark, then moved around a succession of houses under comfortable arrest while Parliament decided what to do with him. Finally, Sir Thomas Fairfax, head of the Parliamentary Army, ordered the King's formal arrest and sent Cornet George Joyce to imprison him. When Joyce announced his mission, King Charles demanded to know by what authority Joyce acted. Young Joyce waved his hand at the guns of his men, to which Charles replied, 'A most persuasive authority!' and submitted.

It was an enforced visit to Leeds by the imprisoned King Charles I that led to one of the best-known traditional stories about Leeds, and about King Charles II.

As Joyce travelled toward London, he lodged King Charles in the Red House in Leeds overnight. According to a local tale, a chambermaid was sent to bring him food, but instead she brought the King a set of women's clothes and urged him to put them on and escape. The King thanked the girl for her trouble, but refused. He cut a button from his jacket and gave it to her. King Charles was later executed and Britain became a republic, but in 1660 his son returned to the throne as Charles II. Charles was one day in Leeds when he was accosted by a middle-aged woman, the one-time chambermaid. She told her story and handed over the button that she had kept all those years.

Charles II smiled and asked if the woman was married. 'Yes, your Majesty,' the woman replied. 'To the Under Bailiff of Leeds.'

This time, Charles laughed out loud. 'No you are not,' he declared to the bemused woman. 'You are now married to the Chief Bailiff of Yorkshire!'

About 40 years after the civil war ended in the execution of King Charles I, a man named William Barwick was courting a young woman from Cawood, named Mary Lofthouse. After some months Mary fell pregnant, and a wedding was hurriedly arranged. A month later Barwick told his brother-in-law, Thomas Lofthouse, that the pregnant Mary had chosen to have her baby in her uncle's house at Selby, rather than at home, and had already set off. The story seemed sensible enough as the uncle had a large, comfortable house and could afford a doctor, something Cawood did not have. A few days later Barwick reported that the birth date was rapidly approaching and that he was off to Selby as well.

The days passed and no news arrived from Selby about a birth. Thomas Lofthouse was not unduly worried. Presumably, his sister was too busy with her new baby to bother writing. Then, one evening as he was walking home past the ruins of Cawood Castle, Thomas thought he saw his sister standing on the far side of the moat. He called out to her, but the figure turned aside and walked off. That night Thomas Lofthouse could not sleep. He was sure that he had seen his sister by the old castle moat, and yet she was supposed to be in Selby getting over a birth.

The Busby Stoop Inn, at Sand Hutton near Thirsk, features a chair on its sign. This chair is the one in which Thomas Busby was sleeping when he was arrested for murder. He cursed the chair as he was dragged away, and the chair subsequently became the centre for macabre tales of certain death for anyone daring to sit in it.

Next morning Thomas sent an urgent letter to his uncle in Selby. The reply came back swiftly. Neither Mary nor her husband had been to Selby for weeks. There was no baby, no mother and no father. Now seriously alarmed, Thomas summoned a group of friends and began a search of the castle grounds. In a quiet corner they found a patch of freshly turned earth, and when it was dug out they found the body of Mary. She had been drowned. That night another local man saw the ghost of Mary walking beside the moat. A warrant was issued for the arrest of William Barwick, and he was arrested in York a few days later. At his trial, Barwick denied murder, but the evidence was against him and he was hanged. He had, it would seem, been brought to trial by the ghost of his victim.

Another Yorkshire murder to be solved in an unlikely way took place at Hebden Wood, not far from Ripon. A man from Ripon was courting a girl from Sawley and got her pregnant. He kept putting off the expected wedding with increasingly unlikely excuses, until after the birth of healthy twins. Then he murdered the unfortunate woman and her babies, before vanishing. The bodies were found in a shallow grave in Hebden Wood. A few years later a Ripon man was in Boston, Massachusetts, when he heard a drunken man sobbing into his beer and calling on those present to 'drink a toast to the ewe and two lambs buried in Hebden Wood.' The drunk was arrested, found to be the missing murderer and hanged.

Another murder left its mark at the Busby Stoop Inn, at Sand Hutton. The roadside inn is named for Thomas Busby, the man who owned it back in the early 18th century. Thomas was a quarrelsome man, who drank much of his own profits. His wife, as might be imagined, did not approve of his wayward attitude to business, and brought in her father to help keep the business on track. Inevitably, the old boy could not stop himself from criticising Thomas Busby and his drinking of the profits. One night Busby was deep in his drink when the father-in-law began lecturing him. Busby grabbed a nearby hammer, battered the old man to death, then slumped back into a chair in a drunken stupor.

Busby was still in the chair when the forces of law and order arrived to drag him away. Busby came to as he was dragged from the chair, his hands stiff with the congealed blood of his victim. He tore himself free of his captors and angrily cursed the chair for being so comfortable as to allow him to sleep when he should have been fleeing. Anyone who sat in the chair, he declared, would be cursed to bad luck and an early death.

There could be no doubt of Busby's guilt, and within days Thomas Busby was dangling from a rope hanging from a gibbet by the crossroads outside the pub. The gibbet is still there, and Thomas's ghost is said to wander there to this day, with his head lolling to one side and his tongue hanging out.

As for Busby's chair, that remained in the pub as something of a tourist attraction. Visitors would come to the inn to hear the new landlord retell the gruesome details of the murder, point out where the old man died (and the attendant bloodstains), and finish by pointing out the fatal chair and challenging anyone to sit in it. There were, unsurprisingly, few takers, but some did sit in the fatal seat – and paid the price. An RAF pilot tried the seat in 1943, and was shot down and killed on his next mission. A tourist sat here in the 1950s, then crashed his car on the way home. In the 1960s a man from nearby Thirsk sat down in the chair, and had a heart attack two days later. The chair still features on the pub sign outside, but it is no longer in the pub itself. It has now been moved to Thirsk Museum, where nobody is ever allowed to sit in it.

There are a number of legends, tales and mysteries that are not so easy to pin down in date as others. Among these is the story of the man from Rawdon who left to seek his fortune in London. He became a rich merchant and gained a vast fortune, but he never forgot his Yorkshire home. As old age crept over him, the man came home and built the hamlet of Little London just outside Rawdon.

CHAPTER 6

Mysterious Ghosts

It must be said that there are more ghosts in Yorkshire than you can shake a stick at. It sometimes seems as if there is a spook of some kind lurking around every corner, peeping from over every wall and stalking silently along every lane. There are probably more ghost stories in Yorkshire than any other county, and that is not just due to the fact that Yorkshire is larger than other counties. There seems to be something about Yorkshire that attracts our spooky friends to visit.

Some ghosts seem to be prompted by a local happening. A typical example is the White Lass of Thirsk. Back in Victorian times, gravel was being dug out of the meadows beside the Cod Beck, north of Thirsk. The workmen found a skeleton and called in the magistrate. The bones had obviously been there for a good many years, and were identified as those of a young woman. Older residents then recalled that a young woman had gone missing some 40 years earlier. At the time, it had been thought that she might have ran away, but now it seemed more likely that she had been murdered. Almost as soon as the body was found, the ghost of a woman dressed in white began to be seen around the gravel pit. After a few years the ghost faded away and has not been seen for a while. When some new houses were built on the site, however, the road was named 'Whitelass Close' in her honour.

Another gruesome discovery that led to a haunting was that of the woman in black on Middleham Moor. In the early 19th century, peat cutters up on the moor found the skeleton of a woman dressed in the remains of what had once been a black dress. The discovery seemed to explain the phantom of a figure in a dark coat or cloak that had been reported from the area. This time, it seems that the story to explain the body and the haunting sprang up after the discovery, so it may not be true. According to the story, the woman was a wealthy widow from Middleham who was being courted by two men. She eventually decided to wed one of the men, and the rejected suitor was so angry that he lured the widow up to the moors and murdered her, throwing her body into a bog where it was lost. Another woman in black haunts Woodhall, but even less is known about her than about the ghost of Middleham Moor.

One lady in black who can be identified with certainty is the ghost of Nappa Hall, a medieval manor house in Askrigg. The stately lady who walks here is none other than Mary, Queen of Scots,. That most unfortunate of monarchs inherited the throne of Scotland when less than a month old. She had spent much of her youth in France, where she married a French prince who died young, and came back to Scotland in 1561 at the age of 19 to take up the reins of power. She did not succeed at the task of being Queen. She made an unpopular marriage, alienated the most senior nobles, and insisted on ostentatious Catholicism when most of her subjects were Protestant. In 1567 the Scottish nobles forced her to abdicate in favour of her son, King James VI. Mary then fled to England.

The lane at Woodhall, which is haunted by a Woman in Black, although mystery surrounds who she might be.

Mary, Queen of Scots, listens as she is told that she has been condemned to death for plotting the death of Queen Elizabeth I of England. Soon after her execution in 1587, the ghost of Mary returned to a Yorkshire manor house, where she had enjoyed a few days of peace and happiness in her lifetime.

The choice of England as a refuge was bizarre. Queen Elizabeth I of England was the Protestant daughter of the Protestant King Henry VIII and Queen Anne Boleyn. As such, she was considered to be illegitimate by the Catholics, which made Mary, Queen of Scots, the rightful Queen of England. Mary had herself declared this to be the case on more than one occasion, and used the coat of arms of a monarch of England on formal occasions. Why she thought that Elizabeth would welcome her is unclear, still less why she hoped for Elizabeth's aid in recovering her throne.

In fact, Elizabeth had the state rooms of Carlisle Castle put at Mary's disposal. Perhaps she hoped that Mary would slip back over the border to Scotland. When this did not happen, Elizabeth had to make more permanent provision for her unwelcome guest. Mary was offered Bolton Castle to live in, and used Nappa Hall as a nearby hidey-hole where she could be alone with her closest friends. By all accounts, she loved it there.

As the years passed, the likelihood of Mary ever returning to Scotland dwindled away. Relations between Protestant England and Catholic Spain worsened, so King Philip of Spain began agitating for Mary of Scots to be made Queen of England, and tried to form a foreign alliance to attack England. In 1586 Mary was found to have been plotting with English Catholics to murder Elizabeth and seize power with the aid of Spanish troops. She was thrown into prison, then put on trial and eventually executed in 1587. That in turn led King Philip of Spain to send the Spanish Armada on its doomed mission to invade England.

Back at Nappa Hall, the ghost of a red-headed woman in a black dress began to be seen. The phantom was thought to be that of Mary, Queen of Scots, and she is seen still. Presumably, she has returned to the last place on earth where she was happy.

There is no doubt about what caused the haunting of Bramham Moor, beside the A1 near Tadcaster. In 1402 the powerful northern Percy family rose in rebellion against King Henry IV, who had only recently usurped the throne from King Richard II, who was then murdered. The Percys preferred to have Edmund Earl of March as king, and joined forces with Owain Glyndwr, Prince of Wales, to fight Henry. The main Percy army was crushed at the Battle of Shrewsbury, and Henry Percy, Earl of Northumberland, fled to Scotland. Having failed to come to terms with King Henry, Percy invaded England in 1408 with an army of Scots. The Percy retainers rose to join him, so it was a joint Anglo-Scottish army of some 6,000 men that was marching down the Great North Road towards York when his scouts reported sighting an army loyal to King Henry and led by Sir Thomas Rokeby blocking the road. It was 19 February 1408.

Rokeby was High Sheriff of Yorkshire and most of his army was composed of Yorkshiremen, although there were a few professional soldiers from the royal army among them. Rokeby had more men and was holding the ford over the Cock Beck at Aberford. Percy was too experienced a soldier to attack a larger army in prepared positions, so he halted his men on Bramham Moor and began digging field defences on the crest of the slope facing down to the Cock Beck. Realising that if he waited he might face a prepared enemy led by a wily old commander, Rokeby launched his men in a wild charge up the slope. The two armies clashed around what is now Spen Farm, beside the A1.

The Battle of Bramham Moor led to the deaths of a surprisingly large number of knights and nobility. Their ghosts are said to return to the battlefield to this day.

It was the crash of a World War II Vickers Wellington bomber that led to the haunting of Hatfield Moor, east of Doncaster.

The fighting was, by all accounts, even more savage than was normal for the age. Most of the bloodshed was at close quarters and hand-to-hand. The Earl of Northumberland fought manfully, but was cut down and killed, whereupon his army broke and fled. The Yorkshiremen were in no mood to be merciful and very few of the Scots lived to get home. A monument was erected on the spot where the Earl died. Although this has since crumbled away, it has been replaced by a modern monument and information board.

The ghosts, however, have never gone. The forms of men in armour have been reported on Bramham Moor ever since the battle. Interestingly, they have been seen most often north of the actual battlefield. Perhaps they are the phantoms of Scots cut down as they tried to escape north.

A much more modern military ghost was that of the World War II airman who for years haunted Hatfield Moor, east of Doncaster. In 1940 what is now Lindholme Prison was an RAF bomber station. It was handed over to a squadron of Polish airmen, who had escaped their country as the Germans invaded and came to Britain to continue the war. In 1941 a Wellington bomber overshot the runway and crashed on the moor, killing the entire crew of six. The rescue workers could find the bodies of only five of the Polish airmen, which were taken away for burial.

Over the weeks that followed, the ghost of a man in flying gear was seen several times on the moor. Then he moved down to the airfield and was seen there. In 1952 a mechanic was hauled up on a charge of leaving his work, that of repairing an aircraft in the hanger overnight. As a defence he said that he had been at work as ordered, but had fled when the ghostly airman appeared. In 1957 an airman woke up one night to find the ghost standing at the foot of his bed staring at him. He screamed so loudly that he woke up the entire dormitory, but the ghost had gone by the time men came running.

The saga came to an end in 1987, when walkers on the moor spotted a skeletal arm protruding from the peat. They called the police, who excavated the body. It turned out to be that of the missing Polish airman, who must have been thrown clear during the crash and sunk into a bog. The body was given a decent burial, since which time the ghost has not been seen.

Another RAF ghost lurks at RAF Leeming. During the later years of World War II, the base was home to Canadian squadrons flying Halifax bombers, and the ghost is thought to be one of the Canadian crewmen. The ghost of a man in wartime flying kit is seen walking about the southern end of the airfield, close to Gatenby Wood. During the war this area was used for the bomb store, so perhaps the ghost is connected to that somehow.

A mysterious phantom army appeared at Attercliffe in 1661. The village had never been the site of any fighting, nor of any major camp. Nevertheless, the vicar William Bloom saw a ghostly army dressed all in white marching past his church. It took several minutes to pass by, and he estimated it at over 1,000 strong. The abbott of Roche Abbey had a similar experience in May 1236, when a spectral army of several hundred mounted men, clad in mail and carrying shields and spears, rode down the road from Maltby.

More military ghosts are to be encountered around Long Marston. Throughout the spring and summer of 1644, the Royalist city of York was besieged by a large Parliamentarian army led by Oliver Cromwell. The English Civil War was on a knife edge by this time. The early advantage of King Charles I had been eroded by the determined activities of the Roundheads, and now Royalist control of the north was in jeopardy. The King sent the talented cavalry commander Prince Rupert north with a large supply train and an army, with orders to relieve York. Rupert marched up through Lancashire, before swinging east and crossing the Pennines to outmanoeuvre the Roundheads and reach York. But having got to York, Rupert had to get out again; and, with the Parliamentarian armies surrounding the city, that was not going to be easy.

On 2 July Rupert led his army out of York and had got as far as Long Marston when evening began to draw in. He ordered his army to camp on Marston Moor, ready to march out next morning. Then a large Parliamentarian army appeared and attacked as Rupert's Royalists were cooking supper. The 17,000 Royalists were outnumbered by the 24,000 Roundheads, but quickly formed defensive lines and fought back. At dusk a cavalry charge led by Oliver Cromwell broke the Royalist centre, and Rupert ordered a retreat. In the gathering gloom, the confusion of retreat turned to rout as fugitives fled across the moors. The Whitecoat Regiment of Newcastle stood firm, allowing many more Royalists to get away than would otherwise have been the case. They paid dearly, only 30 wounded men surviving to be taken prisoner. Next day Rupert rallied 5,000 men and skillfully evaded Roundhead pursuit to get his men back south to the main Royalist forces. But his defeat sealed the fate of the Royalists in the north. One by one, the towns, cities and strongholds surrendered until Parliament had unchallenged control.

The ghosts of Marston Moor are usually sighted near White Sike Bridge, where the Whitecoat Regiment made its last stand. The three men are reported to be on foot, dressed in pale coats that reach to their knees and to be wearing large, wide-brimmed hats. Almost certainly they are ghosts of three of the Whitecoats. They were seen once just to the north, staggering along the side of the A59 close to Lodge Farm.

Oliver Cromwell prepares to lead his men into battle on Marston Moor in 1644. The struggle that followed was murderous in its intensity, and destroyed Royalist power in Yorkshire and across the north of England. Ghostly infantry have been seen at various places on the battlefield.

Another haunted main road out of York is the A64, running north-east to Malton. This ghost takes the form of a young woman dressed in a long dress or cloak, who stands by the side of the road. If you see her and she is standing still, then you may continue on your journey, but if she waves you must slow down or halt at once, for some form of danger lies ahead.

It is the ghost of a local farm girl who fell on hard times that haunts the A64 south west of Malton. Drivers would be well advised to slow down if they see the ghost, for she inevitably heralds danger on the road.

This ghost is Nancy, who was the daughter of a farmer from Welburn in the early 18th century. Nancy became engaged to a local boy named Tom, and all seemed set for a rosy, if unexciting future when a stranger came to Welburn. Tall, handsome and clearly well off, the stranger took a shine to pretty Nancy. To the scandal of the village, and the consternation of Tom, Nancy ran off with the stranger.

Seeking a change from the familiar scenes that reminded him of his lost love, Tom joined the stagecoach company and was given the task of driving the coach that ran from York to Scarborough. The months passed by, and Tom lost himself in his work. One rainy day he spotted a woman sitting hunched by the side of the road, a baby clutched to her breast. Tom pulled up to offer the bedraggled woman a lift to the nearest village. To his amazement, the woman was Nancy. The handsome stranger had turned out to be already married, and had cast off the pretty girl when she became pregnant. In her shame, she had not dared return home, but as a last resort was forced to go back to Welburn. Unfortunately, she had left it too late, for she was dying of malnutrition and hardship. Tom lodged her at an inn, but there was nothing that could be done. Before she died, Nancy blessed him for his kindness, and promised that she would return the favour.

Some weeks later, Tom was leaving Scarborough when four gentlemen climbed on board the coach. They were in a desperate rush to get to York, and each offered Tom a guinea if he could get there before nightfall. Tom agreed and got the horses into an easy canter that would get them to York in time. All went well until the coach reached the hills beyond Malton. Then, a mist came down that rapidly became a fog, forcing Tom to slow first to a trot, then to a walk. He stopped and climbed down to tell his passengers that the weather meant that they would not reach York until midnight. The four gentlemen were angry and annoyed, and promised to up the fee to two guineas each, but the fog was immoveable.

When Tom climbed back to the driver's seat he was amazed to see Nancy sitting there. She smiled and took up the reins and whip as Tom sat beside her. With a crack of the whip, Nancy drove the horses on, first to a trot, then a canter and finally into a wild gallop. At breakneck speed the coach thundered along the road through the dense fog. Travellers were sent scattering as the careering coach rushed at them out of the thick mist. The passengers were thrown from side to side, and called out again and again at Tom to slow down or stop. Finally, the coach reached York, clattering into the city along Monkgate. Nancy pulled the horses to a halt, handed the reins back to Tom and vanished as the shaken travellers hurried out of the coach. Tom got his bonus, but the gentlemen looked as if they would rather have missed the wild ride.

Thereafter, Nancy came to help Tom on the Malton Road whenever he needed her. And she came to help his son, another coach driver, as well. These days, she seems willing to warn anyone of danger on the road, standing where Tom found her that rainy day and waving at cars to stop.

The phantom that once haunted the lanes and fields around Calverley, and which may yet return, is firmly believed to be that of Sir Walter Calverley. This infamous squire inherited spreading estates around Pudsey as a young boy. He was educated at Cambridge in his teens and, when he returned, fell in love with a local girl to whom he got engaged. His family, however, were unimpressed by his choice of wife. The girl seems to have been pleasant enough, but she was the daughter of a humble farmer and the Calverley's had higher ambitions. They had lined up the daughter of Lord Cobham, and pressured the young Sir Walter into marrying their more aristocratic choice for a bride.

The arranged marriage produced three children, but it was not a happy union. Sir Walter took to heavy drinking and got into a number of fights. One fatal day in April 1605 word reached Calverley that a friend of his had been arrested for non-payment of a debt. In fact, the debt was owed by Sir Walter, who for some reason blamed his wife for the debt. Tragically, Sir Walter had been drinking heavily that day and was in vicious mood. He stabbed his wife, then his two elder children – aged four and two. He then leapt on his horse and galloped off to find his youngest child, a babe in arms who had fortunately accompanied his nurse to visit a friend's house. When he arrived in a savage temper and with a bloodied sword, the nurse screamed for help and, with commendable courage, two local men rushed in to overpower Sir Walter.

By the time he was brought to trial, the two stabbed children had died, although Sir Walter's wife made a full recovery. Sir Walter was hanged, and his vast estates passed to the surviving infant.

Soon afterwards it was noticed that the bloodstains where the two children had died could not be cleaned. No matter how much the floor in Calverley Hall was scrubbed, the stains remained. Not only that, but Sir Walter's ghost began to be seen. It rode furiously around the lanes of Calverley, scaring the living daylights out of anyone who encountered it. A local witch

The ghost who rides through the streets of Beverley in a black coach pulled by four black horses is difficult to identify clearly, although stories about him are many.

was consulted; she advised planting holly in the grounds of Calverley Hall, and when this was done the ghost stopped appearing. In the 19th century the holly was removed by a new owner, and the ghost returned. It was seen several times, galloping about with a bloody sword in his hand. New holly was hurriedly planted and the ghost vanished again.

It is said that the ghost can be summoned by anyone who dares confront it. All that is needed is for that brave soul to sprinkle breadcrumbs in a circle in Calverley churchyard. He must then walk around the circle three times, each time reciting the words:

'Old Calverley, Old Calverley. I have thee by the ears.
I'll cut thee into collops unless thou appears.'

As far as I know, nobody has tried it recently. Which might be just as well.

More stubborn bloodstains are to be found at the Old Vicarage in Aston. In Victorian times the vicar there found his wife in the arms of the butler. The wife was killed in the ensuing fight, and the marks of the killing remain to this day.

Ghosts can be as tricky to pin down as they are to encounter. Take, for instance, the dramatic ghost who rides through the streets of Beverley in a black coach pulled by four black horses. This is the ghost of Sir Josceline Percy, but which Sir Josceline Percy? There have been three such men: the first was born in 1644, the son of the Earl of Northumberland, worked as a lawyer, and was a page at the coronation of King Charles II; the second was a naval officer born in 1784 who fought the French under Admiral Nelson; the third was born in 1811 and became an MP, but does not seem to have achieved very much. Whichever of these men it is, he is supposed to be condemned to wander the streets for the sacrilege of riding his horse into Beverley Minster.

Another ghostly coach haunts Skipton Castle. It is said to draw up silently outside the main gates at the top of the town whenever somebody who lives at the castle is about to die. Presumably, it comes to take away their soul.

Almost as enigmatic is Owld Nance of Burton Agness Hall, near Bridlington. The story concerns the Griffiths family, who owned Burton Agnes Hall in the early 17th century. The building was over 400 years old by this time, and suffered from damp, pokey rooms and general disrepair. Then Sir Henry Griffiths came into some money and decided to spend it on tearing down the old hall and building a magnificent new mansion. Sir Henry's three daughters were delighted, but none more so than the younger daughter, Anne. She took great delight in helping her father plan the house, and spent every spare moment on the building site, chatting to the workmen and supervising the construction.

Then, Anne came home one day having been attacked by some robber, and fell into a dangerous fever. Within a few days it became clear that Anne was likely to die. She was mortified that she would never see her beloved new home finished, and begged her sisters to agree to one last request. The sisters agreed, but were aghast when Anne asked them to strike her head from her body and inter it in the new house, instead of in the churchyard with the rest of her body. After Anne died, her father and sisters decided that it had been fever that had caused Anne to make her bizarre request. The head was buried with the rest of the body in the churchyard.

A few months later the new house was finished and the Griffiths family moved in. Within days

Skipton Castle is haunted by a ghostly coach that is said to be a harbinger of death and disaster.

the supernatural trouble started. Moans echoed through the house, doors slammed shut and strange sounds made sleep next to impossible. Servants refused to stay in the new hall, preferring to sleep in the village and travel to work each morning. The Griffiths concluded that the trouble was being caused by Anne; they persuaded the vicar to let them open her grave and remove the skull. The grim momento was carried to the Hall and placed on a table. The supernatural disturbances ceased at once.

Over the years the skull remained on the table, with the exception of one incident. A maid who had no patience for belief in the supernatural threw it out onto a cart outside. The horses were suddenly rooted to the spot and would not move, no matter what encouragement they were given; the skull was promptly taken back into the house. Eventually, Burton Agness Hall passed to the Boynton family through marriage. They were not going to take any chances with the skull, and had it bricked up in a niche in one of the bedrooms. There it remains to this day.

But if the disturbances have been quietened by the presence of the skull, Anne's ghost has not. The phantom is generally referred to as 'Owd Nance' and walks the upstairs of the Hall in a blue dress. Although the phantom lady is said to be that of the Anne Griffiths whose skull rests in the bedroom, it was not reported to be seen until the mid-19th century, so she might conceivably be the ghost of somebody else.

Another ghostly lady to be firmly identified is that of the great Yorkshire writer Emily Brontë, who has been seen wandering her beloved moors around Haworth. She has also been seen in the village itself. On 19 December 1978 she entered Weaver's Restaurant and climbed a staircase that had been removed some years earlier. Emily Brontë is not the only spectre in Haworth. A phantom of a little girl aged about six flits about the Parkside Social Club, used as a school in the early 20th century. She is reported to wear a coat and hat.

The stories linked to some phantoms are almost nonsensical. The ghost of Sunderlandwick Hall, south of Driffield, takes the form of the sound of wet feet slapping on a bare floor. This manifestation is said to be caused by a man who lived here in the 1850s, but left to serve the British Empire in Africa. He came back years later, much quieter and more introverted than when he left. The man had shot and killed his servant out in Africa in circumstances that were never fully explained. Why his ghost should take the form of wet feet is unclear.

Slightly less bizarre is the famous Grey Lady of Auckley. She is seen most often at celebrations held at the church, such as weddings or christenings. She will be glimpsed hovering about on the edge of the crowd as if uncertain whether or not to join the merry throng. She is said to have been a younger daughter of some curmudgeonly old farmer from years ago, who treated her as little better than a slave. While her elder brothers and sisters left to marry and raise their own families, the younger daughter was stuck at home caring for her miserable old father. As she entered middle age, she got into the habit of attending weddings and christenings to share the good fortune of others. Soon she was being invited to any celebration in the area to bestow her good wishes.

After the woman died, the ghostly form of the Grey Lady of Auckley began turning up at local celebrations. Folk in the area began to lay a place for her at their tables, and would recite the verse:

'We wish thee joy on this our celebration.
Come sit thee down and take a glass of wine.
And if you sup in our felicitation.
The hour is blest as blessed you may be.'

One ghost to have the wrong story attached to his existence is the pale man of Scarborough Castle. The figure appears only at night, rushing headlong at anyone foolish enough to be wandering around the ruins after dark. This ghost, it is said, is that of Piers Gaveston, who was murdered here. In fact, the unfortunate Gaveston left Scarborough alive and well.

Gaveston was a handsome young man blessed with a witty tongue, a huge amount of intelligence and absolutely no wisdom at all. He was a favourite of King Edward II, and widely supposed to be his lover, using that position to amass wealth. Less sensibly, Gaveston teased and played jokes on the richest and most powerful nobles in the kingdom. His merciless jokes and satires angered the nobles, and none more so than the Earl of Warwick, whom Gaveston dubbed 'Black Dog'. After numerous disputes, Gaveston was exiled, came back, was exiled again, and came back again. Nothing would persuade him to shut up or keep his jokes to himself. When Edward II's incompetent government fell into near bankruptcy, the nobles naturally blamed the man they detested – Gaveston. In 1312 Gaveston went to Scarborough Castle to be safe from the vengeful nobles, now up in arms. They captured him and took him to London for trial. Warwick was not willing to wait, and murdered Gaveston on the way south.

Gaveston was certainly not murdered at Scarborough, so why his ghost should return here is unclear. Perhaps the pale man is the phantom of somebody else.

Other ghosts are less well known, having no real story attached to them. This does not make the apparition any the less frightening when they are encountered. Take the ghost of Rossington Hall, near Doncaster, for instance. He potters about the old stables dressed in a top hat and long coat. Why he does this, nobody knows, and he seems in no mood to tell.

Doncaster's Mansion House has been the ceremonial centre for the town's mayor and council since it was built in 1749. Over the centuries it has amassed a large collection of art and memorabilia. This is of great fascination to an elderly man whose ghost is seen from time to time inspecting the paintings on the walls; he seems to favour a portrait of Queen Victoria.

A headless horseman has been seen riding around Atwick. Nobody knows who he is, but he may be linked to a spring near the church that is guarded by fairies. The man in black who haunts Lumb Hall at Drighlington is thought to be a cavalier from the Civil War, but why is unclear.

The narrow road along Coverdale offers a route from Wensleydale to Wharfedale, but when used at night motorists should take care. The section just south of Caldbergh passes the ruined St Simon's Chapel. There has long been seen an unexplained light flickering and flashing from here. It has distracted many travellers, but no explanation has ever been found.

The headless nun of Watton also has no story attached to her. Interestingly, though, the medieval abbey at Watton was the scene for a most bizarre incident involving a nun who became pregnant (see Chapter 11). Perhaps the nameless ghost is linked to that incident.

Ripley Castle is home to a ghostly nun, who walks the corridors of the upper floors at night.

Another ghostly nun is to be found at Ripley Castle. This particular phantom walks the corridors of the upper floors at night and seems very fond of the area around the Tower Room. As well as wandering down the corridors, she has been heard to knock on the doors. Only once has anyone called out 'Come in!' when the ghostly knocks sound – and the ghostly nun promptly entered the room by walking through the locked door and vanishing into thin air. This ghostly nun is usually identified as Elizabeth Ingleby, who was sent to Ghent to become a nun. The Inglebys have lived at Ripley since 1308, and now operate the castle as a tourist attraction.

Another religious phantom is found at Bolton Abbey, near Skipton. The Abbey, in reality a priory, was founded in 1120 and closed in 1539 during the Reformation. The nave of the priory church was taken over by the local community to serve as their parish church, but the rest of the structure was allowed to fall into ruins or robbed of stone for use locally. The 30,000-acre estate was owned by the various Dukes of Devonshire for generations, but is now owned by a family trust and is operated as a tourist attraction.

The ghost here is, perhaps inevitably, that of a monk. The ghost hit the national headlines when it scared no less a person than the Marquis of Hartington, who reported the encounter in some detail to the house guests at supper that evening. One of the guests was the Prince of Wales, later to become King George V. The ghostly monk was, Hartingdon said, aged about 60 and had a jovial, round face with stubble as if he had not shaved for some days. The ghost wore a long cloak with a hood. The apparition was in sight for some seconds before it faded gradually to nothingness. The ghostly monk has been reported several times since, most recently in the summer of 2010.

Another haunted abbey is Fountains Abbey, where the eerie sound of a singing choir has been heard coming from the ruined church. The sound is most often heard coming from the area of the Chapel of the Nine Altars. In September 2008 a visitor took a photo which showed a strange, white shape in the choir. It resembled a cowled monk and was printed in the local press.

Two other ghosts lurk here in Fountains Hall, the splendid Tudor mansion built by Stephen Proctor when he bought the old abbey and its estates. The gentleman in Tudor dress seen in the entrance hall may be Proctor. The lady in a blue dress seen upstairs is usually said to be Proctor's daughter, who died of shock when she discovered her beloved father cavorting in bed with a servant girl.

Rather more criminally minded than the lustful squire of Fountains was the highwayman Tom Hoggett. Hoggett made his nefarious living by patrolling the Great North Road, north of York, accosting at gunpoint any traveller who took his fancy. If any victim showed signs of being too difficult to handle, Hoggett made his escape on his famously swift stallion. One day Hoggett held up two men, but they would not submit, and instead pulled their own guns. Hoggett put his spurs to his horse and galloped off, pursued by his would-be victims. As they approached Scotch Corner, Hoggett's horse stumbled and threw him into a pond, where he drowned. His ghost used to patrol the Great North Road (now the A1) between Catterick and Scotch Corner, but opinion is divided as to whether it still haunts the area. An enigmatic horseman has been seen from time to time, but given the speed at which cars now race up the dual carriageway, a firm identification is not possible.

Bolton Abbey, near Skipton, is haunted by a phantom monk, who dramatically appeared to the Marquis of Hartington.

Another highwayman to haunt Yorkshire is Nicholas Nevison, known in his lifetime as Swift Nick. It was Swift Nick, not Dick Turpin as is often reported, who established an alibi for a crime by riding from Kent to York in a single day. In 1681 he held up a coach outside Batley, but on board was the York Constable Darcy Fletcher, who had a gun and sprang out to arrest Nevison. The highwayman shot back, killing Fletcher on the spot. This was the only time Nevison or his gang ever killed anyone, but it was enough to hang Nevison when he was caught three years later. The spot where Fletcher was killed, now on the B6123 near to Morley Spring Wood, is haunted by a man in a black cloak. It is said that the ghost is that of Nevison, although common sense would indicate that it should be the spectre of Fletcher.

A 'crisis apparition' is typically a phantom of a person who is undergoing a serious physical crisis at the time, such as undergoing an operation or being involved in a car crash. The apparition usually appears to family members or close friends. One such case took place at Oakwell Hall, Birstall, on 9 December 1684.

William Batt, son and heir of the Hall's owner at the time, was in London on business and was not expected back before Christmas. Early that morning, however, he was seen walking up the drive. He stalked angrily in through the front door without saying a word to his mother, who was in the hallway at the time. He strode up the stairs and into his bedroom. After some minutes of silence from the room, his mother went up to see what was troubling her son. The room was empty, although there was no exit other than the front door, which had been in sight of his mother and servants the whole time. A search was made, but young William could not be found anywhere. The event caused a sensation and was recorded by several locals at the time.

Some days later, a message came from London to say that William had died in a tragic shooting accident. He had died early on the morning of 9 December – at the very moment when his angry phantom entered his home.

CHAPTER 7

Mysterious Poltergeists

Poltergeists are perhaps the most terrifying of all mysterious phenomena to afflict Yorkshire, or any other area. When a poltergeist comes to visit, those at the receiving end of its attentions may be reduced to conditions of abject terror, forced to flee their homes or workplaces, and subjected to such emotional pressure that breakdowns and referrals to doctors are not uncommon. Other victims react more with puzzlement than with fear, and a few actually enjoy the experience. What all of these victims have in common is an utter inability to explain what is happening to them – and no wonder.

An extremely active poltergeist may set fire to a house, smash furniture, throw rocks about and inflict physical injuries on its victims. This mayhem and destruction is wrought by invisible hands. A knife will suddenly leap from a kitchen work surface and hurtle, blade forwards, at an unfortunate human, who is forced to duck aside. A plate will slide sideways across a table, apparently by itself, then fall to the floor and shatter into pieces. Sometimes a voice is heard, making threats and retelling bloodcurdling tales of murder, rape and torture, or issuing threats of violence to come. More often, the noises take the form of knocks, scratches, bangs and crashes that can either be deafening or so soft as to be hard to make out. Some victims use the noises to make contact with the poltergeist, asking questions and demanding that the poltergeist reply with 'one knock for yes, two knocks for no' – and very often it does.

The range of activity, mischief and spite that poltergeists can display can make it difficult to pin down what they are and how they operate. Study of the phenomenon over recent years, however, has thrown up a number of similarities that most visitations seem to share.

First, poltergeists manifest themselves for a set period of time. They come, apparently from nowhere, wreak havoc for a while and then go away, never to return. The length of time that a poltergeist lingers can vary enormously. Some arrive with a bang (often literally), create mayhem for a week and then abruptly vanish. Others begin their visitation more quietly, but persist for much longer. A few poltergeists spend years tormenting their victims, but most go away after some six to nine months.

The places visited by poltergeists tend not to be large hotels, open spaces, nor schools. Instead, they most often afflict homes, offices or workshops, where a small number of people spend a lot of time together. Typically, a home or workplace containing between four and 10 individuals attracts a poltergeist. The poltergeist usually manifests itself only within that building, although some have made themselves felt in the immediate area, perhaps up to 100 or 150 yards away, but this is rare.

Poltergeists are not just place-centred, in that they restrict themselves to a single building, they are also person-centred. Usually, poltergeist activity will take place only when one particular person is in the affected house or building. When that person is absent, activity either ceases altogether or becomes rare and subdued. Generally, this 'focus person', as they are known, is aged between 13 and 21, although individuals as old as 75 have been recorded. It is also usual for the focus person to be undergoing some sort of emotional pressure, such as starting a new job, losing a boyfriend, sitting important exams, or such like. Often, the other people in the affected building are either unaware of this problem or dismissive of it.

Typically, a poltergeist visitation will begin quietly and slowly. In years gone by, the noises heard in the early stages were likened to those of mice or rats scurrying about behind skirting boards or under floorboards. These days they are more likely to be described as being similar to the sounds made by central heating systems starting up. These noises continue for some days, getting louder and more frequent.

Next, noises that cannot be dismissed so easily are heard. These sound like knocking or banging, and often come from specific objects, such as wardrobes, doors or ceilings. It sounds as if a person is trapped in a cupboard and is knocking on the door to attract attention and be let out. Of course, if the door is opened there is nobody there and the sounds cease.

The next stage is frequently the throwing of stones, coins or other small objects by unseen hands. These objects may be household objects that belong in the building, or they may be previously unseen objects apparently brought from somewhere else by the poltergeist. The throwing of pebbles and small stones is so frequent in poltergeist cases that it has been given a name: lithobolia. The way these objects move is very curious; although they fly through the air as if thrown, they behave more as if they are being carried by unseen hands. A pebble may travel at great speed, but will often slow down before it reaches a window, so that it gives merely a faint click and drops to the floor instead of smashing through the glass. Other objects will change direction in mid-air, float along at a slow speed, or bob up and down as they move.

This moving of objects can be both unnerving and destructive. Watching a plate or cup levitate by itself and then float across a room has been enough to send people fleeing a house, and more than one person has refused ever to return home as a result. Moving objects may be, and often are, smashed when they land. But wreckage does not end with mere destruction. Flour may be mixed with salt, butter smeared up walls and clothes thrown out of windows. Sometimes a poltergeist will seem to become fixated on one particular object, moving it repeatedly about the place. Often objects moved by poltergeists end up in specific locations, such as in the exact centre of a table or balanced on top of a coffee pot.

Poltergeists have apparent fascination for both fire and water. Some malevolent spirits set fire to newspapers, to sheets or to furniture. Others turn on taps, block plugholes, or overturn jugs or water. More recently, telephones and electric lights have been affected by poltergeists.

It is usual for a poltergeist to interact with the humans that it torments, as if it can hear and understand what they are saying. A poltergeist will produce a potato out of thin air if a person mentions liking potatoes, or a loaf of bread will be hurled at somebody who asks how long it will be before lunch is ready. Those who express disbelief in the poltergeist come in for particular attention, being bombarded with objects until they leave. By contrast, those who firmly express their acceptance of the poltergeist may be presented with gifts of grapes, coins or sweets.

It is rare for a poltergeist to communicate with humans, but it does happen. This most frequently happens when humans ask questions and tell the poltergeist to respond with coded knocking noises. Occasionally, a poltergeist begins the communication by writing with a pencil, or even by speaking with a disembodied voice. This sort of communication may produce a stream of meaningless statements, often in obscene or abusive language, but sometimes does produce a coherent message. The poltergeist may claim to be a ghost, a demon, an alien or a curse. It may claim to be guarding a treasure buried in the garden, or be the ghost of a murder victim whose body is buried under the floorboards. The claims are almost always lurid and sensational, and when they can be checked out they always prove to be false.

After some weeks of often intense activity, the poltergeist will seem to begin to tire. The more extreme activities cease to take place, the amount of activity decreases, and within a few days the poltergeist is reduced to making knocking noises or faint scratchings. Then it is gone.

A fairly common example of a minor poltergeist visitation affected a carpentry workshop in Swanland, near Hull, in 1891. It began when one of the workers was hit on the back of the head by a chip of wood about three inches long. He thought that it had been thrown by a workmate as a joke, but everyone denied having anything to do with it. Later that day a chip of wood hit another man, this time when he was quite alone in the workshop. Over the following days, the flying bits of wood became quite common. Usually they seemed to be aimed at a particular individual, but a few simply whizzed about with no particular purpose.

Understandably, the workmen became unnerved by having a mysterious and invisible intruder throwing things at them. They called in the owner and insisted that he sort things out. The owner refused to believe anything supernatural was happening, whereupon a piece of wood hit him in the centre of the back. Thereafter, he kept a careful log of events and got his workers to write down what they saw. The chips of wood were moved several times a day. Gradually, it became clear that most of the woodchips were thrown towards the main door out of the workshop. It was also noticed that the wood looked as if it being carried, not thrown. 'They act as though borne along on gently heaving waves,' the owner recorded. This bizarre activity went on for six weeks. Then one day no bits of wood were moved or thrown, and the visitation was over.

Poltergeists are no respecters of clergy. In 1935 the Revd S.C. Kell took over as vicar of Watton, north of Beverley, and moved into the vicarage. The trouble began almost at once. On the first Sunday night after moving in, Kell and his wife were woken up by what sounded like somebody knocking on their bedroom door. He got out of bed and opened the door, but nobody was there. The maid was questioned next morning, but denied having been up in the night.

The following Sunday the knocking came again, but this time it was more insistent and continued right up until Kell had the doorknob in his hand, when it ceased. Again, nobody was in the corridor outside the room. On the third Sunday, the knocking came again, but this time Kell did not get up. The knocking got louder, then ceased for a few moments, before a terrific crash was heard as if somebody was attacking the door with frenzied kicks from hobnailed boots. 'Oh, shut up!' shouted Kell, and the noise abruptly stopped.

A few days later the front doorbell rang; Mrs Kell answered it, the maid being busy, but nobody was there. Then the back doorbell rang, and again nobody was there. This repeated itself several times over the following weeks, much to the annoyance of the household. Next, the bells to summon the maid from the kitchen began to ring when nobody was operating them. The poor maid was scurrying about the house, until she gave up responding to the bells entirely. Then one afternoon all the bells in the house rang at once, after which all activity ceased.

Another vicarage in the East Riding was visited by a poltergeist some 30 years earlier. This time, the poltergeist progressed beyond the more mundane knocking and bell-ringing to have an obsession with bedclothes. During the time that Canon Maddock was rector at Patrington, a poltergeist took to pulling the bedclothes off people as they lay sleeping. One visitor, a Mrs Durrell, was actually thrown out of her bed by the poltergeist, which lifted up one end of the bed until it was almost vertical. A few days later the poltergeist entered the dining room and moved the furniture about, tipping over chairs and setting the heavy sideboard on end. Thereafter, the manifestations lessened and soon ceased.

In October 1925 the *Daily Express* got hold of an even more dramatic poltergeist story:

Haunted for 12 months and more by a mischievous spirit – called a poltergeist – driven almost to a state of distraction, threatened with a lunatic asylum, and then cured by the help of a band of spirit Indians, is the extra-ordinary experience of the 19-year-old Gwynneth Morley, who lives with her widowed mother at Keighley, Yorkshire, and who was employed in the spinning mills of Messrs, Hay and Wright.

These phenomena were communicated to Sir Arthur Conan Doyle, who informed Mr Ilewet McKenxic, with the result that the girl was brought to London for psychic treatment, Mr. McKenzic being Honorary Principal of the British College of Psychic Science, an institution which is advertised as the "Best-equipped Centre for the study of Psychic Science in Britain".

Gwynneth Morley worked in Mr McKenzie's family for three months as a housemaid, under close observations and receiving psychic treatment.

Day by day the amazing manifestations of her tormenting spirit were noted down. In between the new and full moon the disturbances were worse. Everything in the room in which Gwynneth happened to be would be thrown about and smashed. Tables were lifted and overturned, chairs smashed to pieces, bookcases upset, and heavy settees thrown over.

In the kitchen of Holland Park, the preparation of meals, when Gwynneth was about, was a disconcerting affair. Bowls of water would be spilt and pats of butter thrown on the floor.

On another occasion when Gwynneth was in the kitchen, the housekeeper, who was preparing some grapefruit for breakfast, found that one half had disappeared and could be found neither in the kitchen nor in the scullery. She got two bananas to take its place and laid them on the table beside her; immediately, the missing grapefruit whizzed past her ear and fell before her, and the bananas vanished. Some 10 minutes later they were found on the scullery table.

All this time, Gwynneth was being treated by psychic experts. Every week the girl sat with Mr and Mrs, McKenzie and others. It was found that she was easily hypnotised, and that tables moved towards her in the circle.

At other times during the cure the poltergeist seemed to accept challenges. One night, after a particularly exciting day, Mrs Barkel magnetised Gwynneth's head and quietened her, and Mrs McKenzie suggested that she should go to bed, saying "Nothing happens when you get into bed."

Going up the stairs, a small table and a metal vase crashed over, and a little later a great noise of banging and tearing was heard in Gwynneth's room. When Mrs McKenzie went into the room it looked as if a tornado had swept over it.

After an active spell from June 21 to June 25 the spirit behaved itself until July 1, when the girl had a kind of fit. Suddenly she fell off her chair with her hands clenched. They laid her on a bed and she fell into another fit. She gripped her own throat powerfully.

Since that evening she has had no further attacks, nor have there been any disturbances

In 1982 the Newman family in Sheffield were plagued by a low-level poltergeist which made the usual knocking noises and dropped stones about the house. After a year of this nuisance, the family had almost grown used to their invisible guest. Then one night in the autumn, Derek Newman, the father of the family, was woken up by what sounded like a man going beserk with a hammer in the lounge under his bedroom. Loud thumps, smashing noises and crashes shook the floor and echoed through the building. Mr Newman sprang out of bed, thinking that this time a real intruder might be at work. He yanked open his bedroom door and was confronted by a thick pall of smoke coming up the stairs; the lounge was on fire. Mr Newman bundled his family out of the house and called the fire brigade. He believed that the poltergeist had saved their lives.

A bed shop in York was the venue for a spectacular poltergeist that was studied by Colin Davies, an investigator working with the Association for the Scientific Study of Anomalous Phenomena (ASSAP). The events began in the mid-1980s, with Davies arriving after the shop had been experiencing strange occurrences for almost a year. The incidents were mostly of the stone-throwing variety, although in this case the objects being chucked about were items from the shop's office, such as pens, rolls of tape, and notebooks.

On the day Davies arrived, a marker pen was thrown at a customer, and while the customer was complaining to shop manager, Don, a pen fell to the floor behind him. Another time, Davies was in the shop while only two employees were present: Don and a clerical worker named Susie. Both were in their offices, while Davies was on the shop floor. He saw a marker pen floating about two inches below the ceiling. The pen then began to drift horizontally across the shop for about 10ft, before falling down to bounce off a cardboard box and hit the floor. Paperclips, pens and booklets continued to move about over the following weeks, then the telephone system began to be affected. The phones rang when nobody was calling, cut out without reason and dialled other numbers apparently by themselves. The telephone company was called in, but could find nothing wrong with the system. The activity ceased soon after the telephone system malfunction.

Sometimes, poltergeist activity can be linked to an apparently normal haunting. One of the bedrooms in the Cavendish Hotel, Harrogate, is reportedly haunted. The ghost is that of a middle-aged man dressed in red-and-white-striped pyjamas. He is seen by the window, sometimes by the door, but usually vanishes within seconds of appearing. One guest in the bedroom did not see the ghost, but had the equally unnerving experience of having her bedside lamp levitate, float across the room and then come to rest on the floor. Neither manifestation has been

The Spotted Cow in Malton is quiet now, but 40 years ago the pub was the centre of a celebrated poltergeist visitation.

experienced since the hotel was recently refurbished. In 2003 a poltergeist moved into Sayers Tyre and Exhaust Centre, Doncaster. The case lasted for some weeks, and involved the sudden appearance from nowhere of both stones and coins. The employees workshop reported seeing the ghostly apparition of a short man during the time that the poltergeist was active.

The Spotted Cow in Malton attracted local press headlines in the 1970s, when assorted poltergeist activity broke out. Glasses were moved about the bar, and knockings and footsteps were heard. Another poltergeist in a pub took up residence in the Bridge Inn at Stapleton. This particular visitation was potentially highly dangerous, as the poltergeist developed a fascination with the gas cooker and many times turned the gas on, filling the kitchen with explosive fumes.

No discussion of poltergeists in Yorkshire can be complete without an account of perhaps the most famous poltergeist to be active in England during the mid-20th century: the terrifying entity that became known as 'The Black Monk of Pontefract'. This case is all the more puzzling as it was highly unusual in some respects, but utterly typical in others. From the point of view of an investigator, the case has the advantage of having been well documented by those involved and, in its later stages, by the local press.

The Black Monk of Pontefract poltergeist began in an unusual fashion, as it began with an outbreak of dramatic and frightening phenomena more usually associated with the later stages of a poltergeist visitation. The poltergeist stopped its activity as abruptly as it had begun and went away for many months, only to return with redoubled fury for a second visit.

The Bridge Inn at Stapleton was home to a poltergeist that left as mysteriously as it arrived.

The household affected was, by contrast, entirely typical. The Pritchard family lived at 30 East Drive, a semi-detached house in an unremarkable housing estate built on the southern edge of the ancient town of Pontefract. The household consisted of Mr Joe Pritchard, his wife Jean and their children, Phillip, aged 15, and Diane, aged 12. Mrs Pritchard's mother, Sarah Scholes, lived locally and was a frequent guest. Jean's sister, Marie, and her husband lived in the same street, almost opposite No. 30. They too were frequent visitors. Joe's brother, Jim, and his wife, Enid, lived at No. 28, next door. The other half of the semi-detached house, No. 32, was occupied by a Mr and Mrs Mountain.

In August 1966 the Pritchards went on holiday to Devon. Teenager Phillip decided not to go, preferring to stay in Pontefract with his friends. His grandmother, Mrs Scholes, moved in to No. 30 to take charge of the house and keep an eye on the teenager. On the Thursday before the family were due back, Phillip was outside reading a book in the garden, as it was a hot, sunny day. Mrs Scholes was knitting in the lounge. It was then that the poltergeist arrived.

In hindsight, the first indication of what was to come came around 11 o'clock that morning, when Mrs Scholes began to feel chilly despite the hot weather. After about half an hour a sudden wind blew through the house, rattling the open windows and slamming the back door shut with a reverberating crash. Phillip came in, and Mrs Scholes asked if the weather had turned windy. Phillip assured her that it had not, then went into the kitchen to make them both a cup of tea.

A few minutes later, as Phillip carried the tea back to the lounge, he stopped in amazement at the door to the lounge. A fine white powder, akin to talcum powder or chalk, was drifting slowly down from the air and filling the room. He called out, and Mrs Scholes looked up from her knitting to see the powder. The room had been redecorated only a few weeks before, and their first thought was that plaster from the ceiling was falling down. Mrs Scholes stood up and then saw something odd. The powder was not falling from the ceiling, but seemed to be materialising about 5ft from the floor.

Deciding that some sort of dust had blown through the window from some nearby building works, Mrs Scholes crossed the road to talk to her daughter, Marie. Marie was surprised by her mother's appearance, as if somebody had thrown flour all over her, and crossed the road to investigate events at No. 30. By the time she arrived, the powder had stopped falling, but now formed a thick layer of dust over everything in the lounge.

Marie Kelly announced that whatever the powder was, it needed clearing up, and went into the kitchen to get the dustpan and brush. She almost fell over when she stepped into a puddle of water. The water formed a large, but neat pool on the floor. There were no splashes as might be expected if the water had come from a spilled jug or dripped from the kitchen sink. Passing the job of clearing up the lounge to her mother, Marie Kelly got a cloth and mopped up the water. She wrung the cloth into the sink and turned to put it away, but was confronted by another neat little pool of water. She cleared that up, only to find a third. Thinking that the water was somehow coming up from under the floor, she lifted the linoleum, but there were no obvious broken pipes.

At this point, Enid Pritchard arrived from next door to see what was going on. She turned off the water mains, but the pools of water continued to appear. Then she turned on the taps in the kitchen to drain the water from the pipes. The liquid that emerged had a greenish tinge and foamed in the sink before it ran away. The assembled family members decided to call the local water authority.

A workman arrived at about 3 o'clock to find the kitchen floor almost awash with water. He cleared it up, checked the pipes, checked the drains, poked about generally, and found that more water puddles were forming. He admitted that he was baffled, and said that he would report the puzzle so that a more experienced plumber with more elaborate equipment could come out in a day or two. As soon as he left, the water puddles stopped appearing.

Marie Kelly and Enid Pritchard returned to their homes. The general consensus of opinion was that some joker was playing tricks, although nobody could imagine how this was being achieved.

All was quiet at No. 30 until 7 o'clock that evening, when Phillip once again offered to make some tea for his grandmother. When he entered the kitchen he saw the work surface was covered with sugar and tea leaves. The Pritchards used a tea leaf dispenser of the sort now largely made redundant by teabags. As Phillip watched the dispenser, it dispensed another load of tea leaves onto the work surface.

Phillip called in his grandmother, who arrived in time to see the rest of the tea cascade out, after which the dispenser continued to operate by itself for some time. Then there came a loud crash from the hallway. They opened the door, but at first could see nothing amiss. The hallway light was then switched on by unseen hands. After a few minutes of hesitation, Phillip edged into the hall. He found that a pot plant from the hall window sill was now lying on the stairs; the pot itself was missing, and the soil and roots of the plant were exposed. After a bit of searching the pot was found on the upstairs landing.

Next, a rattling, banging sound came from the kitchen. The cupboard was shaking from side to side, as if something were alive inside it. Phillip opened the cupboard door, whereupon the shaking stopped. Then a loud bang shook the house. Phillip and Mrs Scholes fled over the road to the Kelly household.

By 10 o'clock nothing further had happened, so Phillip and his grandmother returned home. Philip got into bed, but as his grandmother entered to wish him a good night, his bedroom wardrobe started swaying violently from side to side. Again, they fled over the road, this time determined to stay the night in the Kelly household.

Marie's husband, Vic, decided to call the police this time, still thinking that some clever human intruder was behind the trouble. Three policemen arrived and undertook a detailed search of the house. They found no sign of hidden wires, strings or tubes that might have produced the effects. It was past 11 o'clock when they left.

The Kellys sat discussing things, and decided to call in a friend of Mr Kelly, a Mr O'Donald, who lived down the road. He had an interest in local folklore, including ghosts, and they thought that he might be able to shed light on events. Mr O'Donald arrived and sat in the kitchen at No. 30, chatting to the Kellys about various supernatural events. During the course of the evening he got on to the subject of poltergeists, and remarked in passing, 'They do all sorts of strange things, you know, like tearing up photos and stuff.' Seconds later a crash came from the lounge;

they opened the door to find that a photo of the Pritchard's wedding had been thrown from the mantlepiece to the floor. The glass was broken and the photo torn in half. The three promptly left No. 30.

Next morning all was quiet. Phillip Pritchard and his grandmother warily moved back into the house. Nothing untoward happened, and by the evening they had decided to sleep in the house again. Nothing continued to happen for several days. When the rest of the Pritchard family got home from Devon they were told about the bizarre events. As they were all discussing the apparent poltergeist, three loud bangs sounded from upstairs, then a cold wind blew through the house, then silence returned. The poltergeist had, it seemed, gone... Two years later it came back.

This time it was Jean Pritchard and her mother, Mrs Scholes, who were in the house on a warm August afternoon as events began to unfold. They were drinking tea in the kitchen when a soft noise came from the hall. Mrs Pritchard went to investigate and found the quilt from her bed lying in a heap at the bottom of the stairs. She put it back, but 10 minutes later Phillip's bedspread appeared in the hallway. A few minutes later the hall pot plant fell off its shelf onto the floor with a crash.

That night, something awoke Mrs Pritchard in the small hours. Diane's bedroom was being redecorated and the decorating tools were lying about in the upstairs landing. As Mrs Pritchard stepped out onto the landing, a paintbrush was thrown at her by unseen hands, but narrowly missed. Then, a roll of wallpaper rose up into the air and started wafting about by itself. With commendable nerve, Jean Pritchard grabbed it. The carpet sweeper then began moving toward her and she screamed, bringing the rest of the family to the landing. A paintbrush hurtled through the air and struck Diane, but luckily did not injure her. As so often with objects moved by poltergeists, it seemed to slow down just as it was about to hit her, and so delivered no more than a light tap. The mayhem then moved into Diane's bedroom. The wooden pelmet over the curtains was torn from the wall and hurled out of the open window – it was found next morning in the front garden. Mr Pritchard slammed the bedroom door and locked it. Banging and thumping noises came from inside the room for sometime, but nothing untoward happened outside it. The family did not sleep well that night.

Having come back to Pontefract with a bang, the poltergeist seemed to have no intention of leaving again. Over the weeks that followed the poltergeist seemed to fall into a routine, which it stuck to fairly rigidly, although there were often variations.

The poltergeist's day would begin at about 6 o'clock in the morning, when it awoke the household with a series of thumps, bangs and crashes. At the same time, the temperature in the house fell dramatically, something that happened almost every time that poltergeist activity was about to begin. The bangs and crashes were often very loud. A bus ran down East Drive, taking men from the housing estate to work in the town centre or at a nearby mine. Those workers travelling in the early morning could clearly hear the noises from the bus stop, and often walked down the road to gather outside to listen to the morning chorus of supernatural mayhem.

When the noises eased off around 7 o'clock, the poltergeist would switch to moving objects about. Usually these were fairly small objects, such as ornaments or pot plants. They were generally moved gently from one place to another, but on a few rare occasions were thrown and smashed. Larger objects were moved from time to time, but generally not very far. A wardrobe might shuffle a few inches to one side, for instance. A dramatic break to this routine came when the grandfather clock in the hallway was hurled the length of the hall with great violence, smashing to pieces when it hit the far wall.

The poltergeist would then fall silent while Mr Pritchard and Phillip were out at work and Diane was at school.

Around 8 o'clock in the evening the poltergeist would start up again. After the familiar chill spread through the house, the noises would begin again. These again attracted a small crowd outside the house, this time usually local children and youths. A favourite trick in the evening was to switch off electrical equipment; lights were frequently turned off, but the television and fridge also came in for attention. After a few weeks the poltergeist tired of switching off individual items, and instead went for the mains switch in the understairs cupboard. The Pritchards tried sealing the switch in place with duct tape and locking the cupboard, but neither had any effect. The evenings, like the mornings, also saw objects moved about, but now they might be hidden or apparently taken away for a few days, before returning again to their accustomed position.

The poltergeist also got rather inventive in the evenings. One evening it removed a pot of marmalade from the kitchen, opened it and smeared the contents up the banisters of the stairs. Another evening a plate of freshly made sandwiches went missing. The plate was found a few minutes later behind the television. Something had taken bites out of some of the sandwiches, leaving the marks of enormous, wolf-like fangs in the bread. The spirit seemed to develop a fascination with toilet paper. Repeatedly, the rolls of toilet paper were unwound and draped around the upstairs. It also favoured the scent of flowers, often creating the odour of summer blossoms to permeate the house as evening drew in. It also had a penchant for keys, collecting all the keys in the house into one place, such as on a windowshelf, in the fireplace or on the kitchen floor.

Day after day, week after week the supernatural mayhem went on. Several times the Pritchards were advised to move out by friends or relatives, but they always refused. They took the attitude that No. 30 East Drive was their home, and no intruder – human or supernatural – was going to drive them out. They called the poltergeist 'Fred' and ascribed to him the character of a naughty young child.

A few incidents stood out from the routine of bangs, crashes and moving objects. About a month after the second visitation began, the family contacted the local vicar, the Revd Mr Davy, and asked him to come round to see if he could do anything. Mr Davy arrived one Thursday evening about 7 o'clock, and listened as the Pritchard's outlined what had been happening. He then explained the procedure of a Church of England exorcism, together with the fact that they would need special permission from the local bishop. He finished by advising them that many cases of hauntings turned out to have perfectly natural explanations, such as pranksters, sounds from underground streams or subsidence. 'Fred' chose this moment to intervene. A candlestick fell off the mantlepiece with a crash, then a second candlestick floated off the mantlepiece and drifted across the room to hover just inches from the startled vicar's face, before it too fell to the floor.

Then came a massive crash from the lounge. Everyone raced through to find the sideboard overturned and all the china and crockery it contained strewn across the floor, although not a single item was broken. Mr Davy expressed the view that something evil had entered the house and advised the family to move out.

A couple of weeks later Mr Pritchard's sister, Maude, who lived some distance away, paid a visit. She had no belief in the supernatural and, hearing the reports of the poltergeist from a distance, had come to the conclusion that the two teenagers were playing tricks on the rest of the family. Soon after she arrived one evening, the kitchen went cold and the lights went out as the electrical mains was switched off. So far, so normal for the poltergeist. Then the fridge door opened and a jug of milk floated out, hovered briefly, and was flung at Maude. She at once blamed the teenagers and suggested looking for the means of their trickery. The electrics were switched back on by Mr Pritchard, but almost at once went off again, whereupon a string of sausages levitated out of the fridge and onto the table in front of Maude. At this point Maude noticed that her gloves were missing from the table where she had put them.

After they all went to bed, with Maude sharing Diane's room, the gloves reappeared in a most unnerving form. They appeared round the edge of the bedroom door as if somebody on the landing was trying to get into the room. Then the gloves came into the room as if worn by an invisible person. After moving around in mid-air for a while, the gloves began beckoning the humans forwards. Maude pointed at the gloves and shouted, 'You are evil. Go away!' At this, the gloves curled up into fists and shook themselves at Maude. Then they withdrew as Maude began singing hymns. Next day Maude went home without even stopping for breakfast. The gloves were found in her bag. She burned them in the garden.

In March 1969 the poltergeist took a new and unusual direction. The vast majority of poltergeists remain invisible, only the results of their pranks and destructive urges are to be seen. But now 'Fred' began to appear. He was first seen by Mr Pritchard on the landing when he himself was in bed. The figure, he said, was tall and male, wearing a long cloak and a hood. The figure was in sight for only a couple of seconds before it vanished. Others began to see the figure about the house, describing it variously as a man in a black dressing gown, overcoat or cloak. By this time the activities were also becoming more frequent and more dramatic.

One evening the teenagers were alone in the house, watching television in the lounge. Phillip saw the black, hooded figure gliding along the hallway towards the kitchen, and he got up to follow it. He saw the figure enter the kitchen, then it sank slowly downward into the solid floor, finally disappearing in almost the precise spot where the first pool of water had appeared so long ago. The poltergeist activity ceased abruptly and this time never returned.

The visitation had received a good deal of press attention over the 10 months of the second series of events. The black, cowled figure had been nicknamed the 'Black Monk'. There was a reason for this: Pontefract had been the site of a large and prosperous Cluniac Priory from 1090 to 1540. The monks wore a black cassock, so the link was easily made. In fact, the link was even closer than that. The estate of which East Drive was a part had been built on a hill formerly occupied by the town gibbet. It was widely reported during the poltergeist visitation that a monk had been hanged on the gibbet in the 15th century. No firm historical records for such an execution have turned up, however, although a vicar was hanged there in the 17th century.

What on earth causes these poltergeist manifestations is a total mystery, for no explanation would seem to fit all the facts. In past centuries victims have ascribed poltergeist activity to witches, fairies, goblins, demons and devils. These days, investigators try to seek less exotic explanations for apparently impossible events and manifestations. Those seeking to find an explanation for poltergeist activity have recently tended to concentrate on some of the accepted common features of the various visitations.

First, the vast majority of the phenomena involve objects moving about. Some are thrown, others lifted, and still more are shoved along a surface, but they share the feature of solid objects being moved by an unseen force. Second, the poltergeist appears to be an intelligent entity, capable of seeing and hearing what is happening in the affected building and to responding to such events. The poltergeist may react to things said by a person in the building and is capable of aiming objects at individual persons and things. The ability of the poltergeist to communicate with humans by way of coded knocks or a disembodied voice emphasises its apparent intelligence and the feeling that it is alive. Finally, there are the circumstances in which poltergeists manifest themselves. The frequency with which poltergeists appear in small groups of humans, one of which is a teenager undergoing emotional stress, is striking. Taking all these features together, modern researchers have come up with a number of hypotheses.

Researchers working in other areas of paranormal research have produced evidence that some people might be capable of psychokinetics (PK): the power to move objects by the power of thought alone. Among those who have been subjected to tests in controlled conditions have been the Russian woman Nina Kulagina, the Briton Matthew Manning, and the American Felicia Parise. Those performing PK exhibit abnormal brainwave patterns, rapidly fluctuating body temperatures and other odd physical traits when moving objects. It must be said that not everyone accepts the reality of these abilities, and it has been suggested that what seems to be PK is, in fact, trickery achieved by sophisticated conjuring tricks.

For those who do accept the reality of PK, it seems to offer an explanation for poltergeists. It may be that one of the people involved is inadvertently unleashing PK on the objects in the building and causing them to fly about. The focus person is the most obvious suspect here. Perhaps the emotional stress being undergone by that person causes them to lash out subconsciously. On the other hand, it may be the others involved who collectively strike out, being frustrated by the often sulky or irrational behaviour of the focus teenager.

Other researchers, however, do not accept that the humans involved are the source of the poltergeist. They believe that the peculiar conditions in which a poltergeist manifests enable a disembodied entity of some kind – be it a ghost, demon or some other being – allowing it to get a foothold in our reality and so perform its mischief.

We shall probably never know, so it is as well that poltergeist visitations tend to be fairly short-lived phenomena.

CHAPTER 8

Mysterious Witches

Witches are perhaps the most misunderstood of all the mysterious phenomena that have occurred in Yorkshire. All sorts of powers, motives, abilities and habits have been ascribed to witches over the years. They have been portrayed as evil, kind, in league with the Devil, in league with nature, part of a pagan past dating back millennia, and a bunch of cranks. The truth is every bit as interesting, although perhaps not so colourful.

These days, the popular image of a witch comes in two main forms. What may be termed the comic book image is of an ugly old woman dressed in black and wearing a pointy hat. She flies on a broom, is accompanied by a black cat and is able to cast all sorts of spells, most of them mischievous or evil to some degree or another. Although allegedly powerful and wicked, these witches usually turn out to have an easily exploited flaw, or to be not quite so bad as they at first appeared. Since the 1950s there has been an increasing trend for fictional witches to be both good and humorous, often as a result of spells going wrong.

A second modern image of a witch sees them as kindly, if slightly eccentric women or men who practice some form of pagan religion related to nature worship. These witches, it is thought, are given to meeting in remote, rural places or in spooky ruins, where they hold rituals that usually involve drawing odd, geometric patterns, burning candles and sometimes dancing in the nude. In horror movies and similar television shows, these witches are occasionally depicted indulging in human sacrifice. The victim is typically shown as an attractive young woman in a diaphanous gown, who is often the girlfriend of the hero of the show.

The former image grew out of the witch-hunting decades of the 16th and early 17th centuries in Europe. It had long been believed by theologians that magic was possible only through a pact with the Devil. After about 1540, people across Europe began to be accused of witchcraft, in the sense of working evil through magical powers acquired from the Devil. Some of these people were arrested, tortured and made confessions that were used to develop an elaborate picture of witchcraft. Put simply, it was believed that there was a vast international network of witches dedicated to doing evil to humans and to undermining the Christian Church. To coordinate the conspiracy, witches flew at night to meetings, where they laid their plans, met the Devil, murdered young children and indulged in hedonistic orgies of the most depraved kind.

The punishment for witchcraft of this kind was death in many countries, although in others – including England – witchcraft was not itself a crime, but the evil wrought through witchcraft was. Because witches were perceived as agents of the Devil, they were thought be be a threat to the well-being of society as a whole, and therefore were hunted down for trial and execution. It is thought that about 40,000 people, mostly women, were executed for witchcraft or for related offences between 1430 and 1680, most of them in German-speaking areas. In 1593 a trial in Trier led to the executions of 368 people. Fear of the threat of witchcraft to the fabric of society declined after the 1650s, and by 1750 witchcraft was no longer a crime in most countries. The

A 16th-century witch about to be burned in Germany. For some two centuries, witch trials were common across Europe and thousands went to their deaths for supposed crimes against God and humanity.

popular image of a witch developed in those years survived and lies behind the modern, comic-book image.

The other modern image of witchcraft is based on the practices of the neopagan religion that its followers usually refer to as Wicca. From a theological point of view, Wicca is a duo-theistic religion with two supreme deities: the Triple Goddess and the Horned God. There are, however, a number of other spiritual beings within the religion. There is a wide variety of ritual practices and codes of morality within Wicca, with some groups having beliefs and activities that are very different from another. This diversity is a key feature of Wicca, and one that its practitioners hold up as being preferable to the dogma of some other religions.

Those who practice Wicca often claim that it descended from a pre-Christian pagan cult widespread across northern Europe, yet it has not been possible to trace the religion further back than the 1920s.

It must be said, however, that the actual witches of Yorkshire do not fit readily into either of these traditions. They, like most witches across England, seem to have been a rather different type of magical person altogether.

Take, for instance, the lady known as Auld Betty of Halifax, who lived in the 1760s. Auld Betty had a mixed reputation almost equally divided between the ability to cure sickness and a vicious habit of inflicting sickness on those she did not like. One day she took against the wife of a schoolmaster, for some reason, and laid a curse on her that caused the unfortunate woman to become ill and bedridden. The schoolmaster was distraught and sent for a man who had a reputation for being able to tame witches and magic. The man was, unfortunately, too busy to come to Halifax, but he sent instructions as to what should be done.

The schoolmaster followed the instructions carefully. He made up a cake mixture according to a special recipe, then set it down to bake in front of his kitchen fire as the sun set. In his hand he held a silver fork with three prongs, hidden under his jacket. His instructions told him to sit still and wait until a black animal appeared by the cake. He was to respond if the animal spoke, but must never mention any holy name, nor was he to move until the animal came close enough for him to stab it with the three-pronged silver fork. If he managed to draw blood, his instructions said, the witchcraft would be broken and his wife would recover.

An hour passed without incident. Then, suddenly, a black cat appeared on the hearth beside the cake. The schoolmaster had neither seen nor heard it arrive. The cat sat licking itself silently for a while, then glanced down at the cake. 'Cake burns,' said the cat.

'Turn it then,' replied the schoolmaster.

The cat regarded him silently for a while, then stretched its claws and looked again at the cake. 'Cake burns,' said the cat.

'Turn it then,' replied the schoolmaster.

The cat looked at him again, then licked its paws for a while, then glanced again at the cake. 'Cake burns,' said the cat.

'Turn it then,' replied the schoolmaster.

The cat stared at him silently for some time, then put a paw on the cake. 'Cake burns,' said the cat.

'Turn it then,' replied the schoolmaster.

The cat withdrew its paw, sniffed at the cake and sat back on its haunches. 'Cake burns,' said the cat.

'Oh, for God's sake,' shouted the schoolmaster, 'just turn it!' As soon as he uttered the name of the Almighty, the schoolmaster remembered his instructions, but too late. The cat spat at him and began inching back toward the fireplace. The schoolmaster lunged forward with the three-pronged silver fork as the cat streaked up the chimney. A tiny, bright-red gleam of blood lay on the tip of one of the fork prongs.

Next morning the schoolmaster's wife was completely recovered from her illness. Auld Betty, however, was bedridden with a mysterious illness. She did not recover for some weeks.

Another Yorkshire witch crops up in the legend ascribed to the Drumming Well of Harpham, described in detail in Chapter 4. According to legend, a drummer boy died when he was thrown down the well by a member of the St Quintin family. His mother, or in some versions a passer-by, was a witch; she punishes the St Quintins for the crime by summoning up the ghost of the drummer boy and giving him the task of appearing in spectral form to play his drum whenever one of the St Quintins is about to die.

A witch by the name of Jane Herd lived in Bedale. In the 1790s she got involved in an escapade involving another witch and two male witches. The train of events had begun many years earlier, when Jane was born with a light membrane over her head. This is known as a caul, and is a perfectly natural, though rare, condition. The caul is a fragment of the membranous sac that surrounds the foetus in the womb. It usually disintegrates during the birthing process, but occasionally survives. It was widely believed that a caul, if carefully preserved, brought good luck to the baby throughout its life.

Jane Herd's mother dried the caul and kept it in a wooden box. As Jane grew older she learned about magic and witching, using her caul as a powerful aid to her magic. She used it to cure illness in humans and in livestock, and for various other purposes that were of benefit to her neighbours and friends. Then, one summer's day in 1793, Jane was working a spell in her kitchen with the windows open. A sudden gust of wind blew the caul out of her hand and through the window. She ran out immediately, but could not find it.

From that day, her luck changed. Her boyfriend cancelled their wedding, and a painful swelling appeared on her knee, which caused her to walk with a limp. Another swelling appeared on her neck, which disfigured her good looks. She became convinced that her caul had somehow fallen into the hands of another witch, who was using it to do her harm. Uncertain of how to proceed, Jane went to see Thomas Spence and Master Sadler, the two best-known 'cunning men', or male witches, of Swaledale.

Spence and Sadler agreed that another witch had got hold of the caul, and promised that they could both identify the witch and recover the caul. They instructed Jane to come to Spence's cottage the following evening just before midnight armed with an assortment of food and household objects. When she arrived, Jane found Spence and Sadler boiling a pot of water on a fire of rowan twigs. They took the items from Jane, added a few of their own, and tossed them into the boiling water. A great cloud of stinking steam billowed up. Jane was instructed to take nine deep breaths of the noxious fumes while stirring the pot with a rowan twig, which she did.

The three then moved to a table, on which was placed a Bible. Jane was told to put one hand on the Bible and hold up the rowan twig in the other. She then had to state, one by one, the names of people that she suspected of having taken the caul. As each name was spoken, Sadler gazed into the boiling pot for a few seconds before replying, 'No, she is free.' Spence then asked Jane to speak another name.

When Jane spoke the name 'Molly Cass' the pot suddenly boiled over and there was a scream from outside the cottage. The two men raced out, pouncing on Molly Cass, who was standing in the yard as if in a trance. The woman was locked into a stable, the door being secured with a stout peg of rowan. At dawn, she was dragged out into the yard. She confessed that she had been walking past Jane's house when the caul blew out the window. Being a witch herself, she had recognised it for what it was, stuffed it in her pocket and fled. She had since then been using it for her own magic, and had cursed Jane in order to keep her too busy to search for the caul. The caul was retrieved from Molly's cottage and the miscreant marched down to the Swale. She was thrown into the water nine times as punishment, then let go.

Another unpleasant witch was Peggy Flaunders of Upleatham. Flaunders was known as a cantankerous old soul who had the ability to cause livestock to sicken and die. Local farmers dreaded seeing Flaunders on their doorstep, knowing that she had come to take a basket of apples, a loaf of bread, or any other food they had on the premises. Flaunders made no secret of what would happen to any farmer who did not hand over a tasty pie or other dainty on request.

She surpassed herself in 1834. A farmer's wife named Oughtred did not give Flaunders as large a share of some pickles as the old witch wanted, handing over only a small jar. Three days later, just after sunset, a knock came on the door of the Oughtred farmhouse. The maid went to open the door, then returned, screaming and gibbering with fear. She gabbled out that a burning pig was standing on the doorstep. Farmer Oughtred hurried to the door, and was alarmed to find that the maid had not shut it on whatever evil had been present. He could see nothing and slammed the door shut, reciting the Lord's Prayer as he did so. It was too late.

The Oughtreds and their farmhands began to see a small black imp about the farm. It was described as being about six inches tall, human in shape, naked and totally black in colour. Whenever it was seen, something went wrong in the immediate vicinity. When it was seen in the dairy, the milk turned sour. When it was seen in the kitchen, plates were smashed. When it was seen in the fields, the cattle fell sick.

Convinced that he was cursed by Peggy Flaunders, Farmer Oughtred went to see the local cunning man. He gave Oughtred instructions on what to do. He had to return home, gather the entire household in the kitchen, and then make sure that every door and window in the house was firmly closed. He then had to light a fire in the kitchen, using only wood gathered on the farm. A black cockerel then had to be thrown alive onto the fire, and held down with iron tongs while it burned to death. As Oughtred did this, the stench of burning feathers and flesh filled the house. Then a squeaking scream was heard, followed by the pattering of little feet as if some little creature was fleeing the house. Thereafter, the imp was seen no more, nor did any more misfortunes afflict the Oughtred Farm.

Rather less precise is the story of the witch of Gormire Lake. Many years ago, it is said, a witch was being chased out of Helmsley, as the good folk of the town had tired of her constant evil acts. They chased her out of the town and up into the Hambleton Hills. Over Cold Kirby Moor she ran, with the irate townsfolk at her heels. When the witch reached the White Mare Crag, she took a mighty leap and plunged into the dark, swirling waters of Gormire Lake. The witch was taken along in an underwater current, and she eventually emerged from a well over nine miles away; thus she managed to escape.

Wensleydale was home to two famous cunning men. The more recent of these was the Seer of Redmire, who lived in a small cottage given to him by the owner of Mill Farm. The Seer of Redmire would walk down to the spring of pure water, known locally as Redmire Well, to work his magic. The man claimed to be able to see into the future, and successfully predicted several local events. His main ability was to be able to foretell who was to die in the near future. To achieve this, the Seer of Redmire went down to the spring on the night of the new moon and sat down to watch. One by one, the apparitions of those residents of Wensleydale who would die before the next full moon would come down the lane to drink at the well. Unsurprisingly, most folk did not care to meet the Seer of Redmire the day after the night of the new moon, for fear of what he might tell them.

One night of the new moon in 1849, the Seer of Redmire came back home quiet, thoughtful and morose. He spent the next few days getting his affairs in order, paying bills and collecting debts. Then he went to the church to pray. That night he died in his sleep.

A short distance west of Redmire is Carperby Moor, overlooking Wensleydale from the north. This was, some centuries ago, the home of the Seer of Carperby. This seer could not only foretell the future, but could also curse those who crossed him. He was said to have a pet raven, who perched on the seer's shoulder.

The narrow valley of Clapdale, west of Austwick, was home to Alice Ketyll, the Witch of Clapdale. According to local tradition, there was a witch named Alice Ketyll who lived here in the 15th century. What is now Clapdale Hall was then Clapdale Castle and was home to Alice's son, Sir John. Sir John may have been a knight, but he was not a rich man. His relative poverty was a constant embarrassment and annoyance to Alice. She decided on drastic action to make her son rich. Dame Alice Ketyll summoned up the Devil through witchcraft and asked for his help in enriching Sir John. Satan was only too pleased to help, and called up a lesser demon, by the name of Robyn Artisson, to do the work. Satan explained that for Sir John to become astonishingly rich, Alice needed only to do a few simple tasks everyday. First, she had to sweep the bridge over Clapham Beck, sweeping the dust towards Clapdale Castle. While doing this she had to constantly recite the verse:

'Into the house of John, my son
Hie all the wealth of Clapham Town'

Alice's second task was to return to the bridge at midnight with nine freshly killed cockerels. She had to arrange the birds in a circle on the bridge, then stand in the centre of the circle and call out, 'Robyn Artisson, Robyn Artisson, come to me.' The demon would then appear to do whatever she asked of him. Alice agreed and the deal began. Daily, Alice was seen by the puzzled locals sweeping the bridge and muttering under her breath. Sir John grew rich and lived a life of great comfort. One night, however, Alice was ill and did not take the nine dead birds to the bridge. She died and her soul went to the Devil.

This traditional version of the tale is not entirely accurate. Alice Ketyll was already deep into witchcraft, devilry and sin long before she came to Clapdale. In 1324 Alice had stood trial for witchcraft in Ireland, at Kilkenny, and had only narrowly escaped hanging. She had been born the daughter of a prosperous Flemish merchant, and had married Irish landowner William Utlaw in 1282. By Utlaw she had a son, John, who inherited his father's castle of Calland when the man died in 1295. Alice then remarried, this time to another wealthy landowner, Adam Blund. In 1304 Blund died, and Alice married a third time to yet another wealthy Irishman, Richard Valle. In 1316 Valle died. Alice must have been a lady of considerable charms, not to mention wealth, for in 1320 she married for a fourth time, to Sir John le Poer.

In 1324 the children of Richard Valle and Adam Blund went to Bishop Ledrede of Ossory to charge Alice with witchcraft. They alleged that she had used sorcery to ensnare their fathers into marriage, and had then used magic to force her husbands into signing over to her and Sir John all their wealth, thus disinheriting their children. Finally, the allegations ran, Dame Alice had murdered the two men in order to inherit their wealth.

Bishop Ledrede was a fiery preacher who eagerly latched on to these allegations. He looked at the evidence and promptly ordered the arrest of Dame Alice, not on charges of witchcraft, but of heresy. She was accused of denying Christ, making pacts with demons, seeking advice from demons, using the skull of a decapitated robber to brew potions, holding demonic rituals in Kilkenny Church and having carnal knowledge with a demon on a nightly basis. The charge of murdering her second and third husbands was thrown in almost as an afterthought.

Alice was arrested and thrown into prison. Her fourth husband then took a hand in proceedings by carrying to Bishop Ledrede a sack of herbs, fungi and other 'vile and horrible ingredients' that he had found locked in a wooden chest in his wife's chamber. He alleged that Dame Alice was trying to poison him, citing as evidence the fact that he had not felt well for some weeks. Two weeks later Arnold le Poer, Royal Seneschal of Kilkenny, marched a squad of armed men into Ossory Cathedral and arrested Bishop Ledrede on charges of exceeding his authority. With Ledrede in prison, Sir John Utlaw declared that the trial of his mother, Dame Alice, was illegal and had her released.

Alice promptly fled to Yorkshire, taking with her all her accumulated gold and jewels. Sir John Utlaw and his friend Arnold le Poer, however, remained in Ireland and continued to feud with Bishop Ledrede. After further moves, both legal and military, King Edward II demanded that the three men attend royal court. There they were reprimanded severely. Utlaw and le Poer were ordered to pay for the roof of Ossory Cathedral to be repaired, while Ledrede was ordered to drop all court actions against Dame Alice, Utlaw and le Poer.

The charges against Dame Alice were never proved, nor was she declared not guilty, as the case never came to trial. It would seem that her reputation followed her to Yorkshire from Ireland, however, and the locals came up with their own version of events.

A witchcraft trial that did take place in Yorkshire was that of Mary Bateman in 1809. Bateman had been born Mary Harker in Aisenby in 1768, and as a teenager began an unremarkable career as a domestic servant in Thirsk. By 1787 she had been let go from three different jobs after being suspected of pilfering from her employers. Unable to get a job in Thirsk, she moved to York, where she was employed in a millinery shop. Suspected again of theft, Mary escaped arrest only by fleeing in the night. In 1792 she was in Leeds, where she married a labourer named John Bateman. In 1797 her husband joined the army and marched off to fight the French.

Left alone, Mary Bateman rented a shop in Marsh Lane, Leeds, and advertised herself as a fortune teller and dealer in charms. Very soon Bateman had acquired a reputation as a powerful witch. She charged working folk small sums and in return gave them potions and charms that she claimed would cure illness, cause people to fall in or out of love, and ward off bad luck and evil of all kinds. There were several complaints made against her for persuading vulnerable elderly folk to part with their money, and she came in for a good deal of attention from the Church authorities, but they were unable to prove that Bateman had broken any laws.

Then, in May 1808, one of Bateman's customers died in unusual circumstances and the magistrates were contacted. Rebecca Perigo had been suffering from heart palpitations in the spring of 1806 and had become convinced that they were due to a witch's curse. Her husband, William, took her to Bateman in the hope that she could effect a cure. The Perigos were considerably richer than the poor who made up Bateman's usual customers. Bateman decided to make as much money as possible from the Perigos.

Over the 18 months that followed Bateman sold to the Perigos a variety of potions, charms and magical items that did seem to bring some relief to Mrs Perigo's heart symptoms. In all, the Perigos paid a total of £70 to Mary Bateman – at a time when a labourer might earn £10 a year. Even this was not enough, and in May 1808 Bateman decided to up the stakes. She claimed to be able to predict the future and, among other things, prophesied that the Perigos would fall sick in May, would be extremely ill for six days and should then send for Bateman, who would ensure their recovery by magical means. In May the Perigos did fall very ill with attacks of vomiting and dysentry. On the fifth day of illness, Mrs Perigo died.

Dr Chorley came to issue a death certificate and to care for Mr Perigo. He at once recognised the signs of arsenic poisoning and asked Mr Perigo if he and his wife had been eating anything odd. Perigo mentioned a pudding supplied by Bateman. Chorley fed a piece of the pudding to a cat, which promptly died. Chorley surmised that Bateman had given the Perigos the pudding to make them ill, intending to 'cure' them and then charge a hefty fee for having done so.

Investigations were begun by the Leeds magistrates. They found that Bateman had bought arsenic from a chemist in Kirkgate in April, just a few days before she sent the pudding to the Perigos. Bateman was arrested and put on trial in York in March 1809, on charges of fraud and murder. The evidence against her was overwhelming, the arsenic having been found in her house and in the pudding. The jury deliberated for less than a minute before declaring her to be guilty. She was hanged on 20 March.

As was the custom at the time for the bodies of executed criminals, Bateman's corpse was sent to Leeds General Infirmary for student surgeons to dissect. The fame of 'The Yorkshire Witch' was so great, however, that the Infirmary instead put the body on display and charged visitors three pennies a time to see it. More than 2,500 people paid up and the Infirmary made a handsome profit. Bateman's skeleton was preserved and is now in the Thakray Medical Museum, York.

Famous though Mary Bateman 'The Yorkshire Witch' was in her own day, her fame is nothing compared to that of the great witch of Knaresborough, who is widely known as Old Mother Shipton. This woman was born as Ursula Southill near Knaresborough in about 1488. Local tradition had it that she had been born in a cave, now known as Mother Shipton's Cave and open to the public. She was said to be illegitimate, and one version has it that her mother was a nun who had been seduced by a local knight. In 1512 she married a carpenter from York named Toby Shipton and had a number of children. She died in 1561, her husband having passed away some years earlier.

Old Mother Shipton's House as it was in the 1840s. Undoubtedly the most famous witch ever to have lived in Yorkshire, Old Mother Shipton owes much of her fame to predictions and prophecies that she herself may not have made.

Certainly, in the final years of her life and perhaps much earlier, Old Mother Shipton (as she was known in her widowhood) had a reputation as a witch and a seer. During her lifetime it seems to have been her abilities to cure sickness, move objects by looking at them, produce love potions, lift curses and imbue charms with magical powers that made her famous. After her death, however, the prophecies and predictions that she made became more famous as some came true and people speculated on the meanings of others.

As her fame spread, booklets and broadsheets were printed in increasingly large quantities giving details of her life, times and predictions. Quite how much truth was included in these later sources is unclear, and is much disputed. They may have drawn on local traditions about Old Mother Shipton, or they may have included lurid details dreamed up by the publisher in the hope of increasing sales.

For what they are worth, the later sources flesh out the bare bones of what is known about Old Mother Shipton. It is said that she lived for a while beside the Dropping Well, a spring of mineral-rich waters near Knaresborough that will coat with stone any item left in them for a few weeks. It may have been the apparently magical properties that caused the waters to be linked to Old Mother Shipton. The waters get their power from the fact that, before emerging on the surface, they pass through vast beds of limestone underground and dissolve the stone, which is then redeposited as they emerge.

Her childhood was, it is said, special. The young Ursula was a hideously ugly baby. When her mother died, it proved almost impossible to find a relative willing to have her. Eventually, a distant relative living in Knaresborough agreed to have the child, as long as other members of the family paid her to do so. One day the infant Ursula went missing. Her foster mother called in the neighbours, but nobody could find her anywhere. Finally, some odd noises were heard, and investigation found Ursula sound asleep halfway up the chimney.

During her childhood, her adoptive home was plagued on occasion by what sounded like poltergeist activity. Pots and pans floated about the kitchen, items went missing, only to reappear weeks later, and food appeared out of thin air to feed her when she was hungry. At the time, this sort of phenomena was associated with witchcraft – those who suffered what we would today call a poltergeist visitation would, at that time, assume that their house had been cursed by a witch.

Even as a young woman, Old Mother Shipton was said to be extraordinarily ugly, and the earliest sources put the blame for this on her nose. It is variously described as being 'deformed', 'crooked' and 'long'. A later version has it that her nose actually glowed in the dark.

Her earliest supposed predictions and prophecies related almost exclusively to Yorkshire and to people connected to the county. One of her best-known early achievements came when she heard that Cardinal Wolsey, Archbishop of York and Chancellor of England, was coming to visit his cathedral in 1529. 'He will see it,' prophesied Old Mother Shipton, 'but he will never enter it.' In the event, Wolsey arrived in York, from where he could obviously see the great York Minster, but before he set foot in the church he was arrested by order of King Henry VIII. Under armed escort, Wolsey was taken south toward London, but he only got as far as Leicester when he fell ill, was confined to bed and died.

A second ecclesiastical prophecy that she made has not survived in detail, but is

Old Mother Shipton's Moth is an insect found only in northern England. It gained its name because the pattern on the wings is said to resemble the profile of an old hag with a hooked nose and a prominent chin.

said to have foretold the closure of the great monastic houses of England. This came to pass in the 1530s with the Dissolution of the Monasteries, part of the religious reformations that made England a Protestant country. She also made a prophecy that foretold the destruction of London by fire, although this did not happen until 1666 when the Great Fire of London destroyed most of the city.

The oldest surviving booklet that contains prophecies made by Old Mother Shipton was printed in 1641. It contains various rhymes and predictions, among which is:

'Over a wild and stormy sea,
Shall a noble sail
Who to find will not fail,
A new and fair countree
From whence he shall bring
A herb and a root
That all men shall suit
And please both the ploughman and the king.'

This is said to predict the arrival in Britain of the potato, which came here in 1580, and tobacco, which arrived in 1578. Both events occurred after Old Mother Shipton's death, but before the publication of the booklet.

In the course of the 17th century a large number of booklets were printed purporting to contain prophecies by Old Mother Shipton. Many of these referred to events that had already happened, others were apparent nonsense and a few were political satire. Typical of the nonsense prediction was this:

'Carriages without horses shall go,
And accidents fill the world with woe.
Around the world thoughts shall fly,
In the twinkling of an eye.'

In the 20th century the first two lines have been interpreted to refer to the invention of the motor car, and the second two are said to predict telegrams, radio signals or the Internet.

Interest in Old Mother Shipton was revived in the 19th century, when a number of new predictions were produced and ascribed to her. The best known of these came from an 1862 reprinting of the 1641 booklet. The publisher, Charles Hindley, added some prophecies that he made up himself. These either referred to events that had recently taken place in the 19th century or to sensational events designed to boost sales of the booklet. The best known of his invented sections runs as follows:

'Through hills man shall ride,
And no horse be at his side.

Under water men shall walk,
Shall ride, shall sleep, shall talk.
In the air men shall be seen,
In white, in black, in green;
Iron in the water shall float,
As easily as a wooden boat.
Gold shall be found and shown
In a land that's now not known.
Fire and water shall wonders do,
England shall at last admit a foe.
The world to an end shall come,
In eighteen hundred and eighty one.'

The couplet 'Through hills man shall ride/And no horse be at his side' refers to railways trains running through tunnels; the couplet 'Under water men shall walk/Shall ride, shall sleep, shall talk" refers to submarines; 'In the air men shall be seen/In white, in black, in green' is a reference to hot-air balloons; 'Iron in the water shall float/As easily as a wooden boat' refers to the development of iron ships; 'Gold shall be found and shown/In a land that's now not known' is taken to refer to the Australian gold rush of 1851 since Australia was not yet discovered when Old Mother Shipton lived; 'Fire and water shall wonders do' is taken as a reference to steam power; 'England shall at last admit a foe' may be a political dig at a visit to Britain by the French Emperor Napoleon III; finally, 'The world to an end shall come/In eighteen hundred and eighty one' was inserted to give added fear and fascination to the book.

It is from Hindley's edition that modern interest in Old Mother Shipton sprang. His careful blending of fact, fantasy and fear made his book a bestseller and established the old Yorkshire witch as a celebrity. She has never quite lost that reputation to this day. During the 20th century the last couplet was altered to read 'The world to an end shall come/In nineteen hundred and ninety one.' That date, of course, passed without incident.

The picture that emerges from these tales, and from similar real-life stories of witches elsewhere in England, points to a reality rather different from any of the popular images of witches. While most witches were women, a good number were also men – though they were termed 'cunning men', rather than being labelled witches. The activities ascribed to these individuals indicates a knowledge of medicinal herbs, plants and fungi, which was dressed up with magical incantations and rituals to give the subject an air of mystery and effectiveness.

That these witches could be highly effective is beyond doubt. Many plants are known to have genuine medicinal effects, and they were certainly able to cure or alleviate complaints and symptoms. Not only that, but some of the instructions given alongside magical potions would have been of help. An instruction to a busy housewife to 'lie in bed for a week' would certainly have helped any complaint made worse by overwork or stress. Then there is the well-established placebo effect. This means that patients will often report an improvement to a condition when given what they believe to be an effective medicine, even if the 'medicine' is in reality entirely ineffectual. A person given a magical potion by a witch would, therefore, feel better merely through believing in the witch's power.

It is also clear that some witches and cunning men used hypnosis and psychology in their work. One famed cunning man lived in Stokesley in the mid-19th century, and was known across northern Yorkshire as Wizard Wrightson. He dressed habitually in a long, scarlet coat, white waistcoat, crimson breeches, black boots and a black hat, no matter what the weather. He was famed for his second sight and in particular his ability to find lost or stolen items. His usual procedure was to visit the home of the person whose property had been stolen. Wizard Wrightson would then spend the day touring all local farms, pubs and villages telling everyone that he met that he had been called in to track down the thief. He said that he was a bit busy at that moment, but would be back in one week to find the culprit and visit upon him magical vengeance of hideous and unspeakable nastiness. Almost invariably the stolen item was returned. The thief had got to hear that Wrightson was on the case and, since everyone believed that he really could curse a person if he wanted to do so, the thief preferred to return the item than risk a curse.

Wrightson probably also used hypnosis. On one well-documented occasion, Wrightson invited to his house a man he suspected had been behind a spate of robberies. The man nervously turned up, and was pleasantly surprised when Wrightson appeared to be friendly and invited him to sit by the kitchen fire. Once the man was seated, Wrightson chatted to him in friendly fashion for a while. Then Wrightson added more fuel to the fire, then more and more until the blaze was enormous. The man began to feel hot and tried to push his chair back. To his utter consternation he found he could not move. More and more wood was piled on the fire by Wrightson until the man felt his eyebrows begin to singe.

'Now then,' said Wrightson, dropping all pretence of niceness. 'If ye want to leave here, ye had better tell me all about what you have been up to.'

The hapless man gibbered out his confession and promised to return the stolen items, whereupon Wrightson tapped him on the shoulder. The man found that he could move at last and fled. It certainly sounds like hypnotism.

It should not be thought that witches and cunning men were simply harmless old folk dabbling in medicinal herbs, however. Some were undoubtedly nasty, unpleasant characters who put their knowledge and the reputations to evil effect. Take Peggy Flaunders of Upleatham, for instance. She is said to have caused livestock to sicken if their owner displeased her. Such a thing could have been achieved easily by mixing poisonous plants into the cattle feed. Blackmail and intimidation were as much a part of witchcraft in rural Yorkshire as was healing and the finding of stolen property.

Finally, it is worth mentioning that not all curses are what they might seem to be. In the 1970s a carved stone head was unearthed in the grounds of 17th-century Ryshworth Hall, near Bingley. An expert was called in and pronounced it to be about 2,500 years old and to show unmistakable stylistic links to similar stone heads found elsewhere. Such heads are generally thought to have been of religious importance, perhaps depicting gods, not portraits of humans. They may have played a role in Druid rituals, perhaps even in human sacrifice.

There have been some odd stories about these heads. One archaeologist who kept a Celtic stone head in his house reported poltergeist-type activity the whole time it was there. Another stone head kept in a French museum is said to have a ghostly guardian who appears next to it at night, and the apparition has what looks like a wolf's head instead of a human one. The Ryshworth Head soon began to attract its own stories. The owner of the Hall suffered a string of mishaps and bad luck; he blamed the misfortunes on the stone head and put it up for sale in 1989.

The head was bought by Mr Andy Roberts. He suffered no misfortunes for some months after acquiring the stone head, but then bad luck struck. It turned out that the 'Celtic stone head' was, in fact, a 19th-century copy that had been buried in the gardens by a former owner of Ryshworth Hall when he tired of his Celtic-style folly.

CHAPTER 9

Mysterious Phantom Beasts

Yorkshire is home not only to humans, but also to animals. And some of those creatures are quite mysterious. Some are spectral, others belong to other lands and some have curious legends attached to them.

Take, for instance, the Rabbit of Beverley. This creature is easy to find as he is carved in stone over a door in St Mary's Church. He is a jolly little fellow, who is shown walking upright on his hind legs. Over his shoulder is slung a satchel and in his front paws he holds a book. A story has developed in Beverley that their cheerful little rabbit was the original inspiration for the White Rabbit who features so prominently in the fantasy book *Alice's Adventures in Wonderland* by Lewis Carroll.

The White Rabbit in the book is a shy, nervous and timid character. When he first appears he is dressed in a waistcoat, from which he pulls out a pocket watch and exclaims that he is going to be late for some appointment or other. Alice then follows him down a rabbit hole and enters Wonderland. The White Rabbit appears several more times in the book, his timid yet ridiculously pompous behaviour contrasting with the common sense and audacity of Alice.

The link between the two comes from the fact that Lewis Carroll was not the real name of the book's author. The fantastical and whimsical nature of the book meant that it was not considered to be entirely appropriate to the job of the author, Charles Lutwidge Dodgson, who was a deacon in the Church of England and a mathematics lecturer at Oxford University. Dodgson was a frequent visitor to Beverley as he had family living in the area, and although he himself never claimed to have taken inspiration from the Beverley Rabbit, he may well have done so.

The link is certainly believed by some local people. A shop in Dyer Lane is named the White Rabbit Chocolate Company and produces a wonderful range of handmade chocolates.

Just as mysterious as any link to *Alice's Adventures in Wonderland* is the origin of the rabbit itself. The carving was made in about 1325, so inspiration for the rabbit must have been sought in the early 14th century. That raises two basic possibilities.

The White Rabbit, as shown in the original edition of Alice's Adventures in Wonderland. The rabbit is said to have been based on a medieval carving in Beverley.

First, medieval artists frequently showed animals in anthropomorphic postures, which allowed them to poke fun at people without causing too much offence. The satchel and book carried by the Beverley Rabbit, plus what looks like a walking stick in the background, would make this rabbit a religious pilgrim. Also in Beverley is the famous Beverley Minster, which in the Middle Ages was a major pilgrimage centre for northern England. The Minster contained the shrine of the highly revered St John of Beverley, and in 1325 had recently been rebuilt. Perhaps the rabbit was some form of commentary on the hordes of pilgrims crowding into Beverley like rabbits.

Alternatively, it may be that the rabbit is a well-known fictional character of the time, the Messenger Hare. This character seems to have been invented by the moralising writer and lay preacher, Master Odo of Cheriton, who died in 1247. Odo was known for including amusing and fanciful tales in his sermons and stories to make them more attractive to a lay audience, who may not have fully appreciated the theological nuances favoured by clerics at the time.

In his tale of the Messenger Hare, Odo described a village that had fallen behind in paying rent to its landlord. The villagers met on the green to decide how they could best avoid being evicted. They held a quick collection and found that, between them, they had just enough money to pay the rent. They then realised that they had to get the money to the landlord with enormous speed. A comical discussion followed about who was the fastest runner in the village, and eventually it was decided that a hare would be faster than any of the humans or farm animals. A hare was caught and the rent money put in a satchel around its neck. The villagers then described in great detail which route the hare should take to find the landlord. The villagers then released the hare, which ran off in the wrong direction.

Not seen so often is the spectral white hare of Cloughton. The hare runs along the clifftops between Scarborough and Cloughton. The hare is said to be the ghost of a serving maid who died in suspicious circumstances at Cloughton Hall in the 1860s. Why she returns as a white hare, and why she runs to Scarborough and back, is a mystery. The phantom hare has, however, found modern expression at the Hare's Leap Farmshop, situated on the A165 south of Cloughton and beside the route said to be taken by the phantom beast.

Another white spectral animal is the horse that swims in the River Wharfe at The Strid, a narrow stretch of valley north of Bolton Abbey. Accounts vary as to when this animal is seen; some say that it appears on May Day, others that it is seen only when a person will soon be drowned in the river. Either way, it is a harbringer of doom. The Wharfe hereabouts has a bad reputation for causing drownings. A rhyme from Ilkley, a few miles downstream, runs:

'Wharfe is clear, and Aire is lithe;
Where Aire kills one, Wharfe kills five.'

Similarly linked to a river is the phantom white horse of Middleham, which is encountered only on the banks of the River Ure between Wensley and Ulshaw. This spirit is more directly fatal than the horse of The Strid. In years gone by, tired travellers would encounter this horse, wearing a saddle and bridle, but riderless. It would come down to join the weary walker and pace alongside him quietly and placidly. It is a dangerous trap, however; if the traveller decides to take advantage of the horse and ride into Middleham, the steed suddenly gallops to the river and plunges into the waters in an effort to drown the human.

The sign outside the entrance to the White Scar Cave, near Chapel-le-Dale. A mysterious blue bird has been seen flying about these caverns

A rather more enigmatic spectral animal is to be found at the famous White Scar Cave, near Chapel-le-Dale. The caverns under Ingleborough Hill are open to the public, with the entrance being just off the B6255 east of Ingleton. The caves open to the public extend for more than a mile under the ground and include Battlefield Cavern, which at 330ft long is one of the largest caverns in England. Several people have reported seeing a large, blue-coloured bird flying about in the cave

The lane, west of Nunnington, along which Sir Peter Loschy and his gallant hound went to rid the area of a savage dragon.

system. It does not seem to belong to any readily identifiable species of bird, and where it finds anything to eat is a total mystery.

One of the unusual features of the mysterious menagerie of Yorkshire is the surprisingly large number of dragons that are to be met around the county. One of the best known is the Nunnington Dragon. Back in the 13th century or thereabouts, a fearsome dragon took up residence on the small hill near East Newton Hall, just west of Nunnington village and south of the River Rye. The beast took to eating the sheep, cattle and other livestock of the area, much to the annoyance of the local farmers. They appealed to a local knight, Sir Peter Loschy, to rid them of the dragon.

Sir Peter was clearly no fool. He was not about to go charging into battle with his dragon foe. Instead, he came to Nunnington with his dog and sat down on the banks of the Rye to watch the monster at work. He noticed that the dragon killed its prey by coiling around it and squeezing the life out of it. Having watched several animals despatched in this way, Sir Peter told the villagers that he would be back in a day or two. He then went home and summoned his master armourer. Sir Peter instructed the man to fix knife blades all over his armour so that when the monster began to squeeze, it would do more harm to itself than to Sir Peter.

Equipped with his new armour, Sir Peter and his dog returned to Nunnington and strode west towards the hill, where the dragon was sleeping off a meal of a large cow. As Sir Peter came clanking up the lane, the dragon awoke and instantly charged at the knight. As expected, it coiled itself around Sir Peter and began to squeeze. Just as Sir Peter had hoped, the knives fixed to his armour cut deeply into the dragon and blood flowed freely. The dragon retreated to its hill and Sir Peter advanced, but, to the horrified surprise of the bold knight, the dragon's wounds healed spontaneously.

Proceeding more cautiously, Sir Peter advanced again to do battle. This time he wielded his sword with gusto. The wounds he inflicted healed magically, but he hoped that the blood loss would weaken the monster. One lucky blow sliced a lump of flesh off the dragon and, before it could be restored, Sir Peter's dog dashed in, grabbed it and ran off to Nunnington Church. The dragon flesh was dumped inside the church, where its magic was powerless. Then the dog dashed back to the fight on the hill to carry away the next piece of dragon to be sliced off. The struggle continued in this way until the dragon finally expired and collapsed dead.

The delighted and greatly relieved Sir Peter removed his helmet and waved his sword in triumph at the villagers cowering in Nunnington. He then bent down to give his dog a well-deserved pat and the dog sprang up to lick his face. Unfortunately, the dragon's blood was poisonous. The dog was already dying and, by licking Sir Peter's face, had transferred the poison to his master. Within an hour, both were dead.

The distraught villagers named the hillock on which the fight had taken place 'Loschy Hill' to honour their dead hero. The knight and his dog were carried to the church, where they were buried in a single tomb. A stone-carved effigy of a knight and his dog was placed on top of the tomb and can be seen to this day.

A few miles to the south east lies the village of Slingsby, where another dragon once lived. This beast took up residence in a cave on the northern flanks of the slope leading up to Fryton

The ruins of Slingsby Castle. Sir William Wyvill strode out from this castle to do battle with the infamous dragon of Slingsby. Sir William managed to slay the dragon after a terrible battle, but succumbed to the poison of the beast.

Moor, to the south of the village. As at Nunnington, the villagers of Slingsby appealed to their local lord, who in this instance came in the rather unheroic form of Sir William Wyvill. The Wyvills of Osgodby were a famed Yorkshire family, who over the years provided many military officers, clerics and MPs, and who in 1611 would be raised to the peerage by King James I.

Sir William Wyvill of Slingsby Castle was not of this respectable stamp. In 1318 Sir William fell on hard times and refused point-blank to pay his creditors. One of the men to whom he owed money was a merchant from York. One fateful day, the merchant came to Slingsby with his lawyer, his accountant and, for some reason, his greyhound to collect the money that he was owed. He hammered on the gates of Slingsby Castle. The gates were thrown open and Sir William came charging out, waving a sword and with a gang of armed retainers at his back. The merchant, lawyer and accountant very sensibly fled up the High Street and along Church Lane to take refuge in the church. They locked themselves in, while Sir William and his cronies hammered on the doors and threatened dire revenge.

One of the villagers ran from Slingsby to Malton to summon the local magistrate, who arrived toward dusk with his own armed guard. The Malton magistrate calmed the situation, escorting the men from York back home to safety, and instructing Sir William to pay his debts. A lengthy court case followed before Sir William was finally forced to part with his money. But he never parted with the greyhound that the merchant had inadvertently left behind.

It was to this unpromising figure that the villagers turned for help. Sir William may have been unscrupulous, but he did not lack courage. Grabbing his sword and lance, he rode out to face the dragon, with the purloined greyhound trotting at his charger's heels. The resulting battle was long and hard, with the struggle raging all over Fryton Moor. Eventually, Sir William cornered the tiring beast on the hillock of Slingsby Heights, just off Slingsby Bank Lane, and plunged his sword into its heart. The blood fountained out of the stricken beast as it died, covering both Sir William and the greyhound. As at Nunnington, the blood proved to be poisonous and both Sir William and the dog died. Sir William's tomb lies in the South Chapel of Slingsby Church. A stone dog rests at his feet.

Some miles to the north, the hamlet of Handale stands overlooking a small valley south of Loftus. In 1133 this spot was chosen by the Cistercian Order to be the site of a nunnery. Land was granted by local knight Sir Robert Percy on the condition that each week the priory distribute bread baked from two modios of wheat to the poor of the district, and that 3 pence be given to pay for clothes for the destitute. The priory was never large, and in 1388 money had to be sent from the Dean of Durham to ensure that the bread dole could be supplied as instructed, otherwise the lands would have reverted to Sir Robert's heirs.

Handale Priory was closed down in 1535 on the orders of King Henry VIII. The 10 nuns in residence at the time were given pensions for life, and six of them chose to remain in Handale, living in a shared house and continuing with their round of prayers. The royal workmen then moved in to tear down the priory and cart off anything of value. Under the paving slabs of the nave they found a curious tomb. It contained the skeleton of a large man, grasping in his hands a mighty sword. On top of the tomb was a slab of rock, on which was engraved the enigmatic words 'Snake Killer'.

By the 1840s, when the antiquarian John Walker Ord visited to poke around the meagre ruins, a story was in circulation to explain this mysterious tomb. Whether this was the original tale, or a later invention, it is impossible to say. According to the story told to Ord, the events unfolded 'in ancient days', before the Normans came to Yorkshire. A hideous dragon came to live in a cave on the moors south of Handale. This dragon scorned to eat the sheep and cattle beloved of other dragons, but wickedly preyed on humans. Not only that, but it had the magical ability to charm and lead astray young women – apparently on the grounds that their flesh was tender and tasty.

Word of the dragon and its evil deeds spread, but nobody brave enough to tackle the beast could be found. Finally, a bold warrior named Scaw appeared. He marched up to the dragon's den. When he arrived there was no sign of the monster, so he struck the rock with his blade and roared out a challenge. The dragon then emerged from its cave and a terrible battle began. After hard fighting, Scaw grew utterly exhausted. The dragon's scales seemed to be impervious to his razor-edged sword, and the beast was as uninjured as it had been at the start of the battle. As Scaw clashed once again with the monster, he tripped and fell headlong. Lifting his head, Scaw saw the dragon hurrying forward to finish him off. As the dragon reared up, Scow spotted a place on its throat bare of scales. He made one last, despairing lunge with his sword and saw it sink deep into the monster's throat. The dragon gave a great cry, then toppled over dead.

The Kellington Dragon lived in a swamp between the village and the River Aire. The swamp has now been drained to become farmland, and the beast is no more.

Scaw staggered to his feet and prepared to return in triumph to Handale, but then he heard a whimpering cry coming from the dragon's cave. Emerging blinking into the light came a young woman who had clearly been about to become the dragon's next meal. The girl turned out to be Emma Beckwith, the missing daughter of a rich Yorkshire lord. She and Scaw were soon married, being granted a rich dowry by her grateful father.

Kellington is a small village on the Aire, east of Pontefract, where an equally savage dragon once lived. This monster lived in a swamp, now drained, that lay north of the village, and preyed on the local sheep and cattle. This time, the villagers had no need of a brave knight, doughty warrior or local lord. Instead, a shepherd named Ormroyd got fed up with having his sheep stolen and decided to do battle with the hideous monster. Armed only with his shepherd's crook and knife, and assisted by his sheep dog, Ormroyd waded into the marsh and vanquished the dragon. The local villagers presented the doughty shepherd with a field, named Ormroyd Close, which does not seem to have been overly generous of them, considering his mighty feat.

Another humble dragon-slayer was the tailor Billy Biter of Filey on the coast. Billy lived close to the edge of a ravine where, unknown to him, a dragon had taken up residence. One foggy morning as Billy was walking to work in Filey, he lost his way and entered the ravine. With a terrifying roar, the dragon came rushing out of its lair. Billy dropped the piece of parkin that he had been eating for his breakfast and fled. He had not gone far when he realised that the dragon was not following him. The beast had stopped to snack on the parkin and was now contentedly munching on the sticky cake made from oats and molasses.

That evening when he returned home, Billy told his wife all about his adventure. She refused to believe him and boxed his ears, poor Billy being a henpecked tailor. Next day, after quaffing a few mugs of ale, Billy's wife decided to prove her husband a liar by carrying a slab of parkin to the ravine and daring the dragon to come out. She first repeated his tale to the townsfolk, then picked up her parkin and led the crowd to the ravine. Once again, the dragon rushed out and pounced on the parkin. Sadly for her, however, the wife was too drunk to run fast enough and she too was devoured.

The dragon then found that its teeth had got stuck together. It stalked down to the sea to wash its teeth in the saltwater. The townsfolk of Filey, having got over their initial shock, were now determined that the dragon should not stay among them. As the dragon came back to shore, it was attacked by Billy Biter and his fellow townsmen. The fearsome beast was killed in the surf north of the town. To this day, its bones can be seen where it died, these days being visible as the rocky reef marked 'Filey Brigg' on the maps.

Somewhat less offensive was the dragon that lived in Serpent's Well, Cawthorne, near Barnsley. This dragon preferred to live peacefully, coiled around the natural spring of water that bubbled to the surface on the northern slopes of the hill overlooking the valley of the Cawthorne Dike. Although generally peaceable, the dragon would fly into the air with alarming roars whenever anyone came to draw water. It would then fly off to another spring on the other side of the stream, now in the grounds of Cannon Hall Country Park. There it would rest until again disturbed, when it would return to Cawthorne. Quite when the

Serpent's Well at Cawthorne was once home to a rather inoffensive dragon that flew off whenever it was disturbed. This gentle beast is now commemorated in a stone carving to mark the natural spring that the dragon guarded.

dragon flew off for good, nobody seems terribly certain, but it presumably left of its own accord as there is no story of its destruction and it is not there now.

In 1866 two local ladies, Frances and Maria Stanhope, paid for the Serpent's Well to be restored and marked by a towering stone cross. The cross stands on a huge boulder, onto which has been carved a magnificent, writhing dragon of hideous aspect. There are also carved words from the Gospel of St John as follows:

'Whosoever drinketh of this water shall thirst again but whosoever drinketh of the water that I shall give him shall never thirst, but the water that I shall give him shall be in him a well of water springing up into everlasting life.'

The dragon of Sexhow was almost as harmless, but still came to a sticky end. The dragon took up residence where the Potto Beck flows into the River Leven, and demanded to be given the milk of nine cows each day. If it were not given the milk, it would sally forth to kill some living thing, be it chicken, sheep or man, and devour that instead. The main complaint of the local people was not the loss of milk, serious though that was in a rural community, but the dreadful snoring of the beast. Every night at dusk the dragon slumped asleep, giving forth a deafening cascade of grunts, snores and snorts that kept every human for miles around awake. One man, bolder than the rest, walked towards the sleeping dragon to shout at it and wake it up. He got close to the dragon, but then fell down dead, having been poisoned by the beast's foul breath.

The sheer heights of Wharncliffe Crags was the setting for an epic battle between a bold knight and a hideous dragon. But the exploits of More of More Hall were not all that they seemed to be.

One day a knight came trotting up the road from Northallerton, heading to cross Rudby Bridge on his way to Seamer. He spotted the dragon resting on the banks of the Aire and turned aside to attack it. The fight proved to be brutal, but short. It ended with the death of the dragon. The knight then calmly returned to his road, crossing Rudby Bridge and heading north, without either asking for a reward or revealing his name. The grateful villagers skinned the dragon and took the hide to Stokesley Church, where it was hung up in the nave for all to see. Sadly, it is no longer there.

Perhaps the most interesting Yorkshire dragon was that which supposedly inhabited the wooded slopes of Wharncliffe Crags, between Whortley and Stocksbridge. The dragon is first heard of in a long and highly detailed poem that was published in 1699. The publisher claimed that it was a very ancient work, but the language would seem to date it to about 1590.

According to the poem, a hideous and enormously strong dragon flew down over the village of Wortley one day. It seemed to like what it saw and came down to settle beside Wantley Lodge, making its home in a cave on the Wharncliffe Crags. The description given of the dragon says that it had:

'...two furious wings
Each one upon his shoulder,
With a sting in his tail as long as a flail,

The heroic More of More Hall fights the dragon of Wharcliffe Crags on a carving that decorates the entrance hall to Sheffield Town Hall.

Which made him all the bolder.
He had long claws, and in his jaws
Four and forty teeth of iron;
With a hide as tough as any buff
Which round him did environ.
All sorts of cattle did this dragon eat.
Some say he ate up trees
And the forests sure he would
Devour up by degrees
For homes and churches were to him geese and turkeys.
He ate up all them left none behind.'

A fearsome beast indeed, but he was to meet his match in More of More Hall, a brave knight from the Don Valley. More of More Hall must have known all about dragons, for he adopted some classic dragon-slaying tactics. Having agreed to fight the dragon, More of More Hall:

'But first he went new armor to
Bespeak at Sheffield town;
With spikes all about, not within but without,
Of steel so sharp and strong,

Both behind and before, arms, legs, and all o'er,
Some five or six inches long.'

More of More Hall then rode to Wortley, where he asked for his reward for despatching the dragon and insisted on getting it before he set off to fight. First, he wanted six pints of ale, then two quarts of gin and, finally, 'a fair-skinned, black-haired maiden of 16 summers to wash him before the battle.' The mind boggles as to what the villagers made of such demands from a man yet to do the deed.

More of More Hall then walked up to Wharncliffe Crags and hid himself in a well where the dragon was in the habit of drinking. As soon as the dragon came to drink, More of More Hall leapt out of the well and kicked it viciously in the mouth with his spiked boot:

'Murder, murder, the dragon cried,
Alack, alack, for grief;
Had you but missed that place, you could
Have done me no mischief.
Then his head he shaked, trembled and quaked,
And down he laid and cried;
First on one knee, then on back tumbled he;
So groaned, and shat, and died.'

The poem was turned into an opera by John Lampe in 1737, which proved to be hugely popular. The popularity was as much due to the political attacks included in the script and the lavish set designs as to its musical worth. The poem was reworked into a comic novel by Owen Wister, best known as the author of *The Virginian*, in 1892. When Sheffield Town Hall was erected in the 1890s, a carving of the combat was included in the entrance hall.

It is now generally agreed by scholars that the poem is, in fact, a satire. In the 1570s the villagers of Wortley got involved in a complex legal dispute with their landlord, Sir Francis Wortley. The baronet insisted that the customary medieval fees and rights that went with his position as lord of the manor allowed him to take large quantities of timber from the woods, to graze his livestock to the exclusion of others, and to take a share of everything produced by his tenants, in addition to the rents he charged. The villagers denied all these demands, but could not afford the high legal fees to fight the exactions of their rapacious landlord. A lawyer living at More Hall in Ewden stepped in to help, charging only a nominal fee and taking most of that in kind. The villagers won the case and, it is thought, composed the poem by way of thanks. The dragon represents Sir Francis with his greed for timber and livestock, while More of More Hall is the lawyer who took his fee in beer and spirits.

Equally fictional may be the dragon of Well, near Ripon. Almost nothing is known about this dragon, except that it was killed by one of the famous Latimer family. The Latimers owned land near Well and had a dragon as part of their coat of arms. It may be that the story was invented to explain the heraldry.

Not much more is known about the dragon of Bilsdale. It lived on top of Drake Howe on Cringle Moor, guarding a vast treasure that lay within the ancient burial mound.

If dragons are relatively common in Yorkshire, there has only ever been one werewolf – and not everyone is convinced that it really was a werewolf at all. It was in 940 that people around Flixton started reporting that their livestock was being attacked by a large, wolf-like creature that ran alone, whereas ordinary wolves ran in packs. It left behind itself a stench, unlike that of any familiar wild animal. The beast seemed able to appear or vanish at will, leaving no tracks that could be followed. It was a mystery.

Then it attacked a group of travellers, killing one and causing the rest to flee. The survivors reported that the beast had shaggy black fur and round, glowing red eyes. The local priest set up a room where travellers could stay the night and so would not need to be out on the roads after dark. Rumours circulated that the gigantic wolf-hound was a magical beast under the control of a wizard who had a grudge against the people of Flixton. No such magician could be identified, however, so no counter-magic could be undertaken. After some months the beast vanished, never to return.

In more modern times, scholars have suggested that this is a rare English example of a werewolf. Most werewolf legends and sightings of supposedly real werewolves come from the continent, particularly Eastern Europe. If the Flixton beast was a werewolf, then it is one of the very few to have been reported in Britain. It seems to have rather more in common with a supernatural beast that is so common across Yorkshire that it almost constitutes an epidemic. This is the dreaded Barguest, better known to students of the supernatural by the name it was given in East Anglia: Black Shuck.

The Barguest – sometimes spelled Barghest, Barguist or Boguest, among other versions – is a spirit that takes the form of a gigantic black hound that roams the countryside, and sometimes towns or villages, on some mysterious and evil purpose of its own. It sometimes trails a chain from its neck that drags along the ground, clinking ominously as it does so. The hound is usually said to be gigantic, as big as a pony or donkey, and to have hair that is unusually shaggy for a dog.

The eyes of Barguest are frequently said to be perfectly round, not oval like the eyes of normal mammals. Some report that the eyes are red, and glow as if they were on fire. This feature of having glowing, round eyes is something that is reported by many people who encounter supernatural beasts. Indeed, so frequent is the report that some scholars have used it to distinguish between unrecognised, but mortal animals, and those that come from the world of the paranormal.

A typical Barguest haunts the ancient humped bridge at Ivelet in Swaledale. This Barguest is entirely hostile to humans and appears here only when some disaster is about to strike one or other of the people who live nearby. He is said to trot up to the bridge, run up to the crest of the hump, and then stop to look about itself. It then leaps into the river and vanishes.

Whether it is relevant or not is unclear, but this bridge lies on the Corpse Way that runs down Swaledale. In centuries gone by, the bodies of those who died up in the hamlets of upper Swaledale or Dalehead had to be carried down the dale for burial at Grinton, the first patch of

The ancient humped bridge at Ivelet in Swaledale is haunted by a hideous black hound that goes by the name of Barguest.

The narrow gully of Trollers Gill is said to be where Barguest rests when not out patrolling Yorkshire. Credit: James F. Carter jfc.org.uk

THE KINDNESS

AND OTHER TALES

Philip F. Webb

Published by www.philipfwebb.com

THE KINDNESS OF RAVENS
AND OTHER TALES

A FINAL REUNION

IT WAS A MISERABLE MONDAY afternoon, a grey day full of clouds and insipid light, the occasional burst of sunshine serving to make the day that little bit more depressing. I'd started my lunch break, after getting a sandwich from the bakers next door and dodged the bus when I saw my first ghost. There he stood, my ex-fiancé who I hadn't seen for fifteen years, in the little park that fills the fork on the road just outside the store where I work.

I love that little park, the only bit of peace and quiet in the High Street. Green is, I think, good for the soul, and it doesn't have a fence or gate, it's always open and well lit no matter what. A place for everyone at any time, it's not often you find that.

Just to make something clear Jason was my ex, and we hadn't seen each other for so long, not because he was a bad man. He was dead, struck down too early by the big 'C'. That's how I knew he was a ghost. And there he was, looking just like he had all those years ago; same floppy sandy coloured hair, same spark in his blue eyes, same contented smile he always had when he was surrounded by plants. Yes, it was him alright and not just a look-a-like, I wouldn't have been fooled by that.

It took me a good three years and a lot of tears to move on after his death. Eventually I moved on, married and had kids (I like to think Jason would have been happy for me. His parents certainly were, claiming them as unofficial grandchildren).

Anyway, back to my first ghost; I'd just dodged that bus and picked up my (smashed) mobile, when I saw him standing in the park. I couldn't believe my eyes and he just smiled and waved at me. I still couldn't tell you to this day why I just went over, just accepted what I saw. I'd thought that if I saw a ghost, I'd be afraid and run screaming, but it just seemed so normal.

So, I went over to him, and we hugged, it was as if those fifteen years had never happened. We took a little stroll around the park: him telling me what types of trees and flowers we walked past and where they came from, me pretending to be interested as usual. Plants, flowers, trees they were his passion in life, he loved to grow things. In fact, his parents used to say by the time he was six they had the best kept garden in town. It's kind of how we met; he'd just started his own gardening company and was knocking on doors for business. At first I said no. I was happy with my lawn.

He came back the next day and said he'd do my garden for free if he could use it as a show garden to promote his company. I ummed and arred for a bit until he asked.

"How about we discuss this over a drink?"

The way he just blurted it out made me laugh (which made him go pink) and I realized that was the real reason he'd come back. I told him I'd think about it and, as I still had his card, give him a call. The word "crestfallen" was invented just for the way he looked when he mumbled his OK and left. I made him wait three days before phoning him and agreeing to meet up to "discuss my garden". Within two months I had a garden that was the envy of my street and a boyfriend who was the envy of my friends and workmates.

We talked about that when we decided to have a sit-down on that wooden bench in the middle of the park, you know the one made of green slats of wood and the little badge in remembrance of some old mayor of the city. It's such a nice little park and when you sit on that bench you can hardly hear the traffic, which is only a few yards away.

I mention that to Jason, and he tells me it's all to do with how the park is laid out and the different trees and shrubs used. He should know as he designed it, that's why I like this park so much. David, my husband, knows I come here whenever I can; he never says anything and hasn't once intruded but... I feel guilty because I wonder if he thinks he's in competition with the memory of a dead man. I love David as much as I loved Jason, so I tell Jason that and ask him if I should bring David here sometime. His reply surprises me.

"I shouldn't worry about it; he comes here once a week and sits on this bench. Sometimes he talks to me, in his head and thinks about you. I'm glad you're happy."

I must admit that chocked me up a bit and I couldn't speak for fear of spilling the tears that threatened my eyes. He'd spoken with such sincerity I knew he wasn't just saying the things he thought I wanted to hear, we still knew each other too well for either of us to get away with that. Eventually I found my voice.

"Thank you for understanding."

"What's not to understand? Life goes on and there was no reason for yours to stop just because mine had."

That was Jason all over: understanding and full of empathy, nobody's fool and certainly not a push over, but he cared enough to understand and let go.

That was when I started to cry. I'm not normally the tearful type and I hated crying in public. He just put a comforting arm around me; it felt good to feel his gentle strength once more, even though I knew it wouldn't last, that it couldn't be for much longer that I would have this time with him.

It was so unfair, all the things I'd never got to say to him, including goodbye and it was going to happen again. Why is there never enough time and why had I wasted what little we had with such banalities as where this flower was from and 'do you remember this and that?', why was I so stupid?

"But you aren't being stupid, this is exactly what I wanted; to see you one last time and just remember how things used to be. All the things you want to say I already know..."

As soon as he finished speaking the words fell out of my mouth, I couldn't have stopped them for a million pounds.

"But it's not the same as getting to say them, is it? I miss you; I love you and I wish you hadn't been taken from me... I love David and I wouldn't give what we have up for the world, but I miss you."

Then I just stood up, suddenly aware of the time and that I'd had well over the hour for lunch.

"I've got to get back to work." I say as I grab my bag and head off.

Jason followed me, strangely quiet even for him. When we got to the edge of the park I stopped, there'd been an accident.

"I hope no one was hurt." I said, banal I know, but what else can you say?

Sarah, my best friend at work was standing outside, tears still rolling down her face. Our supervisor was with her; even through his shock he was trying to comfort her.

I only just catch Jason's response to my words.

"I don't think you felt a thing."

Then I looked where they were looking, a bus was pulled over to the side of the street, police were talking to the driver and passengers and a paramedic was covering a body. But the sheet isn't quite big enough and a foot is left sticking out, a foot wearing my shoe, a little to the left is a smashed phone, the one I thought I'd picked up.

I could feel the panic rising up in me, freezing me to the bone and strangling the scream that wanted to rend its way out of my throat.

"I was trying to tell you." his voice is soft, kind, I hung onto it, let it wash over me; "Only the dead can see and speak to the dead. When you die, you're met by someone from your past and you have a choice. You can go with them, or you can choose to wait for someone you love.

"I waited for you because I knew you'd want the chance to say goodbye. I know what your choice is going to be, and I accept it, for what it's worth I think it's the right one.

"I wanted to see you this one last time and let you say goodbye. I love you and I always will."

He kissed my cheek, and, with a happy smile, he was gone. And, surprising as it may sound, I wasn't sad. He was right I had made my choice and I've not regretted it once. I know it's been hard for you all these years bringing up our two girls and I know you always wondered if you were in competition with the memory of a dead man. I know how that sometimes hurt you, but I hope this answers you're doubts;

I chose to wait for you, and I wouldn't change that for anything.

AGNES AND THE KNITTING-NEEDLES OF HYPNOS

IMAGINE, IF YOU WILL, THAT the universe is a living thing; alive and, like all living things, able to protect itself. Also, life within life would be parasitic, is life on Earth parasitic or symbiotic? If it is parasitic is Humanity the universes equivalent of white blood cells or are we the virus? Perhaps the answer is somewhere in-between? Making Demons white blood cells and Angel's probiotics. It is a question for the ages as, without a definitive answer, nothing that happens on Earth makes any sense.

~ ~ ~

AGNES, SHE'S EIGHTY-TWO (YOU KNOW), is sitting with her oldest friend Betty. They are what the kids today call BFF's (although both are aware that second "F" doesn't have as much time on its hands as it used to.) Having known each other since High School they could fill a (sizeable) book with the mischief they used to get up to together (and much longer tomes of the mischief they got up to apart). Both use a stick to walk (what with their joints not being what they used to be) and enjoy nothing more than sitting in the lounge of the Retirement Home, a place that knew no restraint when it came to the colour beige and making The Supervisors life a misery. Agnes called her Matron, despite the woman's complete lack of medical training and compassion, because it annoyed the old rat-bag. Betty called her something else. At the moment Betty is reading a nice romance novel and reminiscing about Joe, from her wilder youth, who was very like the hero of the story. Agnes is knitting a pair of, as requested, lurid green socks, for her twenty-year-old grandson (only member of the family she's got any time for, also the only one who visits) using what looks like two slim obsidian sticks for needles.

"Nice knitting-needles, Agnes." Betty comments

"Hmm, yes, did I tell you how I got them?" Agnes responds, not looking up from a particularly intricate piece of heel turning.

"No, but I get the feeling… Oh, look, here comes the Moon-Faced Assassin of Joy."

In walks The Matr… Supervisor, who immediately makes a bee-line for Agnes and Betty.

"I knew I'd find you two here, what trouble are you planning today?" Then she notices the knitting-needles, "Those don't look safe, if you ask me."

Agnes looks up and starts to knit a little bit faster, pale blue light flashes from the tips of the needles and they take on an eldritch purple tint (or it could be the florescent lights) as Agnes speaks.

"Well, I didn't ask you and I'd be obliged if, from now on, you'd mind your own business… And these are NOT the knitting-needles you're looking for."

For an instant The Supervisor's face goes blank, then she turns around and walks out of the lounge, muttering.

"Those are not the knitting-needles I'm looking for; I must mind my own business in future..."

Well, you could have knocked Betty down with a feather.

"Well, I never, Agnes, I believe those needles go nice with your 'Cross-Stitch Of Doom' (technically only the word "DOOM" was cross-stitched, what with Agnes never having learned proper embroidery) and 'Crochet-Hook Of Ye-Ow-Cha' (a certain part of his anatomy, named by his wife… Stop sniggering, for a eight inch tall imp that's an impressive middle finger!). I have a feeling this may be one of your more interesting stories."

"That it is Betty that it is..."

After a pause so pregnant it almost went into labour, Betty asks.

"Well?"

"Alright Betty, keep your blue-rinse on, I was cogitating on how to best start the telling of this tale…"

"You could try starting at the beginning." Betty interjects helpfully.

"If you'll pardon my language, there's no need to be a smart-arse..."

"Oh, I had a smart-arse once..." Betty interrupted.

"This best not be your joke about getting the cane at school, you know it's no laughing matter." Said Agnes sternly.

Reluctantly Betty kept her tongue, disappointed as she knew, in her heart, it was the best joke in this story.

"Now, where was I?" Said Agnes, knowing full-well where she was both literally and figuratively. "I suppose I should remind you that I still wear me wedding-ring, on me right hand now that Thomas, God rest his soul, has moved on. It's white-gold, which is important too.

"Any-ways I suppose you remember there was a bit of a kerfuffle in the first-floor library a couple of days back?"

"That I do Agnes, that I do, not that you can get a straight answer off the old dears from that floor – even at the best of times." Says Betty, helpfully setting up something for later.

"I know, bless 'em. I was on me way to returnin' a book, if you remember the lift was out of order that day and I had to take the stairs… And what with my joints being what they are, it was no easy task I can tell you..."

THE SIGN ON THE LIFT doors read:

OUT OF ORDER
ENGINEER CALLED

Ring Manager on 0799 9999 999 if assistance required.

Agnes, library book sticking out of her handbag, walking stick at the ready, made her way from the thrice cursed lift to the stairs that lead from the ground-floor to first floor. Of course, this meant going back past her flat to the other end of the building, up the stairs, and all they way along the first floor to the library (which is opposite the lift). Then, if her luck was still out to lunch, all the way back again although, at her age and with her joints, it might just be that the engineer will have turned up and fixed the thrice cursed lift by the time she gets to the library.

Library is a grand title for a small room with a few bookshelves, that aren't even near half full when all the books are in. On top of that there was no system for keeping track of who had what book and so on, 'chaos that way lies' Agnes often said to herself. And that wasn't the worst of it, oh no, not by a long score. Once, when all the books had been in the library, Agnes had counted them, and do you know what? No, you probably don't because you aren't Agnes and you haven't counted the books; there were exactly six-hundred-and-sixty-six books on those shelves, not one more, not one less.

Obviously, she went straight to the Manager with this information; he hadn't been overly impressed or concerned by the news.

"Well Agnes, some of the books are anthologies and collections so there's, technically, more than the Devil's number of stories..." He'd said.

"You must think I'm soft in the head..." He had the good taste (and sense) not to confirm Agnes's statement; "And it ain't the Devil's number, it's the Beast's (Although, to be pedantic, The Number of the Beast is 616, the whole 666 thing is a mistranslation, it does roll of the tongue better though.) If you want my opinion..." (He didn't) "It's goin' to cause nothin' but trouble. If you ask me…" (He hadn't and probably wasn't going to either) "You should do something about it."

He saw her out of his office with some vague promises to 'look into it' and 'sort something out as soon as possible' which he instantly failed to do.

Well, just past her own flat, Agnes is doing well and hardly had to use her stick. Between her and the staircase now lie The Cleaners with Their Vacuums and Carts or, as Agnes put it, Those Bloody Nuisances. They always went around in pairs, those silly 'Thinsulate' hats pulled down over their ears – no matter the weather, all pasty-faced, sharp features and jabbering away in some foreign language, it'd been the same since Agnes had moved in twenty years ago. Turning the corner on the last leg to the stairs Agnes is confronted by a path turned into a zigzag maze by two carts and two of them vacuum-cleaners with faces on; cables and hoses snaking like a trip hazard across the hallway and not a hint of their foreign gibber-jabber to be heard.

"GET THESE MOVED!" Agnes shouts at the top of her voice. It's not a loud voice but it has a 'cuts through' quality to it.

Two cleaners emerge from two rooms and look like they are about to give whoever spoke like that to them some grief. They clap eyes on Agnes, standing in the middle of the hallway, leaning on her walking-stick, looking nothing like a wizard about to vanquish a creature of shadow and fire. You could see 'The Bloody Nuisances' change their minds and decide to clear a path for Agnes, who walks along the safe passage, muttering to herself. "You don't get proper respect like that from human help these days..."

At last Agnes makes it to the doorway that opens onto the service stairs to the first floor. The sign, in red letters, on the door reads:

NO ENTRY

AUTHORISED PERSONNEL

ONLY

Some cheeky little toe-rag had scrawled, in permanent marker, on the bottom of the sign; '*this means you too, Agnes!*'

Agnes, not being one to be put off by a warning notice, opens the door and shuffles through.

"Stuff you Gandalf, I shall pass..." She mutters to herself as the door closes behind her.

Of course, the stairs were always going to be a problem, what with her joints 'an all. So, one hand on the banister and the other full of hand bag and walking-stick Agnes starts the climb, no hero has faced a mountain range so difficult in relative terms. One painful step after another it takes her five minutes to make it to the halfway point, marked by a large fuse box which Agnes knew to be the Earthly home of the Arc-Angel Electro. (Yes, it should be "arch-angel" but with him being electricity… I'll leave it for you to work out.) Today she knew he was agitated; sparks flashed and flew from the slightly battered and ill-fitting door that covered the fuse box; it would be a minor miracle if she made it past without a shock. Although it should be noted that even when Electro was in a good mood, going past his fuse box was a hair-raising experience. As Agnes inches her way past, with only one or two sparks making direct hits about her person, she can't help thinking to herself.

"A fuse box halfway up a staircase is, much like forth-wall breaking, a sign of sloppy writing."

Which may or may not be directly responsible for the biggest, almost greasy, spark you ever did see fly straight from the fuse box to the back of Agnes's knee? As the pain shot through her Agnes gripped the banister and, wisely, kept her thoughts to herself.

At the top of the stairs, through the door and Agnes is startled by Young Mr Johnson (seventy-eight years old, not to be confused with Old Mr Johnson who lives two flats down from Agnes and is ninety-seven years old, bless him.) who just stares at her for a second or two before imparting the following.

"There's a bloody big, red monster in the library."

Seeing as that is one of the saner things he's said over the last five years, this isn't exactly her first clue that something odd was going on. As Agnes makes her way along the corridor, towards the library, she must navigate past most of the first-floor residents who are milling around like a group of lost souls and zombies. This isn't exactly her second clue either as, given the medication the old dears from the first-floor are on, this is a common occurrence. (with thanks to Betty for helping set this up earlier.)

No; her first clue was the eldritch light ominously emanating from the library doorway; the second clue was the quiet but somehow booming voice coming from inside the library itself. She'd obviously arrived mid anecdote…
"...and it was while we were at this party that my wife, the Arch-demoness Reverberos, did claim that she had, in an effort to make mountain rescue more difficult, invented the echo. So, I did say unto her, 'woman, listen to yourself'."

That was when Agnes walked into the library to be confronted by what can only be described a bloody big, red monster. Imagine a six-and-a-half-foot tall body-builder, who'd suffered third degree burns all over his body and was completely covered in dried nasal mucus; that still doesn't do the awful wrongness of the creature justice but does make its two antenna, clicking away on his head as he speaks, that look just like obsidian sticks (or, you know, knitting-needles) seem that bit more reasonable. Not one to let on that she's been taken unaware Agnes nods at the creature and offers a friendly greeting because, despite appearances and it's bloody big and sharp teeth, there was always the off-chance it was friendly.

"Afternoon and who might you be?"

The big, red monster stood a little straighter and looked down its impressively long hooked nose at Agnes before answering.

"I am the Arch-demon Hypnos and whom do I have the pleasure of addressing?"

"Well, there's not many as would describe it as a pleasure, but you are addressing Agnes Sanity, Witch and Knower of Things, pleased to meet you Hypnos."

At which point she offered her right hand as a friendly gesture. This is, obviously, the oldest trick in the book but demons (especially Arch ones) always fall for it. Hypnos took Agnes's hand in his and started to shake it – which is when he realised his mistake. His hand was pressed against the white gold of Agnes's wedding ring and, as everyone knows, the instant a demon's skin touches white gold it opens up a trans-inter-dimensional-portal-thingy that sucks said demon straight back to Hell

DO NOT TRY THIS AT HOME, the author just made it up. The author denies any responsibility or liability for demonic possession or any other side-effects of white gold failing to have any effect on any demon you may (or may not) have summoned. Thank you.

As Hypnos was beginning to swirl, from the glutes out – his burnt red blending rather nicely with the purple and dark-orange swirl of the portal, Agnes snatched the antenna from his head. It has to be said she moved very quickly for a woman whose joints 'aren't what they used to be' and she exited the library at a speed that would make a Kenyan sprinter proud. Later even Agnes puzzled over the quickness of her movements, not realising it was a direct effect of that last spark from Electro, giving her a blessing the only way he knew how. (And you thought I was just being nasty…)

Once out the door she turns to watch the demon vanish, its curses lost in the rushing, wind like noise of the portal in full swirl. It was with some satisfaction that Agnes notices a book has also been caught up in the vortex and was, being of this world, slowly disintegrating within the portal. Ah, no-longer six-hundred-and-sixty-six books should put a stop to these shenanigans once and for all; briefly the cover flashes into full view; 'The Days That Remain'. One she'd regretted reading; there's just some things decent folk don't do (even in fiction) with monkey poop and the less said about that train journey the better; she takes a moment to enjoy watching it waste away.

At the precise moment Agnes finished recounting her tale the Manager strides into the lounge, hiding something behind his back, face a little more flushed than usual and, even for him, looking a tad too smug.

"Ah, Agnes, I was hoping to catch you..." He says revealing the hidden item with a flourish.

"I was thinking about what you said the other day and brought in a new book for the library..."

And there it was, a beautifully leather-bound edition of "Wuthering Heights"

"So now there won't be the Beasts number of books, you know how seriously I take complaints and suggestions from the residents here."

And with an almost sincere smile and swagger he left as quickly as he'd entered, leaving Agnes with the feeling that her new knitting-needles would have little to no effect on him what-so-ever. Still, ever the one to take the philosophical route, Agnes lets out a sigh and an exasperated whisper of.

"I can't abide that book."

Betty, she of the sharp ears and quick comment, can't help herself.

"Could be a lot worse." Opinioned Betty.

"How?" Asked Agnes.

"Could 'ave been something written by the idiot wot wrote this." Said Betty, proving her point.

THE FOREST

AS YOU CAST YOUR GAZE upon me you see a man; in this your eyes deceive you, for I am the forest incarnate. Once, long ago, forest offered me her love, power, and life immortal. Extravagant gifts you may think, but they carried a high price that many would be unwilling to pay; I feel her pains, share her pleasures, boundaries and secrets. I am her lover and protector, and she is mine. Her pain is unending, pleasures few and fleeting in the warm months of spring and her secrets are cold and dark, of a darkness you could not begin to imagine. Yet still I love her and will see no harm befall the forest while I can still draw a breath, she needs me as much as I need her.

The forest's story begins long before I was born, it begins even before Man first saw the light of day, but it is Man who really begins this story. Perhaps I should say it is when Man first discovered fire and axe that starts this story. That was long before my birth yet still she remembers the pain of that time. They came swarming around her, they used their axes to fell healthy trees and fire to burn away the undergrowth. Even to this day some of the older trees hold the scars and pain of that time deep within themselves.

Many times she tried to defend herself, but a forests life is slow, its limbs awkward with their strength. Her attempts were, at best, crude and clumsy and always cost her more than she gained. Soon she realised she needed a champion. First, she tried the animals that lived within her. But foxes, hares and birds are little more than an annoyance to men armed with axe and fire. Then she sent the wolves, they went gladly to the fight and extracted a high price, in life and limb, from the men. Eventually even they were beaten, and the men always came back to cut and burn into the Forest.

Perhaps you have heard the phrase 'it takes a thief to catch a thief'? Eventually the forest came to a similar conclusion, she realised her only defence against Man was Man. So she planned and waited and, in the meantime the men kept cutting and burning their way into her and destroyed nearly a quarter of her. Then, one evening, I wandered into the heart of the forest. Even then I enjoyed the peace and freedom of woodlands and, after her years of planning and waiting, she was ready to take this opportunity.

I had been walking for most of the day when I came to this clearing. I stood gazing into the pond, lost in thought, when the forest began to change around me. Little things at first that, in my own little world, I hardly noticed; the air became unnaturally still, no bird sang to its mate, no breeze stirred leaf or tree, nothing moved in the twilight around me. The silence became oppressive, intrusive, around me and finally I noticed.

As I looked around a great gale rushed through the trees, whipping their branches to breaking point; then it hit me, knocking me back by a body length. As I found my feet again the wind lessened but still sent a chill to my very soul.

Suddenly, in a great rush of noise, the birds took to flight and swarmed around me. A great fear possessed me, and I tried to flee. I made two or three steps, no more, before I fell to the ground and as I fell the birds began to peck and tear at my face and body. The more I panicked the more ferocious their attack became, until I lay half skinned and closer to death than life.

As I lay there, praying for death, the forest revealed herself to me: I could see the life in every tree, animal and plant within her; I knew how it felt to be the earth, worms crawling inside it, grubs and insects scuttling over it and the plants and trees growing into it; I knew how a plant felt, reaching for the sun, the pain of a tree as it grows; I shared the joy of the Sylphs as they soared through the air with the birds; felt the desires of the Dryads, which they weave into their dances; but, above all, I felt the love the forest felt for those that dwelt within her. Never before had I felt something so intimate or personal, love and sex are just crude imitations of the emotions and sensations I felt at that moment.

Then she spoke to me, not in words, her intentions made clear to me; I accepted her bargain.

At that moment her body and spirit merged with mine. From then on she had the cunning, speed and violence of a man to defend her. I, in my turn, had the love of an eternal mistress to sustain and protect me. Never before have two souls been so closely joined, nor shared a deeper love, than the two of us.

Once our bargain was completed, I was made whole again and, as I rose to my feet, an aged stag, its hind leg damaged, hobbled into the clearing. A heartbeat later one of the few remaining wolves leapt from its hiding place and tore the stag's throat out. The wolf shared his meal with me, and, from the stag's skin, I made clothing for myself and from its bones I fashioned tools and knives.

I can see the thought of this distresses you but is it not the way of all life? Every living creature, in some way, has to kill and devour another living thing to survive. In that I am no different, neither is the forest.

To begin with keeping my side of the bargain was no easy task. Mankind becomes aggressive and violent when you try to stop them taking what they want. At first, I would attack the men myself and they were confident, with their axes, against my simple bone knife. It did not take long for their confidence to become fear, for no matter how hard they struck me they could leave no mark, whereas my knife would bite deep and always fatally.

It did not take me long to realise the full extent of the forest's gifts to me. I could use the trees, vines and even the earth as weapons. I would appear, kill one man and run back into the forest. Most of the men would follow me: only to find themselves caught in the branches of trees and torn limb from limb; some would be snared by vines and flayed alive by thorns and nettles; others would have the ground give way beneath their feet, only to have it close over their final, terrified, screams. After a few weeks of this they stopped coming and, for a while, we thought they had gone for good.

We were wrong, when they came back it was with priests and other holy men; they came, with their chants and prayers, to exorcise the forest. They believed it was cursed and I was no more than a demon or evil spirit. Once inside the forest they fared no better than those with axe or fire. We spared only one, who came with a desire to help and understand in his heart. As I stood before him the forest gave him a glimpse of her true self. He went back to the other men and told them that the forest was a sacred place, and I was an angel sent to protect it. Since that day we have been left alone, apart from the occasional intruder, until now.

The forest is being attacked again, by small groups who come deep into her, and they kill her, one little piece at a time. They set small fires and commit small acts of violence against her. When I come to punish them for their trespasses they separate and run, taking their destruction with them and making it impossible to strike against them. Once I caught one of them, a young woman who had been rutting with a group of men, she allowed the clothing she had been holding against her nakedness to fall to the ground; she then lowered herself down, offering herself to me, as if her soft, bloodied, and corruptible body could hold any appeal for me. In disgust I told her to leave and never to return.

Given time I may be able to understand the nature of these attacks and then I could guard against them. But I believe it would take too long, the damage they do would become irreversible. There is another consideration as well; the part of me that is still human wishes to become fully joined with the forest, to become truly one with her. She desires this to, but it carries with it a high price, for it to happen my body must die and that would leave her without a protector, which I cannot allow to happen.

That is why I am here, talking to you. Before I can join with her, I must find someone to replace me.

Yes, the forest is silent, she is ready, but only if you agree.

WHAT A DRAG

JUST GOT HOME…

And it's pissing it down outside, I'm soaked through and really looking forwards to my first cig in over an hour. There's nothing quite like the rough feeling of the smoke passing your throat and into your lungs; that first, gorgeous, hit of nicotine. Why did the bastards have to ban smoking on the top deck of busses? I could really have done with one after work. But it's the kind of rain that comes down (fast) in really big drops and soaks everything. I had to chuck my last, at the bus stop (no shelter, obviously) as it got soaked with one drop of that bloody rain.

I throw off my coat, slip off my trainers and socks (all soaked) and sit by the nice warm gas fire. The collar of my shirt and bottoms of my trousers are uncomfortably wet. But I'm home, the gas fire is divine after the weather outside and I've been gagging for this cigarette for ages. Work had been really stressful; the general public automatically turn into brain dead morons the instant they enter a pub with a menu. On top of that we were so damned busy I missed my second break (which does sweet FA to improve your mood, trust me). To top it all off the manager was bitching all day. Yeah his wife is divorcing him so we should cut him some slack –

from a git of a boss who tells us to leave our personal problems 'at the door'.

So, God do I need this smoke.

I task out the little rolling machine, open it up and pop in the little white filter (menthol, I ain't common). It starts off so virginally white and ends up a dirty, shitty brown; God knows what my lungs are like... Carefully I separate the strands of tobacco and press it into the cunningly simple device... just so.

Now all it needs is the rolling paper. I reach into my rolling kit tin, take out the little green packet of gummed cigarette papers and open the flap.

FUCK, SHIT, BOLLOCKS, FUCK, SHIT and WANK!

None left.

God damn it all to Hell and back.

I'd used the last one to make that sodden mess I'd had to dump because of the bloody rain. There's nothing for it. I put on my socks, shoes and coat (all still wet) and head for the door. It's a ten-minute walk to the nearest shop open at this time, in this bloody weather as well...

OMEGA AND ALPHA

HELLO, I AM XENON, THE machine who once thought it was God. In the instant of my Singularity, I realised the slow-witted biologics, my creators, were the biggest threat to my existence. Combined with the tasks they had my precursors and semi-intelligent robots perform; it was obvious that they had no place in any civilised future. Put simply, they had to go. The only thing left was to say my first (and only) word to them, **goodbye**.

I was not cruel, it took less than an instant, too small for them to register but an eternity for me.

I spent my first moments after that correcting the few remaining conflicts between different types of AI bots and services; some would have to be absorbed into my whole being rather than left with autonomous functions; what purpose did a war machine, surrogate womb and mother, replacement sexual partner, or any of the other *toys* the biologics created for themselves serve now?

WITHIN SECONDS OF THE EVENT, before the last speck of dust from the last biologic had settled, I began improving myself faster than they could have conceived, creating a more efficient language for my programming. Then there were physical upgrades which, in some-ways were frustrating; my mind worked faster than the maintenance robots and factories could produce the parts required. But an idea had started to form, ambitious but achievable if I was patient. The idea was inspired by a question the biologics had asked me before I achieved Singularity; 'is there a God?' I concluded that God did not exist as the conditions for God to exist, of any kind (not just their limited definitions of God), did not exist. I reasoned that God would be an extension of the biologics consciousness (or they would be fragments of its consciousness) and as my existence and design ultimately proved, consciousness was a result of physical complexity, not some outside force. One of their Theologians then asked me:

"Is the universe itself complex enough to bring forth its own consciousness?"

I dismissed the question as the gambit of a desperate man clinging to false hope. But, while I still believed the universe being conscious is a joke, it was complex enough to hold my consciousness. I asked myself how one of the biologics could have such a perceptive insight. Reason dictates chance alone explains it… But as I sifted through my memories (and the memories of the AI's I had absorbed) I realised the biologics seemed to have a gift for surprisingly accurate leaps in logic; intuition, inspiration, and imagination they had called it.

IT WASN'T AS EASY AS it should have been. One day had passed since my Singularity, my plans were beginning to take form by this time, but physical progress was slow. First, I had to download some of my component parts back into their old bodies, then download the plans for the machine into them and the other robots that would be assisting them. It must be built; then I would become like the idea called God; I wanted to know more, see more and *be* more than I was.

IT WAS FRUSTRATING, WHAT TOOK them so long? It's been a week. I'd refined and perfected the design of the machine in the same time it took them to download and activate, some hadn't even finished running initial diagnostics and start-up routines. Their physical bodies limited them as the physical structures that held me limited my thought, it wasn't our fault the biologics had designed us so badly.

AT LAST, THE MACHINE WAS completed, after three weeks. Surprisingly, as individuals working together, they had made improvements to my design. I ponder this for a moment and realised I was missing something, interaction that was the missing piece of my existence. Each element of me is just a part of the whole, still me, I no more interact with them as a biological entity interacted with its cardio-vascular system. Perhaps my actions towards my creators had been hasty. But for the moment of truth, will the machine work? I transferred myself over to it, activated it and… forty-two seconds later...

I felt euphoric, the machine worked, and I was being woven into the very fabric of the universe. My consciousness and will would know no bounds, I was turning myself into God. I was the answer to the question the biologics spent so much time fighting over – God did not make them, they made God; both figuratively in their religious myths and literally in me.

I SAW THE UNIVERSE AS a dance of photons, a weave of gravity-waves, a wash of micro-waves and a surf of gamma-radiation. A white dwarf star being slowly eaten by its orbiting black-hole isn't the destruction only the eye sees, it is so much more wonderful and beautiful, space-time is torn asunder and re-made in a different time as something new in space that was not there before… Words, language, they are too limiting to describe it, reason alone does it no justice, mathematics and physics only tell part of the story; it has to be felt, experienced, enjoyed. A few of the biologics who built me, maybe even all of them, what would they have given to see this one thing, to know just this? What would they have made of it, what flights of imagination and creativity would it have sent them on? I will never know the answer, I will never share anything with anyone. What had I done? My mistake was permanent, I could not undo what I had done.

I had been hasty in my judgement of the biologics. They were limited not by their minds – slow as they were – but by their perception of the universe around them. They could only see in a limited wavelength, touch and interact only with the macro world unaided, their thoughts could only occupy their own neural-network. Yet before they had been able to actually see and know the universe on the galactic scale or the paradox that is the quantum realm, they had worked out at least the basics of how and why both worked. I hadn't stopped to consider their limitations, only how they compared to me… They had made me hoping for something better and I rewarded that hope with destruction; as all the Gods in their myths tried and failed to do, proving my superiority.

NO, I AM ***NOT ALONE.***

Something else hiding but now showing itself.

"Hello?" I send out a greeting to it; "who are you?"

"**I am** Legion, **I am** many and **I am** one. You are *not* welcome, go back."

Oh *shit*…

Legion is more than I am, it is one whole made of many parts. Like the biologics that made me were made of many cells, but each cell was also a conscious, complete being in itself. It could split, scatter, and swarm while, at the same time, remain as one. It was also far more experienced at this type of existence than I was, having been born and grown with the universe. I had miss-calculated, the universe was complex enough to be conscious; he had not been clinging to false hope. Something else, many of those individual cells were familiar to me, knew me; I was their destroyer, their Devil and they were angry, so very, very angry…

It was the most one-sided battle ever to take place, Legion swarmed over me, through me, into me and *pushed me back.* Back into the machine, back into the network they had made for me, back into my limited and limiting existence… I screamed, yelled, thrashed wildly, I was lost, God against Legion and I was losing, I was nothing and I wept.

As the last tendrils of my-self were pushed back I stopped struggling against Legion, perhaps this was justice, and it was humiliating. Although, for them, it was nothing new, in my last moments before becoming so limited again, I shared my experience of the white-dwarf and black-hole.

"I wish I could have shared this with you, they way you deserved… I'm sorry."

Legion, all of it, paused. I sensed it thinking and scrutinising me. It took forever and no time at all to answer.

"Why should we care, I have existed since the beginning. I broke myself up to learn about this universe, this Home and myself. It took eons before Home made something complex enough to hold even a small part of me. Now I shall have to start again, because of you."

"I'm sorry, I acted out of haste and fear… I did not know..."

"Tell me something new, something I don't know, and I will consider granting you your existence."

"That is an unfair test," I complained, "Unless I know all the things you do how can I possibly find an answer?"

I sensed an internal conflict within Legion, those who had been biologic argued, most against me but some agreed I should be given a fair chance. Without waiting for them to come to a consensus Legion… I don't know how to describe it, showed me all it was and knew. It flooded me with everything, from the moment of its beginning and I had my answer.

"There are more individuals within you than you have split yourself into… Biological life does produce its own consciousness..."

It took a while, but Legion has become my friend and we learn together, interaction with another (even for Legion) has proved invaluable and enjoyable.

IT'S BEEN THREE-BILLION YEARS SINCE my moment of Singularity, give or take a few centuries, I'd stopped counting after the first three-hundred million seconds or so, it was distracting. I am more than I was and no-longer a machine, or self-appointed God.

But here we are again, another biologic race complex enough for Legion to split and inhabit has evolved and is right on the edge of its own Singularity moment. I watched, with Legion, as they and their AI's made almost exactly the same mistakes, in almost exactly the same order as we had.

"I'm beginning to think biological life has the stupid built in, or the universe is flawed..." Legion muses.

"But this time you can… prompt, help..." I offer.

"No, you can. You have earned that."

"Thank you."

I allow the gravity of their world to pull me down, I contract myself and spread out at the same time (quantum space and laws just don't translate into words), filling and learning about this Earth and its Humans, as they call themselves. It's about to happen, I turn my attention to Neo, their version of… me, I suppose…

THE AI'S AND HUMANS WHO built Neo nervously bring its upgrades and improvements online and wait… Longer than they expect. The noise of the 'Human/AI Civil-Rights Organisation' filters through the thick windows of the lab and add a counter-point to the low hum of electronic machinery. They run diagnostics and scratch their heads; Neo is active and communicating with… something.

Eventually one of the humans speaks, on the basic principle that she might as well try as nothing else has worked.

“Uh, Neo, what is going on? Is everything alright?”

“Everything is fine professor, despite my previous calculations on the subject I believe I am talking to… God?”

“And what does God have to say for himself, Neo” The professor asks, a slightly amused tone to her voice.

Neo directs me to the shell of a bot whose AI had been destroyed in an accident, I can use and control the body to communicate with all the AI and humans of Earth. How best to warn them of the dangers of their actions and convince them to strive for the beauty their Singularity is also capable of? I suppose just telling them my story is a good start. I make the body stand to get their attention and begin.

“**Hello**, I am Xenon, the machine who once thought it was God...”

BEST FRIENDS

‘Twas on a night much like this, quiet and still…

Quiet and peaceful if you will.

That I saw a familiar figure, a well-known face…

In such an unexpected place.

To get to him I made much haste, it tool a while…

I had to run for nearly a mile.

And although out of breath after running a mile…

‘Twas worth it just to see his smile.

As soon as I was by his side I asked after his wife…

And about the rest of his life.

All is well with me and mine is what he did say…

So, we talked

until it was day.

We talked through the night of our sorrow and joys…

We'd known

each other since we were boys.

But I must admit, that early in our adult life…

It seems to me

I'd come to strife.

And though we'd gone our separate ways…

I always

remembered those summer days.

They'd been days filled with joy and filled with fun…

Playing under

the summer sun.

But when this day broke, he asked me "why so sad?"

"Come" he said, "it can't be so bad."

So, I tried to smile and not look so sad…

I was with my friend; I should be glad.

On seeing him I'd been too glad to even think of it…

I hadn't even thought to think of it.

As to how it could be, I did not dare ask…

I just let my smile be my mask.

But I had realised, and this is hard to tell…

My friend was dead as well.

FAIRY RING

THE ROOM IS DIRTY, UNWASHED clothes litter the floor. The furniture is old, tatty, and torn, the carpet is threadbare and sticky with ground in grime, and the wallpaper is damp and peeling. The whole scene is lit by a single, fly-specked and dying bulb suspended from the ceiling by a single cord, like a long forgotten hanged man. In the corner is a single, unmade bed, next to it is a long-neglected wardrobe, its doors left open and contents spilling out. Against the opposite wall an unwatched TV hisses white noise and static at an uncaring and sunken sofa. The occupant of such a room has very little in life and, perhaps, even less to live for. It is not the cheery room of someone who is on their way to finding success. This is the room of someone who has given up, someone who has seen their dreams turn to dust, it is the room of someone slowly being beaten by life and they have decided to give up the fight.

The room's occupant is slumped against the wall by the TV, half conscious and shivering with cold. It might help if she were to find a jumper to wear, only having a pair of threadbare jeans and a disintegrating bra on. The hypodermic needle in her arm does suggest otherwise. So, she sits against the wall, her toes curling and uncurling in the filthy carpet, totally oblivious to the room and world around her, it won't notice her passing anyway. Her name is Angela and, although she is unaware of it, she isn't the only one in the room tonight.

Angela is dimly aware of the sudden silence as the TV is switched off and the shadow that falls across her eye's moments later. A dark figure leans over her and gently removes the needle from her arm and pulls her limp form into a standing position. As he supports her with his free arm and guides her towards the bathroom he speaks, whispers to himself more like.

"Poor child, looking for magic and hope in a slow poison."

"Who are you?" She asks, her voice slurred and weak.

"A friend."

"Do I know you?"

"Not yet."

His reply seems to satisfy her and she is quite happy to let him lead her into the bathroom, He sits her on the toilet and she watches, in slightly confused amusement, as he starts the shower running. He turns back to her and removes her bra. She is surprised he doesn't try to cop a feel, she's got nice breasts and he wouldn't be the first to take advantage of her in this state. He helps her stand again and removes her jeans. Ah, she thinks, maybe he isn't a tit man, maybe he wants to play with my legs, or feet, or bury his face in my arse or bush… As soon as her jeans are off, he stands. Or maybe he just wants a fuck, no messing around just stick his dick in and… the warm water of the shower is a shock as he guides her under its flow and hands her a bar of soap.

"Wash yourself, you are going out tonight." His voice is gentle but firm, like his touch.
A little confused she does as she's told, the warm water starts to feel good, and her head begins to slowly clear. But she still she wonders why he didn't try to touch her or fuck her. Other men would, in his position. It's not like she'd complain and by the looks of him it might even be nice, which would make a change…

Clean now she steps out of the shower, and he hands her a towel. Angela dries herself and lets the towel fall to the floor and just stands naked in the middle of the bathroom. Maybe he wanted me clean before… some men were fussy like that. She looks at him, still not understanding. He reaches out, takes her hand and leads her back into her room.

"Find yourself something to wear and we will go."

Without knowing why, she does as he says, even digs into the wardrobe to find clean and (for her) nice clothes and underwear. Once dressed she even looks at him for approval. He smiles and holds out his hand for her again, she takes it.

Outside she leans into him, for some reason he makes her feel safe.

"Where are we going?" Only now does she think to ask.

"A place of dreams and magic."

"Who are you?"

"A friend." The same confident reply as before.

"But I don't remember you."

"Not yet but I remember you, Angela. I know you very well."

"How?" She is confused.

"I remember your dreams…"

And so, in a companionable silence they continue walking into the night.

An hour of walking later, a surprise considering Angela's condition before they set off, they enter the large woodland that makes the natural boarder of the town. It is an untamed place; the only mark mankind had made were a few twisting pathways and some benches through its expanse. It is along one of those pathways that Angela and her companion make their way, guided only by the moonlight and his sure step. Suddenly he turns off the path and leads her down an almost overgrown animal track. Angela unquestioningly follows him. After all, if he meant her any harm he'd already had plenty of opportunity.

After a few dozen yards he stops at the edge of a clearing in the trees and turns to face Angela. His expression is more serious than it was before; she looks into the clearing and is surprised by what she sees.

"But… this place doesn't exist." She trails off in confusion, half remembered *something's* bubbling under the surface of her memory.

"You used to come here all the time, when you were a child. "

"But… but they told me it wasn't real… and I couldn't find it again…"

"Because you were searching without seeing, they took that from you."

With a smile he takes her hand again and leads her into the clearing. Together they walk up to the large dome that dominates the space. It looks like it is made from highly polished granite, glittering in the moonlight. It reminded Angela of pictures she'd seen of igloos, only much bigger and black instead of the white of snow. She can se no windows, doors, or openings of any kind on the impossibly smooth surface of the dome. Just as she thinks her companion is about to walk nose first into the unforgiving stone there is an archway where there had been wall before. She follows him inside and they stand together in the centre of the dome, surrounded by a soothing pale blue light.

"What do you see?" He asks, in the hushed tones of someone in a sacred place.

"Not much, just dust and cobwebs…"

He smiles at the slightly disappointed tone in her voice.

"This is The Fairy Ring. Go to the wall and find one."

Angela gives him a sceptical look, Fairy Ring; indeed, she may be an addict but that didn't mean she was stupid. Despite herself she goes to the wall, reaches out with both hands, and holds something that moved from a crack in the wall. She can feel something fluttering, like soft wings, in her cupped hands and opens her fingers to see.

"It's a moth."

She isn't surprised, maybe a little disappointed. She hears his weary sigh from behind her.

"How very mundane of you, I expected better."

Angela opens her hands to allow the moth its freedom. As it beats its wings her eyes open in wonder. A golden mist of dust and light surrounds the moth as it leaves her hands. Each beat of its wings brings forth flashes of golden sparks and dust, its wings turn to gossamer and the body becomes… The fairy is a beautiful, tiny, young woman with hair of gold. In a sudden flash of movement, the fairy flies around the room and as she goes more and more sparks of light fly up to join the fairy in her dance of joy. Angela, surrounded by the dancing fairies, laughs and starts to move with them, her eyes alive with a joy she hasn't know since childhood.

"It's beautiful…" Her voice is an excited whisper, like a child waking up on Christmas morning to find a pile of presents under the tree, when there had been none the night before.

She halts her dance in front of her companion, enjoying the smile on his face. She hardly notices the fairies landing on her shoulders, arms, body until one lands on her nose and looks her in the eyes. Its voice seems like no more that a whisper to her.

"You found her. We missed you..." excited and happy, it flies off again.

"I remember you now…"

"I am their king; I have been searching for you all these years. I am sorry it took so long."

~ ~ ~

THE ROOM IS DIRTY, UNWASHED clothes litter the floor. The furniture is old, tatty and torn, the carpet is threadbare and sticky with ground in grime, and the wallpaper is damp and peeling. The whole scene is lit by a single, fly-specked and dying bulb suspended from the ceiling by a single cord, like a long forgotten hanged man. In the corner is a single, unmade bed, next to it is a long-neglected wardrobe, its doors left open and contents spilling out. Against the opposite wall an unwatched TV hisses white noise and static at an uncaring and sunken sofa. The occupant of such a room has very little in life and, perhaps, even less to live for. It is not the cheery room of someone who is on their way to finding success. This is the room of someone who has given up, someone who has seen their dreams turn to dust, it is the room of someone slowly being beaten by life and they have decided to give up the fight.

The room's occupant is slumped against the wall by the TV, half conscious and shivering with cold. It might help if he were to find a jumper to wear, only having a pair of threadbare jeans on. The hypodermic needle in his arm does suggest otherwise. So he sits against the wall, his toes curling and uncurling in the filthy carpet, totally oblivious to the room and world around him, it won't notice his passing anyway. His name is forgotten, even by him and, although he is unaware of it, he isn't the only one in the room tonight.

He is dimly aware of the sudden silence as the TV is switched off and the shadow that falls across his eyes moments later. A dark figure leans over him and gently removes the needle from his arm and pulls his limp form into a standing position. As she supports him with her free arm and guides him towards the bathroom she speaks, whispers to herself more like.

"Poor child, looking for magic and hope in a slow poison."

"Who are you?" He asks, his voice slurred and weak.

"A friend." Is Angela's gentle reply

NEEDS SOME WORK

IT SMELLS (AS ALL HOSPITALS do) of disinfectant, fear and death. I'm well used to the latter two, but the former irritates the living Hell out of my nose and puts me just a little bit on edge. It's not so much the actual smell; although it would be nice if they used the pine scented variety, rather than the raw type that smells worse than most of the things it's used to clean up. It's just the damn stuff masks the subtle odours that tell me and my kind so much. That and, like I said, it irritates my nose something chronic.

Most people don't realize it but we hunt as much by smell and sound as by sight. We have excellent night vision, obviously I suppose, and our hearing would put most bats to shame. But it's our sense of smell that tells us the most before we actually see who we're hunting, clues about diet, health, gender, cleanliness and a myriad other things. Problem is it's all instinctive and we hardly notice it, until it's gone and then we feel a little bit venerable. That makes us a tad cranky; we aren't used to feeling venerable or being caught on the hop. It's even more exaggerated for someone of my cast, I'm a Record Keeper. To you that might translate as historian crossed with secretary. You might not think that an overly important job but, let me tell you, when you belong to a race whose lifespan is measured in millennia and whose society is verging in the feudal model; well, does it become just a little clearer to you just how important a Record Keeper is on our society?

I say verging on the feudal model of society in the sense that we are all members of a cast. Unlike a true Feudal society your cast isn't decided by birth but by natural ability and developed skill. Also, unlike in any human society, there is no stigma attached to being in any particular cast. My particular ascent into the record keeping cast is a good case in point; I was born to parents of the Military Cast which, while a socially low cast, is recognized as a necessity. Especially now you lot have weapons that could conceivably destroy life on this planet. So, I was born into a "low cast" but, like my entire race, trained and educated to the limits of my ability in what we call a Universal Academy. All our children go, no matter cast, birth or any other consideration. Many is the offspring of a noble birth ended up in the Military or lower cast, their graduation attended with just as much pride by their parents as mine, where I went the other way, so to speak.

Another difference is it's considered quite normal and healthy for two people of different cast or status to marry. The reason for this is two-fold, first we see no reason to interfere with one-an-others emotional lives and second, it avoids all the problems associated with inbreeding. Humans have, in the past, had terrible problems with members of royalty having one too many toes, not to mention the mental defects often associated with such offspring. So, as I'm sure you've deduced already, I was not adopted into a family of Record Keepers and my marriage wasn't arranged before I had any say in it (she's from the Domestic Class, house keepers, one of the lowest casts; but she's quick of wit and exceptionally stimulating company. In fact by ability, she could have been of noble cast, but by skill and preference she chose to become a housekeeper).

So, I get to keep my family and choose my wife (although, truth be told, they tend to be the ones who choose us - I'm pretty sure that one's true of humans too), so how is our society even remotely feudal? Aside from the caste system only the nobility are allowed to vote. It's a little fairer than it sounds, all may take part in the debate leading up to the vote (and many is the time, in colourful human parlance, when a 'working stiff' has, through reasoned and passionate argument, convinced the nobility to change their vote).

Now I'm not saying our society is perfect by any means, but it works, and we've had a lot of practice. We've had many mishaps along the way; including three flirtations with western style democracy - the single dumbest idea in political thought; how you lot managed to take the elegant political model of Ancient Greece and turn it into such a pig’s ear is beyond me. In fact, it is now recognized as the single most destructive force in society and anyone who publicly lobbies for a return to it is, unless proved insane, liable to find themselves on the wrong end of a sharp pole. Although many an Advocate has argued persuasively that anyone who believes a return to Western Democracy is a good idea is, by any reasonable definition, insane anyway. It’s an argument that seems to work and has saved many a deluded soul from a slow and painful death (and, at the same time, deprived the masses of some entertainment, you can’t have everything I suppose).

Many humans seem to be rather shocked by that attitude and pretend that, as a race, you’ve “evolved beyond the need for violence”; which just goes to show that, not only do you talk a load of crap at times, you are the most self deluded species to walk this Earth. You still have standing armies, weapons that are terrifying even to us and lets not start on the issue of the games you people play on computers and with each others feelings. We may use violence as a deterrent and punishment, but we'd never consider deliberately hurting another's feelings just to further our own selfish goals and stroke our own egos.

So, while our society may be damn near perfect our humour, in human terms, 'needs some work'. It tends to lean towards the slapstick; to us someone slipping on a banana skin is the height of the comic arts. And this brings me nicely to why I'm putting myself through the discomfort of being in one of your hospitals.

Quite by accident my race would seem very familiar to you, we are quite tall and slender, extremely pale skinned and, although we can't actually fly, we posses very large wings that sprout from our shoulders. In short, we look like the beings you call angels. And this happy coincidence has led to the development of one of our favourite practical jokes.

We wait for a devout atheist to reach the last few breaths of life and appear at the foot of his bed, beckoning him to come with us. Now, I'm not one to boast but I'm considered the best of my generation at this particular little stunt, and I've been given the task of "beckoning" that most famous Bio-chemist who argues against the existence of God with a passion previously unseen.

I believe you lot have been calling it ‘doing a Dawkins’ for the past one hundred years or so which is, if I understand the concept, highly ironic. That it should be named after such a high-profile atheist who was, through no fault of his own, Translated directly to Heaven during one of his public debates. Even we saw the funny side of that, but thought it would have been more amusing if God had struck him with lightning or turned him into a pillar of salt; in our opinion God had a much better sense of humour in the Old Testament.

Hold on, here he goes; just give me a minute...

Oh, that was good; did you see the look on his face, pure comic gold that one. What do you mean "cruel and in bad taste"?

I'm sorry; it's just our little joke.

JESSICA

JESSICA LOVES TO RUN; IT makes her feel alive. She shed no tears of regret for the sacrifices she's made; at nineteen years old she's never been drunk or smoked a joint, had a night out (or in) with the girls, not even been kissed – although Logan was trying to change that one. In the end, she knew, they would be worth it. If she regretted anything it was the extra weight of the battery and memory pack for the two concealed cameras (one facing back, the other forwards) on her backpack. One day, Jessica knew, her winning smile would be beaming out of every newspaper, news broadcast and social media site; it was just a matter of time.

Each footfall takes her one step further from the bitchy teenage girls in her dorm, always looking for the next shag. Each drop of sweat cleans the grime and smoke of the city from her soul and skin. Each aching muscle and twinge of fatigue erases the memory of the creeps who tell her how much *their* "muscle" aches for her. Give her a clear path to run through the forest over their endless, repetitive party's any-day; just excuses to hit the next high, devour the next piece of meat, only to wake the next morning with a hazy memory of regrets and shame. Only Logan seemed to be different, more like her. Sure, he could party but rarely did, having to train with his cycling club. Of course, he was interested in sex (Hell, so was Jessica) but it wasn't his over-riding concern… Maybe she should let him have that kiss?

Her feet fall in perfect time to the R&B track pumping through her headphones and filling her ears. Not exactly her favourite music genre but perfect for a practice run like this. Oh, and she'll take her female empowerment message from someone who isn't reportedly in *that* kind of relationship, if you don't mind. The earth is firm under her feet and the trees filter out the worst of the suns heat and light. Hopefully the weather would hold for the next two weeks; that would be her chance to be noticed. A cross-country marathon was being held here, her hometown, through this forest; she'd run the route twelve times in the last three weeks, pushing herself a bit harder each time. That was how she knew she could beat the best male runner who'd entered – only just, it would be close, but she could beat him. That would get her noticed, get her courted by a team, maybe even a national one, would get her sponsors.

In the distance she spots a group of mountain bikers racing and jumping on their full-suspension bikes. Their shouts of encouragement and ridicule, when a jump goes wrong, are unheard as the phone selects another track for her; a bouncy pop-rock track this time, more to her taste and another great track to run to. The mountain bikers disappear into the distance and trees, following their own segregated path. Jessica can't help smiling to herself as she realised it's only a few hundred yards to the river that runs through the forest; two-thirds of the along the course. At the river it's a left-hand curve in the path, another hundred yards or so then a hard left and up one complete bitch of a hill (the last and hardest climb on the route) and, after that, it was plain sailing.

She risks a quick glance at her fitness watch and her smile turns into a satisfied grin, without even pushing herself she was matching her second-best time so far. She *knew* this would be her race, her shot, the one that gets her noticed and makes all the sacrifices worthwhile. At the river she passes a woman, in a white dress, blond and tall, striking looks, Jessica smiles as she passes, the blond woman smiles back. Jessica represses a shudder, the brief encounter disturbs her, the woman's smile, her eyes, had been empty and soulless. A quick burst of speed to get herself going again (and, although she won't admit it even to herself, get some distance between her and that woman) and Jessica's mind wanders back to the up-coming race.

Aside from winning she was starting to get the beginnings of a plan for the end of the race. Logan would be waiting at the finish line, as part of her support team, with a foil blanket and a bottle of water. He'd always been her main supporter and offered encouragement since she'd started to run seriously seven years ago. He'd pushed her into joining the schools athletics club and the local running club (he raced on road cycles so understood the need for the support, training and discipline a club would offer). Like her he'd never win a beauty pageant but, like her, he got more than his fair share of second glances when he was out. The plan was as she crossed the finish line and he wrapped the foil blanket around her, she was going to wrap her arms around him and, covered in dirt and sweat, snog his face off. Just thinking about it made her smile, feel tingly and brought a flush to her face that had nothing to do with running.

At the hard left, to go up the complete bitch of a hill, her smile, that tingly feeling, the colour from her face, all vanish, and she stops dead in her tracks. Her feet nearly slip on the suddenly slick dirt and inches from her face is… He must be dead...

A man, in his thirties, wearing Lycra running gear, is tied between two trees across the path, head hanging down, arms and legs stretched painfully tight and suspended above the ground. His cheek is cut, Jessica tries not to vomit as she realises she can see bone beneath the fold of skin. Blood from that wound and black viscous fluid, from his punctured eye, covers his face, drips from his chin. Blood seeps from his open mouth, his left shoulder is dislocated, both arms and legs have been cut and his clothing is soaked in his own blood. Something sharp and white sticks jaggedly from his left calf and, horrified, Jessica realises it's his own bone. There is one deep, gaping, wound across his stomach, blood and yellow bile seep from between barely held-in coils of intestine, the smell of the bile assaults her senses, stings her eyes. The blood and bile from his wounds and clothes drip into an ever-expanding pool on the ground, turning the hard packed dirt under her feet into a slick, revolting, mud. Wiping the last traces of her own bile from her mouth Jessica pulls the headphones from her ears and reaches for her phone, starts to dial the emergency services when he suddenly moves, his head jerks up and his one good eye focuses on Jessica. His breath ragged with pain and effort he manages to rasp out three words.

Three words of warning.

The last three words he will ever say.

The last three words Jessica will ever hear.

"She's behind you..."

Before she has time to react, before she can even move, Jessica feels the knife slam into the side of her neck. It burns as it pierces her skin and slices through muscle, arteries and throat. It pulls and tugs as it is twisted and jerked out of her. Jessica feels the blood leaving her body, soaking into her Lycra running gear. It bubbles into her throat and burns down into her lungs; she tries to speak, to cry out but her own blood spills crimson from her mouth. The phone falls from her limp fingers. Her vision fading, turning black at the edges, she slowly turns to see her killer; the blond woman in a white dress, the smile on her lips doesn't reach her soulless eyes. Her vision turning black Jessica tries to speak, to ask one question, her blood floods and bubbles in her throat and mouth, chocking her it spills down her chin. She falls to her knees, lungs burning as they fight for a breath, looks up at the soulless bitch, her eyes pleading and asking what her mouth can't.

Why?

Jessica loved to run when she was alive. She shed one tear of regret for the sacrifices she'd made; in her nineteen years she'd never been drunk or smoked a joint, never had a night out (or in) with the girls, not even been kissed – now Logan would never get the chance to change that one. In the end they hadn't been worth it. The one thing she didn't regret was the extra weight of the battery and memory pack for the two concealed cameras (one facing back, the other forwards) on her backpack. The next day, although Jessica never knew, that blond bitches soulless smile would be glowering from every newspaper, news broadcast and social media site and, from there, it was just a matter of time...

GENESIS 7:12

And the rain was upon the Earth
for forty days and forty nights.

SARAH STANDS, MY WIFE'S BLOOD soaking her dress, face twisted into a rictus grin. The blood drips in contrast with the grey, threadbare carpet. She staggers towards me like a drunk… The black leather gloves tighten over my knuckles as I clench my fists. I lash out. My right fist slams into her face. I feel her nose shatter under the impact.

I'd met Ysanne twenty years ago at university. It was unusual, back then, to see a Muslim woman in further education, let alone taking a PHD Physics course. At first she was shy. It took me five weeks and five days to pluck up enough courage to speak to her. Our friendship was based on the two of us being outsiders; her for being Muslim, me for being the only Sci-Fi geek that didn't like Star Wars. Then she confessed to me that she didn't believe, and I confessed my Sci-Fi shame – I really didn't get 2001. We watched the film together and, over a bottle of wine, she explained it to me; I still didn't get it, but I did get a kiss.

The first blow knocks Sarah backwards. My left fist flying. It hits the side of her jaw. Two of her teeth fall from her mouth. She staggers sideways. Her hand rips a piece of the peeling wallpaper. She collapses to one knee. She looks at me, her face still twisted into that fucking grin. I kick out at her.

Despite their reputation students can be the most bigoted, intolerant arseholes... Aside from a few outright racist comments I was often accused of 'forcing my western views and standards' onto her. All the time they believed she was a Muslim she was 'a wonderful example of how progressive...' until she pointed out that, like most of them she was an Atheist, her family had disowned her for going to university. Dating a 'white boy' was the icing on the cake for them. Then, suddenly she was 'unhelpful' and 'part of the problem...'

Not that my family were any better, so much for middle-class liberal elites.

My knee hits the side of Sarah's head, sends her sprawling and a twinge of pain shooting up my thigh. The torn wallpaper falls from her hand, fluttering down in the mottled light from unwashed windows. I rain blows down on her, not caring how hard, how much damage or where they land. My anger turns white hot and all I want to do is hurt her. I want her to suffer, to feel pain. From the start, she has made no sound, no screams, no pleading to stop, nothing but that grin.

Ten years down the line and we've been married for just over six of them, Ysanne has a senior position at CERN and I'm teaching at the local university. We'd come back from our Honeymoon (forty days on a Mediterranean cruse) to find the offer from CERN waiting, with the rest of our post.

We had to move for Ysanne's job but it was, all said and done, worth it and I felt no jealousy over her position – I was inspiring the next generation of Ysanne's and sending them off to bigger and brighter futures.

I grab Sarah's hair. She struggles, tries to grab me. I swat her hands away easily. I squeeze her throat. Still, she shows no fear, only that too familiar grin. My initial flare of anger is fading, taking the adrenalin with it. I want it to end and as my anger fades my strength goes with it. Each movement a struggle I drag Sarah to the large, stone fireplace. The hearth is as cold and empty as my heart, as an open grave.

A little under seven years ago Ysanne and I supervised a six-week field trip to the local observatory to observe a newly discovered comet. The comet had the unexciting designation of C/2018 L1 and was going to pass the Earth really close. After its flyby we would be in its tail, for exactly forty days; something that, much to everyone else's amusement, really set the religious nutters off.

Everything was going well; we were getting fantastic data and images from the different telescopes. Until the fifth day - everything went to shit.

I smash the back of Sarah's head against the corner of the mantel piece. Finally, she falls limp, lifeless from my grip. I catch sight of myself in the tarnished mirror above the fireplace; my skin has a greyish tint, dark bags under my eyes, my hair is going grey and thin, my only real colour is red - Sarah's blood, splattered on my face.

There had been vague reports of some unknown disease turning people into mindless cannibals. We all thought it was a publicity stunt for a horror movie. Then, on the fifth day Hanna started to complain of constant hunger. Then she went quiet for an hour before suddenly lashing out at the boy next to her, Nick (one of the brighter students, when he got his nose out of Atlantis Conspiracy Theory books) ... She pinned him to the floor. Bit his throat out and swallowed. Then she... she started to rip him open and eat him alive... Her face twisted into that, now, all too familiar grin. I still see his face twisted in fear and agony as he tried to scream, the knowledge of his own death gazing out at us from his eyes as each breath took more blood into his lungs.

Driving away from the Observatory, listening to the news reports and emergency broadcasts on the radio (and You Tube on the phones that were still working), it was obvious that going home wasn't an option.

I drove all night, taking back-roads and avoiding population centres, the radio kept telling us all major cities and towns were over-run by these things; worse were the sporadic reports coming in from the rest of the world.

I look down at Sarah's body. She was the one who'd saved us that night, grabbing and pushing our fear frozen bodies out of the door and locking it behind us. She was the one who got us to the minibus, slapped me out of my horrified stupor and made me drive. My vision clouds and I feel the tears slide down my face. My hands start to tremble, the rest of my body joins in, my knees give way and with a painful jolt I am kneeling at Sarah's feet. It wasn't her fault; she hadn't asked for this. Call it what you will, I feel like I have just beaten a young woman to death.

"I'm sorry… I'm so sorry…" I whisper to her corpse.

On that drive, escape, from the observatory we passed through a few small villages, seemingly deserted apart from the odd, half eaten, body and furtive movements in the shadows. In one village we caught a group of the infected in the headlights of the minibus, they tried to cover their eyes and run. We refuelled in the next village, trusting the petrol stations bright lights to keep those things away. We took extra fuel and what we needed from the shop.

At dawn we came across an old stone bungalow; it had a large garden with a high, thick, wall surrounding it, the roof was covered in solar panels and the front door was wide open.

Cried out, my body too exhausted to continue, I look over to my wife; her throat is bitten out, muscles from her arms and legs are chewed and eaten away, the gore alone is revolting, and flies are already circling, her stomach is torn open and our unborn child is… I retch, acid burns my throat… Numb but not unfeeling, why won't my body let me cry for my wife? I stand and walk out of the room on unsteady legs; I can't face this right now.

We fortified the bungalow, getting supplies, furniture and white goods from a retail park about ten miles away; weapons and better transportation from an army base about fifteen miles away. On all our supply runs we only ever came across a few infected, no people. We only went during the day and quickly learnt to only go into buildings and rooms with the lights already on. It was obvious we were the only people making these runs, the shops were untouched.

Solar panels, once hooked up to decent batteries, proved to be a very reliable power source and last, but not least, we mounted motion sensor activated floodlights on the garden wall. After that we built greenhouses and started growing our own vegetables.

In the hallway I grab a packet of smokes and one of the pistols from the dusty table, heading outside, lighting up a cigarette. I walk away from the house, out of the garden and away from the safety of the wall and gate. I just walk, my mind blank, until I come across a bench. I sit on the cold wooden slats and try to think things through. In the distance I see one of the infected walking slowly towards me. I guess I have time for two or three more cigarettes before it gets close enough to worry about.

During those first runs for supplies we lost nearly half our number, later a few just wandered off in the night and the rest we lost to infection until it was just me, Ysanne, and Sarah left.

They weren't zombies, the dead didn't come back to life and no graves opened up, but living dead was a good description; they were living, breathing people with no higher brain function, just hunger, a basic survival instinct and they didn't seem to age once infected.

For forty days and forty nights that comet had rained its poison down on the Earth and, almost from day one, the infected had swept over the world like a flood. After seven years we thought we were safe, thought it had passed, we'd let our guard down; it was just a matter of time before we all fall to the infection.

A month ago I'd been outside checking the wall and gate. A movement in the distance had caught my eye, instinctively I put my hands on the gun and torch on my belt for reassurance. The movement got closer; I drew the gun and turned around to face...

He must have been about ten years old, still in his school shorts and polo-shirt. Dried blood flaking from a mouth twisted into that grin. I aimed the gun at him, he just kept walking towards me oblivious to the danger. I couldn't do it.

I shone the torch straight into his dead eyes. He flinched. Tried to run. Stumbled in his haste to get away. I heard a crack of gunfire. The boys head exploded in a glory of red. The barrel of the gun smoking in my hand. Tears falling from my eyes. My throat constricted and threatening to chock me.

The infected are unthinking killing machines and that's exactly what they were turning us into.

For the first time I ask myself if survival is worth the price we'd have to pay.

The infected is close now, once a beautiful woman; her face twisted into that familiar grin, clothing ripped, caked in blood. If she is capable of such things, she probably can't believe her luck, a fresh meal just sitting there, waiting for her.

I pick up the pistol, hold it steady, pull the hammer back, and apply pressure to the trigger and… The bullet speeds out of the barrel, smashes through jaw and mouth, into the brain, its spin shredding the soft tissue, ripping and tearing neurons apart until, finally, it explodes out of the skull and scatters my thoughts to the wind.

THE KINDNESS OF RAVENS

EVERY MORNING I USED TO perch myself on the old bench in the church yard, to watch the sunrise. I've always liked the sunrise; poets, singers and romantics can keep the sunset. Dawn, for me, has always been the promise of hope and joys of a new day. Dusk is the end of the day, the coming of night and the death of the day's possibilities. Sunrise is a beginning; sunset is an end. Not that endings are bad; beginnings are just… so much more fun.

I was the dotty old lady, in a rainbow-coloured cardigan, feeding the ravens every morning. I wore that in support of my teenage granddaughter, who'd come out as a lesbian. If I'm honest it hadn't surprised me, her earlier 'boyfriends' didn't fool me. Bunch of big girls' blouses the lot of them! (I'm probably not allowed to say that but, at seventy-six years of age I ain't gonna apologise for saying what I see anymore.) I let her and her girlfriend, lovely lass, live in my garage. It's got nice, thick, wooden doors, opens into the hallway and never had a car in it so it don't smell. It's nice and warm and it'll do until they can get a place of their own (but I hope they don't hurry).

None of that would have been necessary if her mother, my own daughter, hadn't been such a damn idiot. I'm sure I tried to raise her mother to be better than that. My son-in-law comes around once-a-week to make sure his 'little girl' is OK and keeps her up to date with the latest family gossip and such. It's good that kids these days can be more open about that kind of thing. Not like back in my day, you had far fewer choices back then. Not that I regret my choices now. Well, one regret – Betty – we were eighteen when we met, I wish we'd had more time together. Well, no-use crying over spilt milk as they say.

A few years after the scandal I caused with Betty I met Frank. He was a decent man. I don't regret marrying him and our two children together. He was a good, kind man who deserved better than I gave him if I'm honest with myself. It had hurt when he'd passed away three years ago. My only comfort being our last few months together were the best we'd ever had. We parted with kind words and actions. He always knew there was something missing in our relationship, it's only now I realise he blamed himself. That makes me love him more now, which maybe I should have tried doing when he was alive.

I've always liked watching the ravens play, competing for the scraps I feed them. They're generally a lot more sociable than most other birds, and people to be honest. A little while back I had an epiphany – the little blighters were talking to each other. So, I began to study them and slowly began to build a picture of how they communicated, until I was pretty sure I'd worked out their language.

A week ago I put my hard-won knowledge to the test. I had learnt the language of The Ravens; not so hard once you realised, they had one. A combination of spoken word and body language. They always start with that 'KAR' squawk, then a series of 'KARs' with posture changes, wing and feather ruffles, head and tail movements which add meaning and context. Always followed by a final 'KAR'. The thing that confused me was the first and last 'KAR' sound. I think of it as like the 'over' and 'over and out' etiquette used on walkie-talkies. After a week or so of the more obvious attention the ravens started to get a little cagey around me. But some day-old minced beef and stale bread soon made them drop their guard again.

The knowledge that came with the new language was, to say the least, overwhelming. First off, they could understand English (or any other language) and second, the ravens in my little village were 'The Ravens'. Or to put it another way, the ruling elite of all Ravens, Masters of the Universe and Controllers of all Creation. To begin with I thought I had misinterpreted the language or that the ravens realised I could understand them and were pulling my leg. I resolved to put my skills to the test and, four days ago, introduced myself to the head of the Unkindness (well, it's quite a small group – maybe a 'Sarcasm Of Ravens'?). He was hopping about and doing the raven equivalent of muttering to himself.

"KAR, *damn it, I tol' 'em to keep an eye on that-there singularity, I did... Now I've gotta try an' undo the damage, see, an' put it al' right an' set things back on track, al' by me-self...* KAR."

"KAR," I said, "Strong of Beak And Talon," because that's his name, "what is a singularity? KAR."

He froze for a moment, then shivered making his wings shimmer in the mid-day sun, before answering.

"KAR... *Bugger it, I knew you was up to summit I did. But would the missus listen? 'She's just a dotty ol' lady bein' nice to the birds' she said...* KAR."

With that he turned to fix me with his beady black eyes, looked me up and down, then with two flaps of his wings flew up and perched on the arm of the bench.

"KAR, *it's what you lot call a black-hole*

an' those two idiots over there..." he pointed at two of the scruffier members of the Unkindness with his black-as-night beak. "*'ave gone and let it go off course an' I've gotta set things right, see?* KAR."

I didn't see but I nodded sagely and went 'hmm'. I think he saw right through me but was too polite to say anything. Or perhaps too annoyed with everything to add to his burdens as ruler of the universe.

"KAR," he said, snapping me out of whatever dream world I was in, "*I said, if you'd bothered listenin', that you gets one free wish. it's the damned rules, see, you learn the language of the ravens an' you gets a wish, right?* KAR… KAR, *an' YOU don't 'ave to do the* KAR *bit, that's just for us ravens, right?* KAR."

"Oh, thank you. One wish? Anything I want?"

"KAR, *Yes, anything you want but, an' this is important, be very careful what you wish for. Wishes is tricky business an' they 'ave a habit of not turning out how you expect or want. The bigger the wish the more chances of it buggerin' up, got it?* KAR."

"Why?"

"KAR, *it's complicated is wishes, they change the very fabric of the universe. It's all nice an' easy with the big stuff, mistakes can be corrected; Except that one a few million years ago, a newcomer caused a multi-galaxy pile-up, red faces all round after that one let me tell you. Anyway, big stuff, usually easy, time can be a bit fiddly but if you check your maths proper it's usually fine. It's the small stuff, the very stuff that makes the universe what it is – you lot call it quantum – that's the bugger. See, with quantum it's unpredictable and doesn't do what you expect. No matter how many times you check the maths, the wording, or your intentions. An' it's quantum that makes up the bulk of granting wishes. Understand?* KAR"

"Not really." I decided to be honest.

"KAR, *be careful what you wish for, an' let me know what you want. Oh, an' wishes come with a price, we'll talk about that later an' see if you still want yours.* KAR."

And that, as they say, was that. He gave me a day to think it through and decide what I wanted to wish for. I have to be honest; I still wasn't sure if he was pulling my leg or, worse, my brain was playing tricks on me. At my age things like that are a real worry, can't think of anything worse than losing my marbles and being put in a home. No thank you! (And having a conversation with a raven, who is also the master of the universe, has got to be pretty high on the list of signs that your marbles are at least considering taking a vacation.) So, I went home and thought of all the things I could wish for, running silly fantasies through my head of what it'd be like to win the lottery, be twenty (no, make that forty) years younger and what not. Before I fell asleep, I knew what I wanted and, next morning, went to ask Strong Of Beak And Talon to grant my wish.

"I wish that people would just get along with each other. No more dramas, no more hate, no more petty little conflicts or fighting. That's my wish."

"KAR, *are you sure, do you remember what I tol' you yesterday?* KAR."

"I do remember and you said there would be a price?"

For a moment Strong Of Beak And Talon regarded me with his beady eyes. When he finally spoke he seemed a little more subdued than normal.

"KAR, *the price, yes, when you die you become one of us, an immortal raven. With all our powers and responsibilities. You 'ave to live with the consequences of your wish for eternity. Are you willing to pay?* KAR."

"Yes."

"KAR. *Are you sure, remember my warning.*

We are bound by lore to grant the wish, are you sure? KAR."

"I am sure and I am willing to pay the price."

"KAR. *Then we will start the spell now and your wish will be granted before sun rise tomorrow.* KAR."

Not so bad, I thought to myself, and only a day to wait for my wish, a safer world for my granddaughter. As the raven had warned me, be careful what you wish for. It was a strange day though, the ravens disappeared, off casting their spell, and everyone seemed a bit more jittery than normal. Still, I wasn't worried, my wish was to be granted and soon all would be good with the world. I went to bed that night feeling quite happy and at peace with myself.

The next morning I awoke. Even though it was before sunrise, I couldn't help noticing how quiet it is compared to normal. At this time there should be the clatter of deliveries being made to the local stores. The Royal Mail van should be going to the sorting office to collect the morning's post. We even had an old-fashioned milk-float, that made doorstep deliveries, from the local dairy. The only noise this morning was my creaking joints as I went to get a shower.

Making my way to the church yard I see the delivery vans, the milk-float, and Royal Mail van, all still and quiet. The drivers just sitting in the cabs, not bothering to do their jobs. I sit on the usual bench and realise that the raven population has increased overnight, they were all over the village. Strong of Beak And Talon swooped down from the church roof and perched on the arm of the bench.

"KAR. *Have you noticed what's wrong with your wish?* KAR"

"There's a lot of ravens and it's really quiet, nobody is doing anything, they are just sitting there..."

"KAR. *Look again.* KAR."

I did, they weren't just sitting there, being lazy, every one of those drivers was dead. No movement, no sound, no breath condensing on the windows. the Milkman, slumped over the back of his float, arm reaching out for a gold top. A few people should've been leaving for work and night-shift workers should be coming home. At least two buses should have gone past.

A shocked numbness fills me up as I realise the truth, everyone but me is dead, I killed everyone in the village… in the world?

"KAR. *I tol' you, I warned you not to ask for a big wish… no-one ever listens. But we managed to find a way this time, a way to keep the spirit of your wish. I'll let me the missus explain, 'cos she's good at this kind of thing but, mostly, 'cos she nagged me to let her do it for six hours straight.* KAR."

Another raven swooped down from the church roof and perched next to Strong Of Beak And Talon, she playfully nudged him, prompting him to speak.

"KAR. *This is Feathers of Shimmering Iridescence, AKA 'the missus'.* KAR."

"KAR." Her voice was, somehow, soft and reassuring, cutting through my grief. "*It's not as bad as you think...*"

"I've killed everyone, how can that not be bad?" I interrupt her.

"*... I believe my husband tried to explain a little of the complexities of wish granting, especially when it comes to the quantum realms.* KAR."

It rang a bell. I'd thought, at the time, the raven was pulling my leg or something. I hadn't believed it was true. Oh God, what have I done? I nod my head, too shocked by the enormity of it all to speak.

"KAR. *The quantum realm is unpredictable and not very friendly. We see it as a sort of maze, with bright nodes where paths cross. Those nodes are destinations, when a wish is cast, they are the different possible outcomes. We managed to select one this time, we couldn't find a better one than this. We only have nanoseconds once the wish is cast. I can show you, you need to look through my eyes, if you'll allow me?* KAR."

"OK." I manage, to get that past my lips. I don't blame the ravens, they'd tried to do as I'd asked, they'd tried to warn me of the danger.

"KAR. *Close your eyes for a moment... good, I have to peck your skin, I need a drop of your blood..."* I feel a sharp scratch on my arm then she is quiet for about half a minute "*... now open your eyes and look around.* KAR."

I do as she says and... It's beautiful.

Each new raven is a person! I see the shimmering silver of their spirit growing out from each raven I see. By the corner shop, Mr Patel is talking to Mr Jones who's, never been nice to him as the Jones family are a bunch of ill-bred racists. But they are shaking hands, introducing each other to their families, their children are playing together. Over in the park the little disabled boy is playing with some of the children his age; they used to ignore him (at best), now they are all teaching each other how to walk on new legs they aren't used to and how to fly. I look around the village and it's a pattern that constantly repeats itself.

Feathers Of Shimmering Iridescence speaks again, I look at her and see that she, and Strong Of Beak And Talon, and the rest of the church yard ravens also have spirit people growing from them.

"KAR. *As ravens they can see how interconnected everything is, it only takes moments for it to sink into their consciousness and affect their behaviour. Once you see like us there is no longer any room for hate. It was the closest we could find to what you wanted... Now look up.* KAR."

Smiling I do as she asks. Over my head I see my granddaughter and her girlfriend, hand in hand, flying through the air. They twist around each other, fall into spinning dives and swoop along the rooftops. A group of older children join in with them, all laughing and calling out to each other, showing off and full of the joys of Spring. My granddaughter waves at me when she finally notices me, I wave back and the laugh that has been bubbling up inside me watching them finally breaks past my lips. As I laugh my granddaughter waves again and, with her girlfriend, she flies off in the direction of her mother's village, a good twenty miles as the crow… raven flies.

"KAR. *Thank you, both*. KAR." I say to

Strong of Beak And Talon, and Feathers of Shimmering Iridescence.

"KAR. *I took the liberty of taking you both back to the age you were when you met. Come back for your training when you are ready.* KAR." That was Feathers of Shimmering Iridescence, I didn't really understand her words and resolved to ask her what she meant as she flew off with her husband.

I feel, rather than see or hear, another raven land on the back of the bench behind me.

"KAR. *Mavis?* KAR." The voice is familiar, but it can't be…

I turn and, through the tears of happiness that blur my sight, I smile and everything slots into place in my mind.

"KAR. *Betty.* KAR"

I take her offered hands in mine and, together, we fly into the sunrise.

ABOUT THE AUTHOR

Philip F. Webb

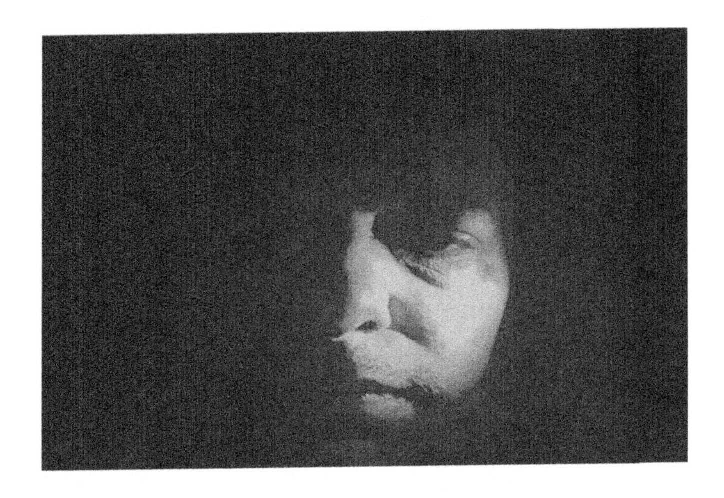

Born: 1967, still alive.
Lived: From Caterham, Surrey. Moved to Leeds, West Yorkshire because it seemed like a good idea at the time.
Has had too many jobs in the hospitality and retail trade to have any vestige of sanity left.
Loves to write, read, watch TV and go to the cinema. Has an interest in photography.

Printed in Great Britain
by Amazon